OXFORD WORLD'

THE BLACK TULIP

ALEXANDRE DUMAS was born at Villers-Cotterêts in 1802, the son of an innkeeper's daughter and one of Napoleon's most remarkable generals. He moved to Paris in 1823 to make his fortune in the theatre. At 28 he was one of the leading literary figures of his day, a star of the Romantic revolution, and known for his many mistresses and taste for high living. He threw himself recklessly into the July Revolution of 1830 which he regarded as a great adventure. Quickly wearying of politics, he returned to the theatre and by the early 1840s was producing vast historical novels at a stupendous rate and in prodigious quantities for the cheap newspapers which paid enormous sums of money to authors who could please the public. His complete works were eventually to fill over 300 volumes and his yarns made him the best-known Frenchman of his age. He earned several fortunes which he gave away, or spent on women and travel, or wasted on grandiose follies like the 'Château de Monte Cristo' which he built to symbolize his success. In 1848 he stood unsuccessfully in the elections for the new Assembly. By 1850 his creditors began to catch up with him and, partly to escape them and partly to find new material for his novels, plays, and travel books, he lived abroad for long periods, travelling through Russia where his fame had preceded him, and Italy where he ran guns in support of Garibaldi's libertarian cause. Without guile and without enemies, he was a man of endless fascination who lived long enough to see his talent desert him. He died of a stroke at Puys, near Dieppe, in 1870.

DAVID COWARD is Senior Fellow and Emeritus Professor of French Literature at the University of Leeds. He is the author of studies of Marivaux, Marguerite Duras, Marcel Pagnol, and Restif de La Bretonne. For Oxford World's Classics, he has edited eight novels by Alexandre Dumas, including the whole of the Musketeer saga, and translated Dumas *fils*'s *La Dame aux camélias*, two selections of Maupassant short stories, Sade's *Misfortunes of Virtue and Other Early Tales* and Diderot's *Jacques the Fatalist*. Winner of the 1996 Scott-Moncrieff Prize for translation, he reviews regularly for the *Times Literary Supplement*.

OXFORD WORLD'S CLASSICS

*For over 100 years Oxford World's Classics have brought
readers closer to the world's great literature. Now with over 700
titles—from the 4,000-year-old myths of Mesopotamia to the
twentieth century's greatest novels—the series makes available
lesser-known as well as celebrated writing.*

*The pocket-sized hardbacks of the early years contained
introductions by Virginia Woolf, T. S. Eliot, Graham Greene,
and other literary figures which enriched the experience of reading.
Today the series is recognized for its fine scholarship and
reliability in texts that span world literature, drama and poetry,
religion, philosophy and politics. Each edition includes perceptive
commentary and essential background information to meet the
changing needs of readers.*

OXFORD WORLD'S CLASSICS

ALEXANDRE DUMAS

The Black Tulip

Edited with an Introduction and Notes by
DAVID COWARD

OXFORD
UNIVERSITY PRESS

OXFORD

UNIVERSITY PRESS

Great Clarendon Street, Oxford OX2 6DP

Oxford University Press is a department of the University of Oxford.
It furthers the University's objective of excellence in research, scholarship,
and education by publishing worldwide in

Oxford New York

Athens Auckland Bangkok Bogotá Buenos Aires Calcutta
Cape Town Chennai Dar es Salaam Delhi Florence Hong Kong Istanbul
Karachi Kuala Lumpur Madrid Melbourne Mexico City Mumbai
Nairobi Paris São Paulo Singapore Taipei Tokyo Toronto Warsaw

with associated companies in Berlin Ibadan

Oxford is a registered trade mark of Oxford University Press
in the UK and in certain other countries

Published in the United States
by Oxford University Press Inc., New York

British Library Cataloguing in Publication Data

Data available

Library of Congress Cataloging in Publication Data

Dumas, Alexandre, 1802–1870.
[Tulipe noire. English]
The black tulip/Alexandre Dumas; edited with an introduction by
David Coward.
p. cm.—(Oxford world's classics)
Translation of: La tulipe noire.
Includes bibliographical references.
1. Witt, Johan de, 1625–1672—Fiction. 2. Netherlands—
History—1648–1714—Fiction. 3. Tulip mania, 17th century—
Fiction. I. Coward, David. II. Title. III. Series.
PQ2229.T8E5 1993 843'.7—dc20 92–19029
ISBN 0–19–283750–8

3 5 7 9 10 8 6 4

Printed in Great Britain by
Cox & Wyman Ltd.
Reading, Berkshire

CONTENTS

INTRODUCTION

Dumas lived in an age which had a taste for heroes and grand gestures. Brought up on the Napoleonic legend, he and his generation had chafed at the ultra-conservatism of the 1820s. They had climbed on barricades in July 1830 and acted as midwives to their very own Revolution: Dumas himself single-handedly overwhelmed the bemused garrison of a gunpowder store at Soissons. But the new regime of Louis-Philippe, the bourgeois king, scarcely lived up to their expectations. If the struggle against oppression generated excitement, the practical problems facing a large nation, just beginning its industrial revolution, were dull and prosaic. Romantic writers and artists, never comfortable with ordinariness, looked elsewhere for the excitement they needed. They found it in imagination and emotion. But many, eager to escape the eternal dullness of the present, also took to the past which they thought as fascinating and exotic as any foreign land. They did not so much discover history as invent it.

'History', said Vigny, 'is a novel written by the People.' Readers did not need to be told twice. They were fascinated by the recent past—Napoleon had generated far more history than they had been able to digest—and, after 1815, when tensions between conservatism and liberalism seemed to revive the struggles of the 1780s, they were curious to know more about the events and the personalities which had made the Revolution of 1789. But their interest quickly spread to all parts of French history, and especially to those epochs which featured conflict, high drama, and sensational turning-points. Even in serious historians like Michelet and Guizot they found a strong narrative drive and an exalted sense of the forces which had created the modern French nation. Naturally publishers were only too eager to supply the new demand, and in the 1820s began reprinting vast collections, some running to hundreds of volumes, of obscure, forgotten memoirs, journals, correspondence, and chronicles which, unprocessed by historians, seemed to be History itself.

In the theatre, the practice of dramatizing the past had been part of the playwright's stock-in-trade for centuries, and Dumas first made his name with historical subjects. In the novel, a newer form of writing which was to grow in strength and popularity as the century advanced, Walter Scott had already shown the way. He filtered out the dullness and gave his readers a spangled view of the past and his many imitators a formula. He was read avidly in France, where his practice of inserting sympathetic, enterprising characters into the company of real kings and queens was taken as a model. Scott turned history into a pageant and Vigny, Mérimée, and Hugo followed where he had led. Dumas, also a great admirer, set out to do for the French what the author of *Waverley* had done for the British. Though many of his romances, like the *Count of Monte Cristo* (1844–5), had a contemporary or near-contemporary setting, he wrote cycles of novels grouped around three distinct periods of French history: the political and religious strife of the sixteenth century; the Musketeer trilogy which covered forty years of the seventeenth century; and a series which dealt with the end of the *ancien régime* and the French Revolution.

Dumas's education scarcely fitted him for the task he set himself. The son of a general who had fallen from Napoleonic grace for his outspokenness, he finished his schooling by the age of 14 and worked in a lawyer's office at his native Villers-Cotterêts, fifty miles north-east of Paris. In 1823 he moved to the capital which he was determined to conquer. By 1829 his historical drama, *Henri III and his Court*, had made him famous. He confirmed his place as a leader of the new school of Romantic writers with a flow of high-impact melodramas which expressed the now-obligatory emotionalism and overwhelmed audiences in both Paris and the provinces. In 1832 he began to diversify and that year sold *Isabel de Bavière*, a medieval tale of love, war, and chivalry, to the *Revue des Deux Mondes*, the house-journal of Romanticism. It was the first of a series of 'Chronicles of France', but made no significant impact. The reason, as Dumas cheerfully confessed in his *Memoirs* (vi. 100), was that until 1831 he knew no history at all: he had found the plot of *Henri III* ready-made in a stray paragraph of an odd volume of a sixteenth-century diarist which he had not bothered to read to the end. But he now became a passionate student and began an affair with History which was to last the rest of his life. To his natural gift for dialogue and narrative—which he admitted possessing 'to the highest degree'—he was to add his own unique ingredient: *la verve amusante*.

In 1833, his liberal opinions became suspect and he went briefly into exile in Switzerland. Never keen to waste material, he wrote the first of his series of travel books which are as companionable as they are unreliable: Dumas was one of nature's cavaliers, always liked a good story, and was perfectly capable of inventing one when life failed him. On returning to Paris he continued to write plays, but by the end of the 1830s was increasingly struck by the possibilities of fiction. His 'Chronicles of France' may not have achieved the success of plays like *Kean* (1836), but instinct told him that there were many stories waiting in the wings to be rescued from the dust.

Moreover, fiction was beginning to offer richer rewards than the theatre. In 1836, a new breed of publishers revolutionized the press by using revenue from advertisements to reduce the price of newspapers. They found that serialized fiction had a marked effect on sales, and offered large advances to writers who could turn out sensational stories at high speed to strict deadlines. Quality novelists, like Balzac, either wilted under the pressure or else failed to supply the excitement and thrills demanded by the new readers of the new, cheap papers and magazines. But Frédéric Soulié, a friend of Dumas, had the knack, and his *Memoirs of the Devil*

(1837–8) demonstrated what rich pickings could be made. Soon the exuberant Eugène Sue, probably the most widely read of all nineteenth-century French novelists, was making his name—and a fortune—with *The Mysteries of Paris* (1842–3) and *The Wandering Jew* (1844–5), both of which first appeared in serialized form.

Dumas, who had developed a taste for high living and fast women, always spent everything he earned and more besides. When approached by newspaper editors, he signed up immediately. His motives were not entirely mercenary, however, for he brought to his fiction all the passionate curiosity about human nature which had been the strength of his plays. He was a keen observer of contemporary manners, but an even keener consumer of history. He was less interested in historians than in chronicles and memoirs which contained dramatic, spicy revelations about the personal lives of the makers of history and brought the past to life. He did not read: he trawled. He was no antiquarian, wedded to accuracy, but used history to stimulate his imagination. It was an exploitable resource and he exploited it.

Although he was not much given to theorizing, he made at different times a number of contradictory statements about his ambition 'to raise the novel to the dignity of history'. He always respected the facts, he said, and avoided 'interpretations' of personalities and events. Yet he was not always as true to such claims as he was in his first and most faithful attempt at fictionalizing history, *The Chevalier d'Harmental* (1842), which sets a dramatic love story against an accurately drawn picture of early eighteenth-century political intrigue. He also claimed that he usually began by inventing a story and then searched for a period in which to set it, a process which inevitably led to distortions of the facts quite inconsistent with his stated pieties. In practice, Dumas was a romancer who followed his nose, his imagination, his heart, and his instinct. His habit of presenting history in terms of personalities observed in situations rooted in conflict encouraged caricature and black-and-white judgements. The reader is in no doubt where Dumas's sympathies lie: he stands for Good against Evil, underdogs against tyrants, and we have no difficulty in telling which is which. Ultimately History was for him, as he provokingly remarked, 'the nail on which I hang my novels'.

Dumas's natural impatience and his colossal writing commitments left him little time for personal research, and he relied on a string of collaborators to the point where he was accused of passing off as his own the work of other hands. It seemed to many of his contemporaries quite impossible that any one man could have written, or even dictated, all the books which appeared under his name. In 1845 a journalist said in print what many were thinking: Dumas was no more than the squalid proprietor of a 'fiction factory'. Dumas sued and won his case. He admitted to using the services, not only of secretaries who corrected his punctuation, spelling, and inconsistencies, but also of what would now be called 'researchers' and 'script-consultants'. But he always acknowledged the help he was given and paid for it as regularly as his nonchalant attitude to money allowed. Albert Vandam, who knew him well, recalled in *An Englishman in Paris* (London, 1892) that, 'though for forty years Alexandre Dumas could not have earned less than eight thousand pounds per annum; though he neither smoked, drank, nor gambled; though, in spite of his mania for cooking, he himself was the most frugal eater . . . it rained writs and summonses around him, while he himself was frequently without a penny'. He was known to all the bailiffs in Paris, and of his earnings, 'a third went to Dumas's collaborateurs, another third to his creditors, and the rest to himself'. No one could be angry with the open-handed Dumas for long. He had his detractors, but was a man without enemies.

He left much of the historical spadework to his collaborators. Under his direction they furnished substantial plot outlines which it was his practice to rewrite completely, adding the 'Dumas touch' with which he stamped his personal, unique mark on the published product. It is in this sense that he claimed, rightly, to have been the author of all the books he signed. However, there were occasions when looming deadlines curtailed his involvement, and paragraphs, pages, and probably whole chapters were sent to the printer unchanged and, it was said, unread. Dumas was as careless with literary property as he was with money. But such was his charm—Vandam reckoned he suffered from chronic optimism—that none of his collaborators ever sustained a charge of plagiarism against him, though Maquet, his most consistent collaborator, took him to court twice in the 1850s for his failure to pay agreed royalties.

Dumas first met Auguste Maquet, a former history teacher with literary ambitions, in 1838. Maquet approached him with a much-rejected play which Dumas obligingly rewrote as *Bathilde*. It was performed in 1839 under Maquet's name. In the same way, Dumas turned Maquet's short novel *Le Bonhomme Buvat* into the four-volume *The Chevalier d'Harmental*, which he signed as his own at the insistence of the publisher: Dumas's name could sell anything. The pattern of their collaboration was thus set early in their relationship. Maquet focused the historical background and wrote first drafts of narratives agreed with Dumas, who then rewrote Maquet, expanding his text, inventing new twists, and adding those touches of humour, drama, and suspense which are his hallmark. The nature of their collaboration is clear enough from what remains of the manuscript materials of *The Three Musketeers* (1844), which shows the published novel to have been a vast, virtuoso orchestration of Maquet's bald and rather dull draft.

In 1847 Dumas, already the most famous living Frenchman, opened his own playhouse, the 'Théâtre historique', and moved into a grand house at Marly, the 'Château de Monte Cristo', which he had built to symbolize his success. But the political temperature rose in Paris and in February 1848 the bourgeois monarchy of Louis-Philippe was overthrown. Dumas was no socialist and his republican sympathies, though strong, coexisted with a snobbish regard for monarchs and the honours they gave: he eventually assembled a large collection of medals and decorations, some of which he bought himself. He now decided to enter politics. He made an approach to the town of Saint-Germain-en-Laye with a view to becoming its representative but was turned down: he was thought too immoral. Undaunted, he persisted in his ambition and stood in four elections and by-elections. In September, at Joigny in Burgundy, he thumped the republican tub and hecklers with equal vigour. 'A parliamentary candidate', remarked Vandam, 'however eloquent, who flings his constitutents into the river when they happen to annoy him, must have been a novelty even in those days.' Dumas was not elected, and in December he voted for the new Republic in the person of Louis-Napoleon.

But the upheaval had been disastrous for Dumas and for literature. Takings at his theatre fell dramatically and newspapers could now no longer afford to pay him the huge fees he had commanded before the Revolution. Moreover, distracted by his excursion into politics, Dumas wrote comparatively little in the course of 1848. He still worked with Maquet on the last novel of the Musketeer saga, *Le Vicomte de Bragelonne* (1847–50), and probably on his other ongoing serials, including *The Queen's Necklace*. But the strain in their relationship was beginning to tell. By 1850 Dumas was besieged by creditors. In the autumn he was forced to sell the Théâtre historique and the Château de Monte Cristo. To raise money he had started newspapers, turned his most famous novels into plays, and in general tried to write himself back to solvency. He failed and eventually, in December 1851, fled to Belgium, not to escape the consequences of the *coup d'état* which turned France back to the right, but more mundanely to avoid his creditors.

It should not be thought that the irrepressible Dumas regarded bankruptcy as much more than a rather annoying inconvenience. Its most serious consequence was to be the final break with Maquet who, angered by Dumas's reluctance to keep to the financial arrangement they had made, decided to launch out on his own. But in 1850 the break still lay in the future—they shared equal billing for *Urbain Grandier*, staged in March 1850—and it was probably Maquet who primed Dumas's imagination in the usual way for *The Black Tulip*, which was not serialized but published in three volumes in November 1850.

Dumas's attention had been drawn to the shocking fate of the De Witte brothers, accused in 1672 of having conspired against William, Prince of Orange, when he travelled to Holland for the coronation of William III in May 1849. The German composer Flotow, who had turned *Henri III and his Court* into an opera in 1840, claimed that it was the king himself who mentioned the story to him, though the suggestion may have come from another of his friends, Prince George de Waldeck. The facts were not difficult to unearth, for the affair was amply documented. Dumas knew no Dutch, but the history of Holland and of the campaigns of Louis XIV were widely available in French accounts, which were not as discreet as that of David Hume, who drew a veil over 'indignities too shocking to be recited' (*The History of England*, 1789, xi. 189). The tale had been told notably by P. A. Samson (*Histoire de Guillaume III*, 1703), Jacques Basnage (*Annales des Provinces-Unies*, 1719–26), and Paul Pellisson-Fontanier (*Histoire de Louis XIV*, 1749). Nearer Dumas's day, accounts of the slaughter of the De Witte brothers and the rise of William of Orange were available in the multi-volume histories of Louis XIV by Capefigue, Mignet, and others. The most detailed version was contained in a manuscript history of the Netherlands written by Abraham de Wiquefort, a close contemporary observer of events, to which Dumas or one of his collaborators may have had access through antiquarian friends like Paul Lacroix or Paulin Pâris. It seems likely that Basnage and Wiquefort were the primary sources for the events described in the first four chapters of *The Black Tulip*.

As was his habit, Dumas ignored all dull preliminaries and translated history into excitement, horror (he was fascinated by decapitations and other forms of violent death), and above all, personalities. Simplifying a complex situation, Dumas turned the events into a conflict between the brothers, portrayed as decent republicans, and the wily, even sinister, William of Orange. Under John de Witte, the United Provinces had become a strong political and commercial federation. The Stadtholdership had been cancelled and the Seven Provinces were run like a republic, a model of political organization which hardly appealed to neighbouring monarchs. Rivalry with England had led to serious skirmishing, while Louis XIV was eager to press his claims to sovereignty of the Netherlands through his Spanish-born queen. War was declared in May 1672. The French advanced rapidly and by the middle of June were halted only by a last resort: the Dutch breached their dykes and flooded vast tracts of their land. The blame for their predicament was laid squarely by the Dutch on John de Witte and his brother Cornelius, his staunchest supporter. Attempts were made on their lives, and when the 22-year-old William was proclaimed Stadtholder their position became untenable. Ignoring the political background and siding with two men who stand for right, justice, and true patriotism, Dumas, as was his custom, plunges his reader *in medias res* with a date: 20 August 1672. John may have been the senior partner, but Dumas was more interested in Cornelius. His fate was much more gruesome.

In 1670, William Tichelaer, a barber-surgeon from Pulten Island, had been found guilty of using threats and violence against a woman who refused to marry him. On 8 July 1672 he approached Cornelius de Witte, who was *Ruart* (or Steward) of Pulten, to ask that the fine against him be set aside. According to Tichelaer, Cornelius had agreed but only on condition that he also undertake to assassinate William, Prince of Orange, for which service he would be richly rewarded. There were no witnesses to the conversation, but though Tichelaer was a known trouble-maker, such was the feeling against the De Wittes that charges were brought against Cornelius on 23 July. He was escorted from Dordrecht to the Hague on 25 July. An investigation was set in train immediately and on 16 August the court, satisfied that the required 'half-proof' of guilt had already been obtained, ordered that he should be put to the question. He was tortured for three-and-a-half hours. His feet were crushed by the 'boot', after which a fifty-pound weight was hung from his toes: even the executioner, who was instructed to remain silent, was appalled by the severity of the torture applied. Cornelius's judges, lacking the confession required to justify the death penalty, stripped him of his offices and sentenced him to exile.

As Tichelaer left the court-house on 20 August, he stirred the waiting crowd against the leniency of the judgement. Cornelius's jailer urged him to go while he still could but, unable to walk, Cornelius sent to his brother's house on the nearby Kneuterdijk for a coach. The message was carried by the jailer's maid and John, who was suspicious, waited for confirmation but eventually went. When the two brothers attempted to leave the Gevangenpoort they were prevented from doing so by an angry mob, which eventually broke into the prison, dragged them out, and cut them down as a crowd of a thousand looked on and cheered. The bodies were hung by the feet and mutilated. Ears, fingers, and other trophies were sold as souvenirs while a few of the crowd roasted parts of the bodies and ate them.

Dumas found the fate of the brothers irresistible and he wrote it up with relish. Unfortunately, the story ended rather abruptly and was good for a mere four chapters. Of course, it may be that he viewed the episode simply as an ideal curtain-raiser: a number of his novels (*The Memoirs of a Physician*, say, or *The Queen's Necklace*), start with an epic bang before settling into a less exalted mode. Certainly, some readers have felt that Dumas suddenly loses interest in History altogether as he shifts our attention to the inoffensive Van Baerle. Yet there is nothing inconsistent in Dumas's proceeding. To his mind, the personal values of his mild-mannered tulip-fancier are closely related to the political ideals of the De Wittes, and the drama of the amazing 'tulipa negra' enacts, on a smaller scale, a second clash between individual will and collective tyranny. Van Baerle, 'the real hero of this tale', is also a victim of the kind of oppressive state which William is intent on creating and which Dumas found anathema to his own generous spirit. Van Baerle is a mirror held up to the De Wittes. But his predicament, and the sticky-sweet love story which articulates it, also illustrate a more general moral idea: the vulnerability of the pure. To state his case for the good against the wicked, Dumas resorted to another phenomenon of history, the Tulipmania which raged in Holland in the 1630s.

The tulip was first introduced into Holland in 1571 from Turkey. It caused a sensation, since nothing recognizable as tulips had been mentioned by the writers of antiquity, nor had they figured in the illuminations or paintings of the Middle Ages. Henry Lyte (*A Niewe Herball*, 1578) preferred the name 'Lily-narcissus', and twenty years later Gerard's *Herbal* remarked upon the efforts to breed new varieties, 'all which to describe particularlie were too roule Sisiphus stone or number the sands'. By this time it featured widely in the gardens of Holland and botanists like Clusius experimented with colour, size, and shape. During the first years of the reign of Louis XIII tulips became fashionable at the French court, and the illustrated *Hortus Floridus* (1614) of Chrispijn van de Pas spread the reputation of the flower throughout Germany, northern France, and the Netherlands. Demand spawned suppliers, and the Dutch, especially in the towns of the province of Holland, found their soil and climate ideally suited to the cultivation of new varieties. In 1623 a single bulb of 'Semper Augustus' was selling for thousands of florins and the economic potential of the trade became apparent. Amsterdam, Haarlem, Hoorn, Utrecht, and Rotterdam were the centres of the new trade, and surrounding areas were given over almost entirely to the new crop. The unpredictable 'breaking' of the tulip multiplied varieties: there were new groups of Admirals and Generals, six kinds of Marvels, seven Tournais, and thirty Paragons. Marque-trines with four or five colours in their petals were particu-larly valuable.

By the 1630s the extension of the trade to cheaper varieties intensified the traffic in tulip futures. Professional florists, who published illustrated catalogues, were joined by weavers, street porters, chimney-sweeps, barge skippers, and turf-cutters, who planted bulbs in every available space in the hope that they might be lucky and produce one of the new variegated blooms which changed hands at astounding prices. 'Collegiums' were set up by growers who formed syndicates with elected officials to regulate the trade. They met in taverns, held auctions, and transacted extraordinary deals. At the height of the mania bulbs were bought and sold for huge sums without ever leaving the ground, and prices rose daily. For one Viceroy, a farmer is said to have paid 2,500 florins in the form of 2 carts of wheat and 4 of rye, 8 fat pigs, 4 oxen, a dozen sheep, 2 oxheads of wine, 4 tons of butter, 1,000 pounds of cheese, some furniture and clothes, and a silver beaker. Such speculators were known as *kappisten* ('the hooded ones') after the hoods worn by the mad, and no social group or religious sect was immune. Prints, pamphlets, and songs satirized the craze and moralists denounced this new instance of human folly. Eventually speculation in tulip bulbs reached such heights that the States of Holland intervened in February 1637 and effectively ended the trade. Many were ruined in what is regarded as the first docu-mented example of stock-market fever.

Countless stories were told of bulbs mistaken for onions and expensively eaten, of fortunes won and lost, and Dumas probably found his theme in one such tale of the shoemaker in the Hague who had produced a tulip which was entirely black. He was approached by a syndicate of Haarlem florists who offered to buy it. He refused, but finally agreed when the price reached 1,500 florins. But the moment he handed the bulb to the purchaser, it was dropped on the floor and crushed out of existence. When the shoemaker protested he was informed that the Haarlem florists had produced a black tulip of their own and would have paid 10,000 florins to stifle the competition. The shoemaker took to his bed and immediately died of chagrin.

There is no way of telling just where Dumas found the story, but he admits to knowing Charles La Chesnée Monstereul's *Le Floriste françois* (1654), which he consulted on tulip lore. He derived a few names of blooms from Monstereul but little else: he cheerfully allows Rosa to plant a bulb in late April which flowers in mid-May. Nor, curiously, was his imagination fired by the Dutch Tulipmania, a subject fertile in the treasons, stratagems, and spoils which were his stock-in-trade. But the thought of a tulip which was as black as soot clearly appealed to him, since he makes it, and not the characters, the true and only hero of his tale. Moreover, the time was ripe: the tulip was back in fashion throughout Europe. Charles Malo's *Histoire des Tulipes* had appeared in 1821. New varieties were produced, and one, the 'Citadel of Antwerp', was sold on the international market for £650 in 1836. In England the years between 1840 and 1855 were the heyday of tulip shows and tulip clubs, and the National Tulip Society was founded in London in 1849. Tennyson evoked 'Deep tulips dash'd with fiery dew' in *In Memoriam* in 1850. A tale from the pen of Dumas which had 'tulip' in its title could scarcely fail.

When the fury of the first chapters has died away, Dumas gives us a dreamy hero, a plucky heroine, and a simple tale of love. Forsaking his epic style, he chose to work on a small scale and produced a novel which is not symphonic or operatic like his grander works, but is cast more in the chamber mode. The tone is intimate and the mood romantic: here again Dumas expresses his generation's fascination with prisons, the power of love, and the beauties and mystery of nature. The Dutch landscape is rather perfunctorily evoked, for Dumas wrote much too quickly to stake any great claim as a stylist (unlike Fromentin, who was to paint much finer word-pictures in his book on the Dutch painters, *Les Maîtres d'autrefois*, in 1876). Dumas's style is to be defined by his ability to conjure suspense and to involve us closely in the fate of his characters. Even so, some readers have found the story all too predictable and familiar: the love of a jailer's daughter for a prisoner is part of every nation's history. Others have found the hero altogether too unworldly, the heroine too cloying, the villains too wooden, and the whole much too sugary a confection. Moreover, Dumas is careless even by his dashing standards: not only does he end the Dutch Wars five years early, but would have us believe that, at 28, Van Baerle has not only put a career as an entomologist behind him but has packed astounding achievements into remarkably few seasons.

Yet such criticisms scarcely do justice to the strengths and subtleties of this far from simple tale. At its heart is an affirmation of civilized values. Van Baerle is no daydreamer but a man of ideals, determined to protect the black flower not because it will make him rich and famous, but because it is a triumph of art over ignorance. He may be less doughty than d'Artagnan, less steely than Monte Cristo, but he is no less committed than they to the struggle to ensure that right prevails against impossible odds. It is his defenceless idealism which attracts Rosa, who is clearly a sister to d'Artagnan's Constance. She is bolder and more enterprising than he. For love and a flower, she dares to stand up against the envy of Boxtel, the grovelling cowardice of her jobsworth of a father, and even the might of the State. Their cause transcends the circumstances of the plot, for what they achieve is Justice.

Their final victory at Haarlem does not simply furnish a happy ending to their valiant struggle. It also redeems the De Wittes. It has been said that Dumas exploited the brothers' gory fate for its shock value and then grew bored with them. He has been accused of rewriting history by making William the prime mover in their deaths. In reality, public and private events are the two faces of the same struggle for right which is resolved in a wider dimension in the shadowy character of William. The first sight we have of him shows a cold, ambitious, and ruthless political realist. The last is of a mature statesman who knows that power without justice is not only unsustainable but wrong. Thus, *The Black Tulip* both articulates Dumas's unshakeable belief in the human spirit and teaches a sharp political lesson. Gryphus, whose savagery is tamed, is a cipher for the mob who killed the De Wittes as eagerly as they cheer Van Baerle and Rosa. Boxtel dies, as all selfish schemers deserve to. But the message is plainest when applied to Dumas's own day: in just over a year Louis-Napoleon was to overthrow the Republic and turn France into a materialistic Empire. Dumas, the temperamental republican, devout liberal, and the future admirer of Garibaldi (for whom he was to run guns in 1860) here fires a warning-shot over the bows of a ruler who was following the opposite path to William.

This political dimension may now have lost its urgency, but there is still much more at stake in this deceptively slight tale than two lovers, a handful of cardboard villains, and a bulb. The black tulip brings out the best and the worst in people, for in Dumas's hands it acquires a talismanic power. It makes the good happy, halts the wicked and makes kings human. Van Baerle's passion for the flower has a symbolic value just as it had for Monstereul, the author of *Le Floriste françois*:

As it is seen that among animals Man wears the crown; among the Planets, the Sun holds the first rank; and among precious stones, the Diamond is of greatest price, so it is certain that of all the flowers the Tulip holds pride of place, being the object upon which Nature has lavished the greatest of her Beauties and the Instrument through which Nature reveals to the eyes of all the world the most handsome of the ornaments with which she had been endowed by her Divine Creator.

Two centuries later Dumas makes the black tulip an emblem of justice and right, which are Nature's ultimate gift to ungrateful mortals.

NOTE ON THE TEXT

The publication of *La Tulipe noire* was announced in the *Bibliographie de France* on 8 November 1850. Two separate editions appeared in French in New York in 1850, and the first translation into English, by Fayette Robinson, was published there before the end of the year. Meanwhile, no fewer than six separate editions, all dated 1850, of a pirated version appeared in Belgium hot on the heels of the first French edition. The Belgian text was slightly abridged (it is approximately 5 per cent shorter), the most visible changes being the substitution of 'Van Herysen' for 'Van Systens' in Chapter 25 and the loss of Dumas's long description of Haarlem at the start of Chapter 31. The first British translation, by Franz Demmler, was published in London in 1854 and was based not on the original French text but on the pirated version. It was subsequently reprinted many times by Routledge.

American editions of *The Black Tulip*, with very few exceptions, have either reprinted or revised Fayette Robinson's translation of the first French edition. British publishers, on the other hand, have continued to adopt or update Demmler's version—itself heavily indebted to the American translation—of the Belgian text, though Dent, through its association with Little, Brown of Boston, reverted to the fuller version in its Everyman series (1906). The text of 1854 has therefore been the translation which generations of British readers have known for a century-and-a-half.

The decision to follow Demmler and continue the British tradition is not based on historical considerations alone, but is amply vindicated on aesthetic grounds. The cuts constitute a desirable form of the pruning which Dumas, who never lost the habit of stretching his material to fill pages and thus maximize the financial return on his labours, was always too busy to undertake. With so much padding removed, the novel gains significantly in pace. The Explanatory Notes at the end of this volume restore a handful of significant omissions, however, and the interested reader is referred to them.

SELECT BIBLIOGRAPHY

Unlike most of Dumas's novels, *The Black Tulip* was not serialized before publication. It appeared early in November 1850 (Paris, Baudry, 3 vols.) priced 22 *frs.* 50. The first translation into English, by Fayette Robinson, appeared as: *The Black Tulip: A Romance* (New York, Burgess, 1850, 2 vols.). The first British translation, by Franz Demmler, *Rosa; or, the Black Tulip* (London, Hodgson, 'The Parlour Library', 1854), adopted one of the numerous pirated versions of Dumas's novel printed in Brussels, and is the version followed in the present edition. The first and only critical edition was prepared for schools by Paul Blouet (London, Hachette, 1882). The fullest study to date is the preface by Richard Garnett to a translation by A. J. O'Connor of *The Black Tulip* (London, Heinemann, 1902; repr. 1923).

Readers wishing to follow the complex printing history of Dumas's voluminous writings in French may usefully consult Douglas Munro's *Dumas: A Bibliography of Works published in French, 1825–1900* (New York and London, 1981). *Alexandre Dumas père: A Bibliography of Works Translated into English to 1910* (New York and London, 1978), also by Douglas Munro, is the best guide to British and American editions.

Dumas's autobiography, *Mes mémoires* (1852–5; ed. Pierre Josserand, Gallimard, 1954–68, 5 vols.; English trans., London, 1907–9) is an engaging but far from reliable account of his life to 1832. The best French biographies are those of Henri Clouard, *Alexandre Dumas* (Paris, 1955), André Maurois, *Les Trois Dumas* (Paris, 1957; English trans., London, 1958), and Claude Schopp, *Dumas, le génie de la vie* (Paris, 1985; American trans., New York and Toronto, 1988). Isabelle Jan, *Dumas romancier* (Paris, 1973) offers the fullest study of the novels.

Among the many books in English devoted to Dumas, very readable introductions are provided by Ruthven Todd,

The Laughing Mulatto (London, 1940), A. Craig Bell, *Alexandre Dumas* (London, 1950), and Richard Stowe, *Dumas* (Boston, 1976). Michael Ross's *Alexandre Dumas* (Newton Abbot, 1981) gives a sympathetic account of his life. The most balanced and comprehensive guide, however, is F. W. J. Hemmings' excellent *The King of Romance* (London, 1979).

The historical and floricultural background to *The Black Tulip* is richly explained into two excellent books: Simon Schama's *The Embarrassment of Riches* (Collins, London, 1987) and Herbert H. Rowen's *John de Witt, Grand Pensionary of Holland, 1625–72* (Princeton University Press, 1978).

A CHRONOLOGY OF
ALEXANDRE DUMAS

1762 25 March: Birth at Saint-Domingo of Thomas-Alex-andre, son of the French-born Marquis Davy de la Pailleterie and Marie-Cessette Dumas. After returning to France in 1780, he enlists in 1786 and rises rapidly through the ranks during the Revolution.

1802 24 July: Birth at Villers-Cotterêts of Alexandre Dumas, second child of General Dumas and Marie-Louise-Eliza-beth Labouret, an innkeeper's daughter.

1806 26 February: Death of General Dumas. Alexandre is brought up in straitened circumstances by his mother. He attends local schools and has a happy childhood.

1819 Dumas, now a lawyer's office-boy, falls in love with Adèle Dalvin who rejects him. Meets Adolphe de Leuven, with whom he collaborates in writing unsuccessful plays.

1822 Visits Leuven in Paris, meets Talma, the leading actor of the day, and resolves to become a playwright.

1823 Moves to Paris. Enters the service of the Duke d'Orléans. Falls in love with a seamstress, Catherine Labay.

1824 27 July: Birth of Alexandre Dumas *fils*, author of *La Dame aux camélias*.

1825 22 September: Dumas's first performed play, written in collaboration with Leuven and Rousseau, makes no impact.

1826 Publication of a collection of short stories, Dumas's first solo composition, which sells four copies.

1827 A company of English actors, which includes Kean, Kemble, and Mrs Smithson, performs Shakespeare in English to enthusiastic Paris audiences: Dumas is deeply impressed. Liaison with Mélanie Waldor.

1828–9 Dumas enters Parisian literary circles through Charles Nodier.

1829 11 February: First of about 50 performances of *Henry III and his Court*, which makes Dumas famous and thrusts him into the front ranks of the Romantic revolution in literature. Dumas meets Victor Hugo. He consolidates his reputation as a dramatist with *Antony* (1831), *La Tour de Nesle* (1832), and *Kean* (1836), which are all landmarks in the history of Romantic drama.

1830   May: Start of an affair with the actress Belle Krelsamer. Active in the July Revolution: Dumas single-handedly captures a gunpowder magazine at Soissons and is sent by Lafayette to promote the National Guard in the Vendée (Aug.).

1831   5 March: Birth of Marie, his daughter by Belle Krelsamer.
17 March: Dumas acknowledges Alexandre, his son by Catherine Labay.

1832   6 February: Start of his affair with the actress Ida Ferrier.
15 April: Dumas succumbs to the cholera which kills 20,000 Parisians.
29 May: First performance of *La Tour de Nesle*: Gaillardet accuses Dumas of plagiarism.
July: Suspected of republican sympathies, Dumas leaves Paris for Switzerland. After the spectacular failure of his next play, he begins to take a systematic interest in the literary possibilities of French history.

1833   Serialization of a book of impressions of Switzerland, the first of his travelogues.

1834–5   October: Dumas travels in the Midi. From the Riviera, he embarks on the first of many journeys to Italy.

1836   31 August: Dumas returns triumphantly to the theatre with *Kean*.

1838   Death of Dumas's mother. Travels along the Rhine with Gérard de Nerval who introduces him to Auguste Maquet in December.

1840   1 February: Dumas marries Ida Ferrier, travels to Italy, and publishes *Le Capitaine Pamphile*, the best of his children's books.

1840–2   Dividing his time between Paris and Italy, Dumas increasingly abandons the theatre for the novel.

1842   June: Publication of *Le Chevalier d'Harmental*, the first of many romances written in association with Maquet.

1844   March–July: Serialization of *The Three Musketeers* in *Le Siècle*.

August: First episode of *The Count of Monte Cristo* published in *Le Journal des débats*.

15 October: Amicable separation from Ida Ferrier. Publication of *Louis XIV and his Century*.

1845   21 January: Start of serialization of the second d'Artagnan story, *Twenty Years After*, in *Le Siècle*.

February: He wins his libel suit against the journalist Jacquot, author of *A Fiction Factory: The Firm of Alexandre Dumas and Company*, in which he was accused of publishing other men's work under his own name.

27 October: First performance of *Les Mousquetaires*, an adaptation of *Twenty Years After*. Beginning at 6.30 p.m., it lasts until 1 a.m.

1846   Final break with Ida Ferrier. Brief liaison with Lola Montès.

November–January: Travels with his son to Spain and North Africa.

1847   30 January: Loses a lawsuit brought by newspaper proprietors for failure to deliver copy for which he had accepted large advances.

11 February: Questions are asked in the National Assembly about Dumas's appropriation of the navy vessel, *Le Véloce*, during his visit to North Africa.

20 February: Opening of the 'Théâtre historique'.

7 March: Completion of the 'Château de Monte Cristo' at Marly-le-Roi.

20 October–12 January 1850: Serialization of the final Musketeer adventure, *The Vicomte de Bragelonne*, in *Le Siècle*.

1848   Dumas stands unsuccessfully as a parliamentary candidate and votes for Louis-Napoleon in the December elections.

1849   17 February: First performance at the 'Théâtre historique' of *La Jeunesse des Mousquetaires*, based on *The Three Musketeers*.

1850   16 October: The 'Théâtre historique' is declared bank-
        rupt. The 'Château de Monte Cristo' is sold off for 30,000
        francs.
        November: Publication of *The Black Tulip*.

1851   Michel Lévy begins to bring out the first volumes of
        Dumas's complete works which will eventually fill 301
        volumes.
        7 December: Dumas flees to Belgium to avoid his credi-
        tors.

1852   Publication of the first volumes of *My Memoirs*. Dumas
        declared bankrupt with debts of 100,000 francs.

1853   November: Returns to Paris and founds a periodical, *Le
        Mousquetaire* (last issue 7 Feb. 1857) for which he writes
        most of the copy himself.

1857   23 April: Founds a literary weekly, *Le Monte Cristo*, which,
        with one break, survives until 1862.

1858   15 June: Dumas leaves for a tour of Russia and returns in
        March 1859.

1859   11 March: Death of Ida Ferrier. Beginning of a liaison
        with Emilie Cordier which lasts until 1864.

1860   Meets Garibaldi at Turin and just misses the taking of
        Sicily (June). Returns to Marseilles where he buys guns
        for the Italian cause and is in Naples just after the city
        falls in September. Garibaldi stands, by proxy, as god-
        father to Dumas's daughter by Emilie Cordier.
        11 October: Founds *L'Indipendente*, a literary and political
        periodical published half in French and half in Italian.

1863   The works of Dumas are placed on the Index by the
        Catholic Church.

1864   April: Dumas returns to Paris.

1865   Further travels through Italy, Germany, and Austria.

1867   Publishes *The Prussian Terror*, a novel intended to warn
        France against the coming Prussian threat. Begins a last
        liaison, with Adah Menken, an American actress (d.
        1868).

1869   10 March: Dumas's last play, *The Whites and the Blues*.

1870   5 December: Dumas dies at Puys, near Dieppe, after a stroke in September.

1872   Dumas's remains transferred to Villers-Cotterêts.

1883   Unveiling of a statue to Dumas by Gustave Doré in the Place Malesherbes.

THE BLACK TULIP

CHAPTER ONE

A Grateful People

ON THE 20th of August, 1672, the city of the Hague, always so lively, so neat, and so trim, that one might believe every day to be Sunday; with its shady park, with its tall trees, spreading over its Gothic houses; with its canals like large mirrors, in which its steeples and its almost Eastern cupolas are reflected; the city of the Hague, the capital of the seven United Provinces,* was swelling in all its arteries with a black and red stream of hurried, panting, and restless citizens, who, with their knives in their girdles, muskets on their shoulders, or sticks in their hands, were pushing on to the Buitenhof,* a terrible prison, the grated windows of which are still shown, where, on the charge of attempted murder, preferred against him by the surgeon Tyckelaer,* Cornelius De Witte,* the brother of the Grand Pensionary of Holland, was confined.

If the history of that time, and especially that of the year in the middle of which our narrative commences, were not indissolubly connected with the two names just mentioned, the few explanatory pages which we are about to add might appear quite supererogatory; but we will, from the very first, apprise the reader—our old friend, to whom we are wont, on the first page to promise amusement, and with whom we always try to keep our word as well as is in our power—that this explanation is as indispensable to the right understanding of our story, as to that of the great event itself on which it is based.

Cornelius De Witte, warden of the dykes, ex-burgomaster of Dort, his native town, and member of the Assembly of the States of Holland,* was forty-nine years of age, when the Dutch people, tired of the republic such as John De Witte,* the Grand Pensionary of Holland, understood it, at once

3

conceived a most violent affection for the Stadtholderate, which had been abolished for ever in Holland by the " Perpetual Edict " forced by John De Witte upon the United Provinces.

As it rarely happens that public opinion, in its whimsical flights, does not identify a principle with a man, thus the people saw in the personification of the republic in the two stern figures of the brothers De Witte, those Romans of Holland, spurning to pander to the fancies of the mob, and wedding themselves with unbending fidelity to liberty without licentiousness, and prosperity without the waste of superfluity; on the other hand, the Stadtholderate recalled to the popular mind the grave thoughtful image of the young Prince William of Orange.*

The brothers of De Witte humoured Louis XIV.,* whose moral influence was felt by the whole of Europe, and the pressure of whose material power Holland had been made to feel in that marvellous campaign on the Rhine which, in the space of three months, had laid the power of the United Provinces prostrate.

Louis XIV. had long been the enemy of the Dutch, who insulted or ridiculed him* to their heart's content, although it must be said that they generally used French refugees for the mouthpiece of their spite. Their national pride held him up as the Mithridates* of the republic. The brothers De Witte, therefore, had to strive against a double difficulty —against the force of national antipathy, and, besides, against that feeling of weariness which is natural to all vanquished people, when they hope that a new chief will be able to save them from ruin and shame.

This new chief, quite ready to appear on the political stage, and to measure himself against Louis XIV., however gigantic the fortunes of the Grand Monarch loomed in the future, was William, Prince of Orange, son of William II., and grandson, by his mother, Mary Stuart, of Charles I. of England. We have mentioned him before as the person by whom the people expected to see the office of Stadtholder restored.

This young man was, in 1672, twenty-two years of age.

4

John De Witte, who was his tutor,* had brought him up with the view of making him a good citizen. Loving his country better than he did his disciple, the master had, by the " Perpetual Edict," extinguished the hope which the young prince might have entertained of one day becoming Stadtholder. But God laughs at the presumption of man, who wants to raise and prostrate the powers on earth without consulting the King above; and the fickleness and caprice of the Dutch, combined with the terror inspired by Louis XIV., in repealing the " Perpetual Edict '"*and re-establishing the office of Stadtholder in favour of William of Orange, for whom the hand of Providence had traced out ulterior destinies on the hidden map of the future.

The Grand Pensionary bowed before the will of his fellow citizens; Cornelius De Witte, however, was more obstinate, and notwithstanding all the threats of death from the Orangist rabble, who besieged him in his house at Dort, he stoutly refused to sign the act by which the office of Stadtholder was restored. Moved by the tears and entreaties of his wife, he at last complied, only adding to his signature the two letters V. C. (*Vi Coactus*), notifying thereby that he only yielded to force.*

It was a real miracle that on that day he escaped from the doom intended for him.

John de Witte derived no advantage from his ready compliance with the wishes of his fellow citizens. Only a few days after an attempt was made to stab him,* in which he was severely although not mortally wounded.

This by no means suited the views of the Orange faction. The life of the two brothers being a constant obstacle to their plans, they changed their tactics, and tried to obtain by calumny*what they had not been able to effect by the aid of the poniard.

How rarely does it happen that, in the right moment, a great man is to be found to head the execution of vast and noble designs; but it as rarely happens that, when the devil's work is to be done, the miscreant is not at hand, who readily and at once enters upon the infamous task.

The wretched tool in this instance was Tyckelaer, a surgeon by profession. He lodged an information against Cornelius De Witte, setting forth that the warden—who, as he had shown by the letters added to his signature, was fuming at the repeal of the " Perpetual Edict "—had, from hatred against William of Orange, hired an assassin to deliver the new republic of its new Stadtholder; and he, Tyckelaer, was the person thus chosen; but that, horrified at the bare idea of the act which he was asked to perpetrate, he had preferred rather to reveal the crime than to commit it.

This disclosure was, indeed, well calculated to call forth a furious outbreak among the Orange faction. The attorney-general caused, on the 16th of August, 1672, Cornelius De Witte to be arrested; and the noble brother of John De Witte had, like the vilest criminal, to undergo, in one of the apartments of the town prison, the preparatory degrees of torture, by means of which his judges expected to force from him the confession of his alleged plot against William of Orange.

But Cornelius was not only possessed of a great mind, but also of a great heart. He belonged to that race of martyrs who, indissolubly wedded to their political conviction, as their ancestors were to their faith, are able to smile on pain: whilst being stretched on the rack, he recited, with a firm voice, and scanning the lines according to measure, the first strophe of the " Justum ac tenacem "*of Horace; and, making no confession, tired, not only the strength, but even the fanaticism of his executioners.

The judges, notwithstanding, acquitted Tyckelaer from every charge; at the same time sentencing Cornelius to be deposed from all his offices and dignities; to pay all the costs of the trial; and to be banished the soil of the republic for ever.*

This judgment against not only an innocent, but also a great man, was indeed some gratification to the passions of the people, to whose interests Cornelius De Witte had always devoted himself: but, as we shall soon see, it was not enough.

The Athenians, who, indeed, have left behind them a

pretty tolerable reputation for ingratitude, have in this respect to yield precedence to the Dutch. They, at least in the case of Aristides,* contented themselves with banishing him.

John De Witte, at the first intimation of the charge brought against his brother, had resigned his office of Grand Pensionary.* He, too, received a noble recompense for his devotedness to the best interests of his country, taking with him into the retirement of private life the hatred of a host of enemies, and the fresh scars of wounds inflicted by assassins, only too often the sole guerdon* obtained by honest people, who are guilty of having worked for their country, and of having forgotten their own private interests.

In the meanwhile William of Orange urged on the course of events by every means in his power, eagerly waiting for the time when the people, by whom he was idolised, should have made of the bodies of the brothers the two steps over which he might ascend to the chair of Stadtholder.

Well, then, on the 20th of August, 1672, as we have already stated in the beginning of this chapter, the whole town was crowding towards the Buitenhof, to witness the departure of Cornelius De Witte from prison, as he was going to exile; and to see what traces the torture of the rack had left on the noble frame of the man who knew his Horace so well.

Yet all this multitude was not crowding to the Buitenhof with the innocent view of merely feasting their eyes with the spectacle: there were many who went there to play an active part in it,* and to take upon themselves an office which they conceived had been badly filled—that of the executioner.

There were, indeed, others with less hostile intentions. All that they cared for was the spectacle, always so attractive to the mob, whose instinctive pride is flattered by it— the sight of greatness hurled down into the dust.

" Has not," they would say, " this Cornelius De Witte been locked up, and broken by the rack? Shall we not see him pale, streaming with blood, covered with shame?"

7

And was not this a sweet triumph for the burghers of the Hague, whose envy even beat that of the common rabble; a triumph, in which every honest citizen and townsman might be expected to share?

" Moreover," hinted the Orange agitators interspersed through the crowd, whom they hoped to manage like a sharp-edged and, at the same time, crushing instrument— " moreover, will not, from the Buitenhof to the gate of the town a nice little opportunity present itself to throw some handfuls of dirt, or a few stones, at this Cornelius De Witte, who not only conferred the dignity of Stadtholder on the Prince of Orange merely *Vi Coactus*, but who also intended to have him assassinated?"

" Besides which," the fierce enemies of France chimed in, " if the work were done well and bravely at the Hague, Cornelius would certainly not be allowed to go into exile, where he will renew his intrigues with France, and live with his big scoundrel of a brother, John, on the gold of the Marquis de Louvois."*

Being in such a temper, people generally will run rather than walk; which was the reason why the inhabitants of the Hague were hurrying so fast towards the Buitenhof.

Honest Tyckelaer, with a heart full of spite and malice, and with no particular plan settled in his mind, was one of the foremost, being paraded about by the Orange party like a hero of probity, national honour, and Christian charity.

This daring miscreant detailed, with all the embellishments and flourishes suggested by his base mind and his ruffianly imagination, the attempts which he pretended Cornelius De Witte had made to corrupt him; the sums of money which were promised; and all the diabolical stratagems planned beforehand to smooth for him, Tyckelaer, all the difficulties in the path of murder.

And every phrase of his speech, eagerly listened to by the populace, called forth enthusiastic cheers for the Prince of Orange, and groans and imprecations of blind fury against the brothers De Witte.

The mob even began to vent its rage by inveighing against the iniquitous judges, who had allowed such a

8

detestable criminal as the villain Cornelius to get off so cheaply.*

Some of the agitators whispered: " He will be off, he will escape from us!" others replied—

" A vessel is waiting for him at Schevening,* a French craft. Tyckelaer has seen her."

" Honest Tyckelaer! Hurrah for Tyckelaer!" the mob cried in a chorus.

" And let us not forget," a voice exclaimed from the crowd, " that at the same time with Cornelius, his brother John, who is as rascally a traitor as himself, will likewise make his escape."

" And the two rogues will in France make merry with our money, with the money for our vessels, our arsenals, and our dockyards, which they have sold to Louis XIV."

" Well, then, don't let us allow them to depart!" advised one of the patriots who had gained the start of the others.

" Forward to the prison, to the prison!" echoed the crowd.

Among these cries, the citizens ran along faster and faster, cocking their muskets, brandishing their hatchets, and looking death and defiance in all directions.

No violence, however, had as yet been committed, and the file of horsemen who were guarding the approaches of the Buitenhof remained cool, unmoved, silent, much more threatening in their impassibility than all this crowd of burghers, with their cries, their agitation, and their threats. The men on their horses, indeed, stood like so many statues, under the eye of their chief, Count Tilly,* the captain of the mounted troop of the Hague, who had his sword drawn, but held it with its point downwards, in a line with the straps of his stirrup.

This troop, the only defence of the prison, overawed by its firm attitude not only the disorderly riotous mass of the populace, but also the detachment of the burgher-guard* which, being placed opposite the Buitenhof to support the soldiers in keeping order, gave to the rioters the example of seditious cries, shouting—

" Hurrah for Orange! Down with the traitors!"

The presence of Tilly and his horsemen, indeed, exercised a salutary check on these civic warriors; but, by degrees, they waxed more and more angry by their own shouts, and as they were not able, to understand how any one could have courage without showing it by cries, they attributed the silence of the dragoons to pusillanimity, and advanced one step towards the prison, with all the turbulent mob following in their wake.

In this moment, Count Tilly rode forth towards them single-handed, merely lifting his sword and contracting his brow whilst he addressed them:

" Well, gentlemen of the burgher-guard, what are you advancing for, and what do you wish?"

The burghers shook their muskets, repeating their cry:

" Hurrah for Orange! Death to the traitors!"

" ' Hurrah for Orange!' all well and good!" replied Tilly, " although I certainly am more partial to happy faces than to gloomy ones. ' Death to the traitors!' as much of it as you like, as long as you show your wishes only by cries. But, as to putting them to death in good earnest, I am here to prevent that, and I shall prevent it."

Then, turning round to his men, he gave the word of command:

" Soldiers, ready!"

The troopers obeyed orders with a precision which immediately caused the burgher-guard and the people to fall back, in a degree of confusion which excited the smile of the cavalry officer.

" Halloa!" he exclaimed, with that bantering tone which is peculiar to men of his profession: " be easy, gentlemen, my soldiers will not fire a shot; but, on the other hand, you will not advance by one step towards the prison."

" And do you know, sir, that we have muskets?" roared the commandant of the burghers.

" I must know it, by Jove, you have made them glitter enough before my eyes; but I beg you to observe, also, that we on our side have pistols, that the pistol carries admirably to a distance of fifty yards, and that you are only twenty-five from us."

" Death to the traitors!" cried the exasperated burghers.

" Go along with you," growled the officer, " you always cry the same thing over again. It is very tiresome."

With this he took his post at the head of his troops, whilst the tumult grew fiercer and fiercer about the Buitenhof.

And yet the fuming crowd did not know, that at the very moment when they were tracking the scent of one of their victims, the other, as if hurrying to meet his fate, passed, at a distance of not more than a hundred yards, behind the groups of people and the dragoons, to betake himself to the Buitenhof.

John De Witte, indeed, had alighted from his coach with a servant, and quietly walked across the courtyard of the prison.

Mentioning his name to the turnkey, who, however, knew him, he said—

" Good morning, Gryphus,* I am coming to take away my brother, who, as you know, is condemned to exile, and to carry him out of the town."

Whereupon the jailer, a sort of bear, trained to lock and unlock the gates of the prison, had greeted him and admitted him into the building, the doors of which were immediately closed again.

Ten yards farther on, John De Witte met a lovely young girl, of about seventeen or eighteen, dressed in the national costume of the Frisian women,* who, with pretty demureness, dropped a curtsey to him. Chucking her under the chin, he said to her—

" Good morning, my good and fair Rosa; how is my brother?"

" Oh! Mynheer John, sir," the young girl replied, " I am not afraid of the harm which has been done to him. That's all over now."

" But what is it you are afraid of?"

" I am afraid of the harm which they are going to do to him."

" Oh! yes," said De Witte, " you mean to speak of the people down below, don't you?"

" Do you hear them?"

" They are indeed in a state of great excitement; but when they see us, perhaps they will grow calmer, as we have never done them anything but good."

" That's unfortunately no reason, except for the contrary,"* muttered the girl, as on an imperative sign from her father she withdrew.

" Indeed, child, what you say is only too true.'

Then, in pursuing his way, he said to himself—

" Here is a damsel who very likely does not know how to read, who, consequently, has never read anything; and yet, with one word, she has just told the whole history of the world."

And with the same calm mien, but more melancholy than he had been on entering the prison, the Grand Pensionary proceeded towards the cell of his brother.

CHAPTER TWO

The Two Brothers

As the fair Rosa, with foreboding doubt, had foretold, so it happened. Whilst John De Witte was climbing the narrow winding stairs which led to the prison of his brother Cornelius, the burghers did their best to have the troop of Tilly, which was in their way, removed.

Seeing this disposition, King Mob, who fully appreciated the laudable intentions of his own beloved militia, shouted most lustily—

" Hurrah for the burghers !"

As to Count Tilly, who was as prudent as he was firm, he began to parley with the burghers, under the protection of the cocked pistols of his dragoons, explaining to the valiant townsmen that his order from the States commanded him to guard the prison and its approaches with three companies.

" Wherefore such an order? Why guard the prison?" cried the Orangists.

" Stop," replied the Count; " there you at once ask me more than I can tell you. I was told: ' Guard the prison,' and I guard it. You, gentlemen, who are almost military men yourselves, you are aware that an order must never be gainsaid.

" But this order has been given to you that the traitors may be enabled to leave the town."

" Very possibly, as the traitors are condemned to exile," replied Tilly.

" But who has given this order ?"

" The States, by George !"

" The States are traitors."

" I don't know anything about that."

" And you are a traitor yourself !"

" I ?"

13

" Yes, you."

" Well, as to that, let us understand each other, gentlemen. Whom should I betray? The States? Why, I cannot betray them, whilst, being in their pay, I faithfully obey their orders."

As the Count was so indisputably in the right that it was impossible to argue against him, the mob answered only by redoubled clamour and horrible threats, to which the Count opposed the most perfect urbanity.

" Gentlemen," he said, " uncock your muskets; one of them may go off by accident, and if the shot chanced to wound one of my men, we should knock over a couple of hundreds of yours, for which we should, indeed, be very sorry, but you even more so; especially as such a thing is neither contemplated by you, nor by myself."

" If you did that," cried the burghers, " we should have a pop at you too."

" Of course you would; but suppose you killed every man Jack of us, those whom we should have killed would not, for all that, be less dead."

" Then leave the place to us, and you will perform the part of a good citizen."

" First of all," said the Count, " I am not a citizen, but an officer, which is a very different thing; and secondly, I am not a Hollander, but a Frenchman, which is more different still. I have to do with no one but the States, by whom I am paid; let me see an order from them to leave the place to you, and I shall only be too glad to wheel off in an instant, as I am confoundedly bored here."

" Yes, yes!" cried a hundred voices; the din of which was immediately swelled by five hundred others; " let us march to the Town Hall; let us go and see the deputies! Come along! Come along!"

" That's it," Tilly muttered between his teeth, as he saw the most violent among the crowd turning away; " go and ask for a meanness* at the Town Hall, and you will see whether they will grant it; go, my fine fellows, go!"

The worthy officer relied on the honour of the magistrates, who, on their side, relied on his honour as a soldier,

" I say, Captain!" the first lieutenant whispered into the ear of the Count, " I hope the deputies will give these madmen a flat refusal; but, after all, it would do no harm if they would send us some reinforcement."

In the meanwhile, John De Witte, whom we left climbing the stairs, after his conversation with the jailer Gryphus and his daughter Rosa, had reached the door of the cell, where, on a mattress, his brother Cornelius was resting, after having undergone the preparatory degrees of the torture. The sentence of banishment having been pronounced, there was no occasion for inflicting the torture extraordinary.*

Cornelius was stretched on his couch, with broken wrists and crushed fingers. He had not confessed a crime of which he was not guilty; and now, after three days of agony, he once more breathed freely, on being informed that the judges, from whom he had expected death, were only condemning him to exile.

Endowed with an iron frame and a stout heart, how would he have disappointed his enemies, if they could only have seen, in the dark cell of the Buitenhof, his pale face lit up by the smile of the martyr, who forgets the dross of this earth after having obtained a glimpse of the bright glory of Heaven.

The warden, indeed, had already recovered his full strength, much more owing to the force of his own strong will than to actual aid; and he was calculating how long the formalities of the law would still detain him in prison.

This was just at the very moment when the mingled shouts of the burgher-guard and of the mob were raging against the two brothers, and threatening Captain Tilly, who served as a rampart to them. This noise, which roared outside the walls of the prison, as the surf dashing against the rocks, now reached the ears of the prisoner.

But threatening as it sounded, Cornelius appeared not to deem it worth his while to inquire after its cause; nor did he get up to look out of the narrow grated window, which gave access to the light and to the noise of the world without.

He was so absorbed in his never-ceasing pain that it had almost become a habit with him. He felt with such delight the bonds, which connected his immortal being with his perishable frame, gradually loosening, that it seemed to him as if his spirit, freed from the trammels of the body, were hovering above it, like the expiring flame which rises from the half-extinguished embers.

He also thought of his brother; and whilst the latter was thus vividly present to his mind, the door opened, and John entered, hurrying to the bedside of the prisoner, who stretched out his broken limbs and his hands, tied up in bandages, towards that glorious brother, whom he now exceeded, not in services rendered to the country, but in the hatred which the Dutch bore him.

John tenderly kissed his brother on the forehead, and put his sore hands gently back on the mattress.

" Cornelius, my poor brother, you are suffering great pains, are you not?"

" I am suffering no longer, since I see you, my brother."

" Oh! my poor dear Cornelius, I feel most wretched to see you in such a state."

" And, indeed, I have thought more of you than of myself; and whilst they were torturing me, I never thought of uttering a complaint, except once, to say, ' Poor brother!' But now that you are here, let us forget all. You are coming to take me away, are you not?"

" I am."

" I am quite healed; help me to get up, and you shall see how well I can walk."

" You will not have to walk far, as I have my coach near the pond,* behind Tilly's dragoons."

" Tilly's dragoons! What are they near the pond for?"

" Well," said the Grand Pensionary, with a melancholy smile which was habitual to him, " the gentlemen at the Town Hall expect that the people of the Hague would like to see you depart, and there is some apprehension of a tumult."

" Of a tumult?" replied Cornelius, fixing his eyes on his perplexed brother; " a tumult?"

" Yes, Cornelius."

" Oh! that's what I heard just now," said the prisoner,

16

as if speaking to himself. Then, turning to his brother, he continued—

"Are there many persons down before the prison?"

"Yes, my brother, there are."

"But then, to come here to me——"

"Well?"

"How is it that they have allowed you to pass?"

"You know well that we are not very popular, Cornelius," said the Grand Pensionary, with gloomy bitterness. "I have made my way through all sorts of by-streets and alleys."

"You hid yourself, John?"

"I wished to reach you without loss of time, and I did what people will do in politics, or on sea when the wind is against them—I tacked."

In this moment the noise in the square below was heard to roar with increasing fury. Tilly was parleying with the burghers.

"Well, well," said Cornelius, "you are a very skilful pilot, John; but I doubt whether you will as safely guide your brother out of the Buitenhof in the midst of this gale, and through the raging surf of popular hatred, as you did the fleet of Van Tromp past the shoals of the Scheldt to Antwerp."*

"With the help of God, Cornelius, we'll at least try," answered John; "but, first of all, a word with you."

"Speak!"

The shouts began anew.

"Hark, hark!" continued Cornelius, "how angry these people are. Is it against you? or against me?"

"I should say it is against us both, Cornelius. I told you, my dear brother, that the Orange party, whilst assailing us with their absurd calumnies, have also made it a reproach against us that we have negotiated with France."

"What blockheads they are!"

"But, indeed, they reproach us with it."

"And yet, if these negotiations had been successful, they would have prevented the defeats of Rees, Orsay, Wesel, and Rheirberg;*the Rhine would not have been crossed, and Holland might still consider herself invincible in the midst of her marshes and canals."

" All this is quite true, my dear Cornelius, but still more certain it is, that if in this moment our correspondence with the Marquis de Louvois were discovered, skilful pilot as I am, I should not be able to save the frail barque which is to carry the brothers De Witte and their fortunes out of Holland. That correspondence, which might prove to honest people how dearly I love my country, and what sacrifices I have offered to make for its liberty and glory, would be ruin to us if it fell into the hands of the Orange party. I hope you have burnt the letters before you left Dort to join me at the Hague."

" My dear brother," Cornelius answered, " your correspondence with Marquis de Louvois affords ample proof of your having been of late the greatest, most generous, and most able citizen of the Seven United Provinces. I dote on the glory of my country; and particularly do I dote on your glory, John—I have taken good care not to burn that correspondence."

" Then we are lost, as far as this life is concerned," quietly said the Grand Pensionary, approaching the window.

" No, on the contrary, John; we shall at the same time save our lives and regain our popularity."

" But what have you done with these letters?"

" I have entrusted them to the care of Cornelius Van Baerle,* my godson, whom you know, and who lives at Dort."

" Poor honest Van Baerle! who knows so much, and yet thinks of nothing but of flowers and of God who made them. You have entrusted him with this fatal secret; it will be his ruin, poor soul!"

" His ruin?"

" Yes; for he will either be strong or he will be weak. If he is strong, he will, when he hears of what has happened to us, boast of our acquaintance; if he is weak, he will be afraid on account of his connection with us: if he is strong, he will betray the secret by his boldness; if he is weak, he will allow it to be forced from him. In either case he is lost,

18

and so are we. Let us, therefore, fly, fly, as long as it is still time."

Cornelius De Witte raising himself on his couch, and grasping the hand of his brother, who shuddered at the touch of the linen bandages, replied—

"Do not I know my godson? have not I been enabled to read every thought in Van Baerle's mind, and every sentiment in his heart? You ask whether he is strong or weak. He is neither the one nor the other; but that is not now the question. The principal point is, that he is sure not to divulge the secret, for the very good reason that he does not know it himself."

John turned round in surprise.

"You must know, my dear brother, that I have been trained in the school of that distinguished politician John De Witte; and I repeat to you, that Van Baerle is not aware of the nature and importance of the deposit which I have entrusted to him."

"Quick then," cried John, "as it is still time, let us convey to him directions to burn the parcel."

"Through whom?"

"Through my servant Craeke,* who was to have accompanied us on horseback, and who has entered the prison with me, to assist you downstairs."

"Consider well before having those precious documents burnt, John!"

"I consider, above all things, that the brothers De Witte must necessarily save their lives, to be able to save their character. If we are dead, who will defend us? Who will have fully understood our intentions?"

"You expect, then, that they would kill us, if those papers were found?"

John, without answering, pointed with his hand to the square, from whence, in that very moment, fierce shouts and savage yells made themselves heard.

"Yes, yes," said Cornelius, "I hear these shouts very plainly; but what is their meaning?"

John opened the window.

"Death to the traitors!" howled the populace.

" Do you hear now, Cornelius?"

" To the traitors! that means us!" said the prisoner, raising his eyes to Heaven and shrugging his shoulders.

" Yes, it means us," repeated John.

" Where is Craeke?"

" At the door of your cell, I suppose."

" Let him enter then."

John opened the door; the faithful servant was waiting on the threshold.

" Come in, Craeke, and mind well what my brother will tell you."

" No, John; it will not suffice to send a verbal message; unfortunately I shall be obliged to write."

" And why that?"

" Because Van Baerle will neither give up the parcel, nor burn it, without a special command to do so."

" But will you be able to write, poor old fellow?" John asked, with a look on the scorched and bruised hands of the unfortunate sufferer.

" If I had pen and ink you would soon see," said Cornelius.

" Here is a pencil, at any rate."

" Have you any paper, for they have left me nothing."

" Here, take this Bible, and tear out the fly leaf."

" Very well, that will do."

" But your writing will be illegible."

" Just leave me alone for that," said Cornelius. " The executioners have indeed pinched me badly enough, but my hand will not tremble once in tracing the few lines which are requisite."

And, really, Cornelius took the pencil and began to write, when through the white linen bandages drops of blood oozed out, which the pressure of the fingers against the pencil squeezed from the raw flesh.

A cold sweat stood on the brow of the Grand Pensionary. Cornelius wrote:

" MY DEAR GODSON—Burn the parcel which I have entrusted to you. Burn it without looking at it and without opening it, so that its contents may for ever remain unknown to yourself. Secrets of this description are death to those with whom they are deposited. Burn it, and you will have saved John and Cornelius De Witte.

"Farewell, and love me,

"CORNELIUS DE WITTE.

"*August* 20, 1672."

John, with tears in his eyes, wiped off a drop of the noble blood which had soiled the leaf; and, after having handed the dispatch to Craeke with a last direction, returned to Cornelius, who seemed overcome by intense pain, and near fainting.

"Now," said he, "when honest Craeke sounds his old coxswain's whistle, it will be a signal of his being clear of the crowd, and of his having reached the other side of the pond. And then it will be our turn to depart."

Five minutes had not elapsed before a long and shrill whistle was heard through the din and noise of the square of the Buitenhof.

John gratefully raised his eyes to Heaven.

"And now," said he, "let us be off, Cornelius."

CHAPTER THREE

The Pupil of John de Witte

WHILST THE clamour of the crowd in the square of the Buitenhof, which grew more and more menacing against the two brothers, determined John De Witte to hasten the departure of his brother Cornelius, a deputation of burghers had gone to the Town Hall to demand the withdrawal of Tilly's horse.

It was not far from the Buitenhof to Hoogstraat*(High Street); and a stranger, who since the beginning of this scene had watched all its incidents with intense interest, was seen to wend his way with, or rather in the wake of, the others towards the Town Hall, to hear, as soon as possible, the current news of the hour.

This stranger was a very young man, of scarcely twenty-two or three, with nothing about him that bespoke any great energy. He evidently had his good reasons for not making himself known, as he hid his face in a handkerchief of fine Frisian linen, with which he incessantly wiped his brow or his burning lips.

With an eye keen like that of a bird of prey, with a long aquiline nose, a finely-cut mouth, which he generally kept open, or rather, which was gaping like the edges of a wound; this man would have presented to Lavater,* if Lavater had lived at that time, a subject for physiognomical observations, which at the first blush would not have been very favourable to the person in question.

" What difference is there between the figure of the conqueror, and that of the pirate?"*said the ancients. The difference only between the eagle and the vulture: serenity or restlessness.

And, indeed, the sallow physiognomy, the thin and sickly body, and the prowling ways of the stranger, were the very type of a suspecting master, or an unquiet thief; and a police-officer would certainly have decided in favour of the latter supposition, on account of the great care which the mysterious person evidently took to hide himself.

He was plainly dressed, and apparently unarmed; his arm was lean but wiry; and his hands dry, but of aristocratic whiteness and delicacy, and he leaned on the shoulder of an officer, who, with his hand on his sword, had watched the scenes in the Buitenhof with eager curiosity, very natural in a military man, until his companion drew him away with him.

On arriving at the square of the Hoogstraat, the man with the sallow face pushed the other behind an open shutter, from which corner he himself began to survey the balcony of the Town Hall.

At the savage yells of the mob, the window of the Town Hall opened, and a man came forth to address the people.

" Who is that on the balcony?" asked the young man, glancing at the orator.

" It is the deputy Bowelt,"*replied the officer.

" What sort of man is he? Do you know anything of him?"

" An honest man; at least, I believe so, Monseigneur."

Hearing this character given of Bowelt the young man showed signs of such a strange disappointment and evident dissatisfaction that the officer could not but remark it, and therefore added—

" At least people say so, Monseigneur. I cannot say anything about it myself, as I have no personal acquaintance with Mynheer Bowelt."

" Well," the young man muttered half to himself and half to his companion, " let us wait, and we shall soon see."

The officer bowed his head in token of his assent, and was silent.

" If this Bowelt is an honest man," His Highness continued, " he will give to the demand of these furibund petitioners a very queer reception."

The nervous quiver of his hand, which moved on the shoulder of his companion, as the fingers of a player on the keys of a harpsichord, betrayed his burning impatience, so ill concealed at certain times, and particularly at that moment, under the icy and sombre expression of his face.

The chief of the deputation of the burghers was then heard addressing an interpellation to Mynheer Bowelt, whom he requested to let them know where the other deputies, his colleagues, were.

" Gentlemen," Bowelt repeated for the second time, " I assure you that in this moment I am here alone with Mynheer d'Asperen,* and I cannot take any resolution on my own responsibility."

" The order! we want the order!" cried several thousand voices.

Mynheer Bowelt wished to speak, but his words were not heard, and he was only seen moving his arms in all sorts of gestures, which plainly showed that he felt his position to be desperate. When, at last, he saw that he could not make himself heard, he turned round towards the open window, and called Mynheer d'Asperen.

The latter gentleman now made his appearance on the balcony, where he was saluted with shouts, even more energetic than those with which, ten minutes before, his colleague had been received.

This did not prevent him from undertaking the difficult task of haranguing the mob; but the mob preferred forcing the guard of the States—which, however, offered no resistance to the sovereign people—to listening to the speech of Mynheer d'Asperen.

" Now, then," the young man coolly remarked, whilst the crowd was rushing into the principal gate of the Town Hall, " it seems the question will be discussed indoors, Captain. Come along, and let us hear the debate."

" Oh, Monseigneur! Monseigneur! take care."

" Of what?"

" Among these deputies there are many who have had dealings with you; and it would be sufficient that one of them should recognise Your Highness."

" Yes, that I might be charged with having been the instigator of all this work; indeed, you are right," said the young man, blushing for a moment from regret of having betrayed so much eagerness. " From this place we shall see them return with or without the order for the withdrawal of the dragoons, and then we may judge which is greater, Mynheer Bowelt's honesty, or his courage."

" But," replied the officer, looking with astonishment at the personage whom he addressed as Monseigneur, " but Your Highness surely does not suppose for one instant that the deputies will order Tilly's horse to quit their post?"

" Why not?" the young man quietly retorted.

" Because doing so would simply be signing the death warrant of Cornelius and John De Witte."

" We shall see," His Highness replied, with the most perfect coolness; " God alone knows what is going on within the hearts of men."

The officer looked askance at the impassible figure of his companion, and grew pale; he was an honest man as well as a brave one.

From the spot where they stood, His Highness and his attendant heard the tumult and the heavy tramp of the crowd on the staircase of the Town Hall. The noise thereupon sounded through the windows of the hall, on the balcony of which Mynheers Bowelt and d'Asperen had presented themselves. These two gentlemen had retired into the building, very likely from fear of being forced over the balustrade by the pressure of the crowd.

After this, fluctuating shadows in tumultuous confusion were seen flitting to and fro across the windows: the council-hall was filling.

Suddenly the noise subsided; and as suddenly again it rose with redoubled intensity, and at last reached such a pitch that the old building shook to the very roof.

At length the living stream poured back through the galleries and stairs to the arched gateway, from which it was seen issuing like water from a spout.

At the head of the first group a man was flying rather than running, his face hideously distorted with Satanic glee: this man was the surgeon Tyckelaer.

" We have it! we have it!" he cried, brandishing a paper in the air.

" They have got the order!" muttered the officer in amazement.

" Well, then," His Highness quietly remarked, " now I know what to believe with regard to Mynheer Bowelt's honesty and courage: he has neither the one nor the other."

Then, looking with a steady glance after the crowd which was rushing along before him, he continued—

" Let us now go to the Buitenhof, Captain; I expect we shall see a very strange sight there."

The officer bowed, and, without making any reply, followed in the steps of his master.

There was an immense crowd in the square, and about the neighbourhood of the prison. But the dragoons of Tilly still kept it in check with the same success and with the same firmness.

It was not long before the Count heard the increasing din of the approaching multitude, the first ranks of which rushed on with the rapidity of a cataract.

At the same time he observed the paper which was waving above the surface of clenched fists and glittering arms.

" Halloa!" he said, rising in his stirrups and touching his lieutenant with the knob of his sword; " I really believe these rascals have got the order."

" Dastardly ruffians they are!" cried the lieutenant.

It was indeed the order, which the burgher-guard received with a roar of triumph. They immediately sallied forth, with lowered arms and fierce shouts to meet Count Tilly's dragoons.

But the Count was not the man to allow them to approach to within an inconvenient distance.

" Stop!" he cried, " stop, and keep off from my horse, or I shall give the word of command to advance."

" Here is the order," a hundred insolent voices answered at once.

He took it in amazement, cast a rapid glance on it, and said quite loud—

" Those who have signed this order are the real murderers of Cornelius De Witte. I would rather have my two hands cut off than have written one single letter of this infamous order."

And, pushing back with the hilt of his sword the man who wanted to take it from him, he added—

"Wait a minute, papers like this are of importance, and are to be kept."

Saying this, he folded up the document, and carefully put it into the pocket of his coat. Then, turning round towards his troop, he gave the word of command—

"Tilly's dragoons, wheel to the right!"

After this he added in an undertone, yet loud enough for his words to be not altogether lost to those about him—

"And now, ye butchers, do your work!"

A savage yell, in which all the keen hatred and ferocious triumph, rife in the precincts of the prison, simultaneously burst forth, and accompanied the departure of the dragoons, as they were quietly filing off.

The Count tarried behind, facing to the last the infuriated populace, which advanced at the same rate as the Count retired.

John De Witte, therefore, had by no means exaggerated the danger, when, assisting his brother in getting up, he hurried his departure. Cornelius, leaning on the arm of the ex-Grand Pensionary, descended the stairs which led to the court-yard. At the bottom of the staircase he found little Rosa, trembling all over.

"Oh! Mynheer John," she said, "what a misfortune!"

"What is it, my child?" asked De Witte.

"They say that they are gone to the Town Hall to fetch the order for Tilly's horse to withdraw."

"You do not say so!" replied John. "Indeed, my dear child, if the dragoons are off, we shall be in a very sad plight."

"I have some advice to give you," Rosa said, trembling even more violently than before.

"Well, let us hear what you have to say, my child. Why should not God speak by your mouth?"

"Now, then, Mynheer John, if I were in your place. I should not go out through the large street."

27

" And why so, as the dragoons of Tilly are still at their post?"

" Yes, but their order, as long as it is not revoked, enjoins them to stop before the prison."

" Undoubtedly."

" Have you got an order for them to accompany you out of town?"

" We have not."

" Well, then, in the very moment when you have passed the ranks of the dragoons, you will fall into the hands of the people."

" But the burgher-guard?"

" Alas! the burgher-guard are the most enraged of all."

" What are we to do, then?"

" If I were in your place, Mynheer John," the young girl timidly continued, " I should leave by the postern, which leads into a deserted by-lane, whilst all the people are waiting in the High Street to see you come out by the principal entrance. From thence I should try to reach the gate by which you intend to leave the town."

" But my brother is not able to walk," said John.

" I shall try," Cornelius said, with an expression of most sublime fortitude.

" But have you not got your carriage?" asked the girl.

" The carriage is down near the great entrance."

" Not so," she replied. " I considered your coachman to be a faithful man, and I told him to wait for you at the postern."

The two brothers looked first at each other and then at Rosa, with a glance full of the most tender gratitude.

" The question is now," said the Grand Pensionary, " whether Gryphus will open this door for us."

" Indeed he will do no such thing," said Rosa.

" Well, and how then?"

" I have foreseen his refusal, and just now, whilst he was talking from the window of the porter's lodge with a dragoon, I took away the key from his bunch."

" And you have got it?"

" Here it is, Mynheer John."

28

"My child," said Cornelius, "I have nothing to give you in exchange for the service you are rendering us, but the Bible which you will find in my room: it is the last gift of an honest man; I hope it will bring you good luck."

"I thank you, Master Cornelius, it shall never leave me," replied Rosa.

And then, with a sigh, she said to herself, "What a pity that I do not know how to read."

"The shouts and cries are growing louder and louder," said John, "there is not a moment to be lost."

"Come along, gentlemen," said the girl, who now led the two brothers through an inner lobby to the back of the prison. Guided by her, they descended a staircase of about a dozen steps; traversed a small courtyard, which was surrounded by castellated walls; and the arched door having been opened for them by Rosa, they emerged into a lonely street where their carriage was ready to receive them.

"Quick, quick, my masters, do you hear them?" cried the coachman in a deadly fright.

Yet, after having made Cornelius get into the carriage first, the Grand Pensionary turned round towards the girl, to whom he said—

"Good-bye, my child; words could never express our gratitude. God will reward you for having saved the lives of two men."

Rosa took the hand which John De Witte proffered to her, and kissed it with every show of respect.

"Go—for Heaven's sake go," she said; "it seems they are going to force the gate."

John De Witte hastily got in, sat himself down by the side of his brother, and, fastening the apron of the carriage, called out to the coachman—

"To the Tol-Hek!"

The Tol-Hek was the iron gate leading to the harbour of Schevening, in which a small vessel was waiting for the two brothers.

The carriage drove off with the fugitives at the full speed of a pair of spirited Flemish horses. Rosa followed them with her eyes, until they turned the corner of the street, upon which, closing the door after her, she went back and threw the key into a well.

The noise which had made Rosa suppose that the people were forcing the prison door was indeed owing to the mob battering against it after the square had been left by the military.

Solid as the gate was, and although Gryphus, to do him justice, stoutly enough refused to open it; yet it could not evidently resist much longer, and the jailer, growing very pale, put to himself the question, whether it would not be better to open the door than to allow it to be forced: when he felt someone gently pulling his coat.

He turned round and saw Rosa.

" Do you hear these madmen?" he said.

" I hear them so well, my father, that in your place——"

" You would open the door?"

" No, I should allow it to be forced."

" But they will kill me!"

" Yes, if they see you."

" How shall they not see me?"

" Hide yourself."

" Where?"

" In the secret dungeon."

" But you, my child?"

" I shall get into it with you. We shall lock the door, and when they have left the prison, we shall again come forth from our hiding-place."

" Zounds, you are right there!" cried Gryphus; " it's surprising how much sense there is in such a little head!"

Then, as the gate began to give way amidst the triumphant shouts of the mob, she opened a little trap-door, and said—

" Come along, come along, father."

" But our prisoners?"

" God will watch over them, and I shall watch over you."

Gryphus followed his daughter, and the trap-door closed over his head just as the broken gate gave admittance to the populace.

The dungeon where Rosa had induced her father to hide

himself, and where for the present we must leave the two, offered to them a perfectly safe retreat, being known only to those in power, who used to place there important prisoners of state, to guard against a rescue, or a revolt.

The people rushed into the prison, with the cry of—

" Death to the traitors! To the gallows with Cornelius De Witte! Death! Death!"

CHAPTER FOUR

Popular Justice

THE young man, with his hat still slouched over his eyes, still leaning on the arm of the officer, and still wiping from time to time his brow with his handkerchief, was watching in a corner of the Buitenhof, in the shade of the overhanging weather-board of a closed shop, the doings of the infuriated mob, a spectacle which seemed to draw near its catastrophe.

" Indeed," said he to the officer, " indeed, I think you were right, Van Deken; the order which the deputies have signed is truly the death-warrant of Master Cornelius. Do you hear these people? They certainly bear a sad grudge to the two De Wittes."

" In truth," replied the officer, " I never heard such shouts."

" They seem to have found out the cell of the man. Look, look, is not that the window of the cell where Cornelius was locked up?"

A man had seized with both hands and was shaking the iron bars of the window in the room which Cornelius had left only ten minutes before.

" Halloa, halloa," the man called out, " he is gone."

" How is that? gone?" asked those of the mob who had not been able to get into the prison, crowded as it was with the mass of intruders.

" Gone, gone," repeated the man in a rage, " the bird has flown."

" What does this man say?" asked High Highness, growing quite pale.

" Oh! Monseigneur, he says a thing which would be very fortunate if it should turn out true."

" Certainly, it would be fortunate if it were true," said the young man; " unfortunately, it cannot be true."

" However, look——" said the officer.

And indeed, some more faces, furious and contorted with rage, showed themselves at the windows, crying—

" Escaped, gone, they have helped them off!"

And the people in the street repeated the fearful imprecations:

" Escaped! gone! Let us run after them, and pursue them!"

" Monseigneur, it seems that Mynheer Cornelius has really escaped," said the officer.

" Yes, from prison perhaps, but not from the town; you will see, Van Deken, that the poor fellow will find the gate closed against him, which he hoped to find open."

" Has an order been given to close the town gates, Monseigneur?"

" No; at least I do not think so; who could have given such an order?"

" Indeed, but what makes your Highness suppose——?"

" There are fatalities," Monseigneur replied, in an off-hand manner; " and the greatest men have sometimes fallen victims to such fatalities."

At these words the officer felt his blood run cold, as somehow or other he was convinced that the prisoner was lost.

At this moment the roar of the multitude broke forth like thunder, for it was now quite certain that Cornelius De Witte was no longer in the prison.

Cornelius and John, after driving along the pond, had taken the large street*which leads to the Tol-Hek, giving directions to the coachman to slacken his pace, in order not to excite any suspicion.

But when, on having proceeded half-way down that street, the man felt that he had left the prison and death behind, and before him there was life and liberty, he neglected every precaution, and set his horses off at a gallop.

All at once he stopped.

" What is the matter?" asked John, putting his head out of the coach window.

" Oh! my masters," cried the coachman, " it is——"

Terror choked the voice of the honest fellow.

" Well, say what you have to say!" urged the Grand Pensionary.

" The gate is closed, that's what it is."

" How is this? It is not usual to close the gate by day."

" Just look!"

John De Witte leaned out of the window, and indeed saw that the man was right.

" Never mind, but drive on," said John; " I have with me the order for the commutation of the punishment;* the gatekeeper will let us through."

The carriage moved along, but it was evident that the driver was no longer urging his horses with the same degree of confidence.

Moreover, as John De Witte put his head out of the carriage window he was seen and recognised by a brewer, who, being behind his companions, was just shutting his door in all haste to join them at the Buitenhof. He uttered a cry of surprise, and ran after two other men before him, whom he overtook about a hundred yards farther on, and told them what he had seen. The three men then stopped, looking after the carriage, being, however, not yet quite sure as to whom it contained.

The carriage, in the meanwhile, arrived at the Tol-Hek.

" Open!" cried the coachman.

" Open!" echoed the gatekeeper, from the threshold of his lodge; " it's all very well to say, ' Open,' but what am I to do it with?"

" With the key, to be sure!" said the coachman.

" With the key! Oh, yes! but if you have not got it?"

" How is that? Have not you got the key?" asked the coachman.

" No, I haven't."

" What has become of it?"

" Well, they have taken it from me."

" Who?"

" Some one, I dare say, who had a mind that no one should leave the town."

34

" My good man," said the Grand Pensionary, putting out his head from the window, and risking all for gaining all; "my good man, it is for me, John De Witte, and for my brother Cornelius, whom I am taking away into exile."

" Oh! Mynheer De Witte, I am indeed very much grieved," said the gatekeeper, rushing towards the carriage; " but, upon my sacred word, the key has been taken from me."

" When?"

" This morning."

" By whom?"

" By a pale and thin young man, of about twenty-two."

" And wherefore did you give it up to him?"

" Because he showed me an order, signed and sealed."

" By whom?"

" By the gentlemen of the Town Hall."

" Well, then," said Cornelius calmly, " our doom seems to be fixed."

" Do you know whether the same precaution has been taken at the other gates?"

" I do not."

" Now then," said John to the coachman, " God commands man to do all that is in his power to preserve his life; go, and drive to another gate."

And whilst the servant was turning round the vehicle, the Grand Pensionary said to the gatekeeper—

" Take our thanks for your good intentions; the will must count for the deed; you had the will to save us, and, in the eyes of the Lord, it is as if you had succeeded in doing so."

" Alas!" said the gatekeeper, " do you see down there?"

" Drive at a gallop through that group," John called out to the coachman, " and take the street on the left; it is our only chance."

The group which John alluded to had, for its nucleus, those three men whom we left looking after the carriage, and who, in the meanwhile, had been joined by seven or eight others.

These new-comers evidently meant mischief with regard to the carriage.

When they saw the horses galloping down upon them, they placed themselves across the street, brandishing cudgels in their hands, and calling out—

" Stop! stop!"

The coachman, on his side, lashed his horses into increased speed, until the coach and the men encountered.

The brothers De Witte, inclosed within the body of the carriage, were not able to see anything; but they felt a severe shock, occasioned by the rearing of the horses. The whole vehicle for a moment shook and stopped; but immediately after, passing over something round and elastic, which seemed to be the body of a prostrate man, set off again amidst a volley of the fiercest oaths.

" Alas!" said Cornelius, " I am afraid we have hurt some one."

" Gallop! gallop!" called John. But, notwithstanding this order, the coachman suddenly came to a stop.

" Now, then, what is the matter again?" asked John.

" Look there!" said the coachman.

John looked. The whole mass of the populace from the Buitenhof appeared at the extremity of the street along which the carriage was to proceed, and its stream moved roaring and rapid, as if lashed on by a hurricane.

" Stop, and get off,' said John to the coachman; " it is useless to go any farther: we are lost!"

" Here they are! here they are!" five hundred voices were crying at the same time.

" Yes, here they are, the traitors, the murderers, the assassins!" answered the men who were running after the carriage, to the people who were coming to meet it. The former carried in their arms the bruised body of one of their companions, who, trying to seize the reins of the horses, had been trodden down by them.

This was the object over which the two brothers had felt their carriage pass.

The coachman stopped, but, however strongly his master urged him, he refused to get off and save himself.

In an instant the carriage was hemmed in between those who followed and those who met it. It rose above the mass of moving heads like a floating island. But in another instant it came to a dead stop. A blacksmith had, with his hammer, struck down one of the horses, which fell in the traces.

At this moment the shutter of a window opened, and disclosed the sallow face and the dark eyes of the young man, who with intense interest watched the scene which was preparing.

Behind him appeared the head of the officer, almost as pale as himself.

" Good Heavens, Monseigneur, what is going on there?" whispered the officer.

" Something very terrible, to a certainty," replied the other.

" Don't you see, Monseigneur, they are dragging the Grand Pensionary from the carriage, they strike him, they tear him to pieces."

" Indeed, these people must certainly be prompted by a most violent indignation," said the young man, with the same impassible tone which he had preserved all along.

" And here is Cornelius, whom they now likewise drag out of the carriage—Cornelius, who is already quite broken and mangled by the torture. Only look, look!"

" Indeed, it is Cornelius, and no mistake."

The officer uttered a feeble cry, and turned his head away; the brother of the Grand Pensionary, before having set foot on the ground, whilst still on the bottom step of the carriage, was struck down with an iron bar which broke his skull. He rose once more, but immediately fell again.

Some fellows then seized him by the feet, and dragged him into the crowd, into the middle of which one might have followed his bloody track, and he was soon closed in among the savage yells of malignant exultation.

The young man—a thing which would have been thought impossible—grew even paler than before, and his eyes were for a moment veiled behind the lids.

The officer saw this sign of compassion, and, wishing to avail himself of the softened tone of his feelings, continued—

" Come, come, Monseigneur, for here they are also going to murder the Grand Pensionary."

But the young man had already opened his eyes again.

" To be sure," he said. " These people are really implacable. It does no one good to offend them."

" Monseigneur," said the officer, " could not one save this poor man, who has been your Highness's instructor? If there be a means, name it, and if I should perish in the attempt——"

William of Orange—for he it was*—knit his brows in a very forbidding manner, restrained the glance of gloomy malice which glistened in his half-closed eye, and answered—

" Captain Van Deken, I request you to go and look after my troops, that they may be armed for any emergency."

" But am I to leave your Highness here, alone, in the presence of all these murderers?"

" Go, and don't you trouble yourself about me more than I do myself," the Prince gruffly replied.

The officer started off with a speed which was much less owing to his sense of military obedience than to his pleasure at being relieved from the necessity of witnessing the shocking spectacle of the murder of the other brother.

He had scarcely left the room, when John—who with an almost superhuman effort had reached the stone steps of a house, nearly opposite that where his former pupil concealed himself—began to stagger under the blows which were inflicted on him from all sides, calling out—

" My brother—where is my brother?"

One of the ruffians knocked off his hat with a blow of his clenched fist.

Another showed to him his bloody hands; for this fellow had ripped open Cornelius and disembowelled him and was now hastening to the spot in order not to lose the opportunity of serving the Grand Pensionary in the same manner, whilst they were dragging the dead body of Cornelius to the gibbet.

John uttered a cry of agony and grief, and put one of his hands before his eyes.

" Oh! you close your eyes, do you?" said one of the soldiers of the burgher-guard; " well, I shall open them for you."

And saying this, he stabbed him with his pike in the face, and the blood spurted forth.

" My brother!" cried John De Witte, trying to see through the stream of blood which blinded him, what had become of Cornelius; " my brother, my brother!"

" Go, and run after him!" bellowed another murderer, putting his musket to his temples and pulling the trigger.

But the gun did not go off.

The fellow then turned his musket round, and, taking it by the barrel with both hands, struck John De Witte down with the butt-end. John staggered, and fell down at his feet, but raising himself, with a last effort, he once more called out—

" My brother!" with a voice so full of anguish, that the young man opposite closed the shutter.

There remained little more to see; a third murderer fired a pistol with the muzzle to his face; and as this time the shot took effect, blowing out his brains, John De Witte fell, to rise no more.

On this, every one of the miscreants, emboldened by his fall, wanted to fire his gun at him, or strike him with blows of the sledge-hammer, or stab him with knife or sword; every one wanted to draw a drop of blood from the fallen hero, and tear off a shred from his garments.

And after having mangled, and torn, and completely stripped the two brothers, the mob dragged their naked and bloody bodies to an extemporised gibbet, where amateur executioners hung them up by the feet.

Then came the most dastardly scoundrels of all, who, not having dared to strike the living flesh, cut the dead in pieces, and then went about in the town selling small slices of the bodies of John and Cornelius at ten sous a piece.

We cannot take upon ourselves to say whether, through the almost imperceptible clink of the shutter, the young man witnessed the conclusion of this shocking scene; but at the very moment when they were hanging the two martyrs on the gibbet, he passed through the terrible mob; which was too much absorbed in the task, so grateful to its taste, to take any notice of him; and thus he reached unobserved the Tol-Hek, which was still closed.

" Ah! sir," said the gatekeeper, " do you bring me the key?"

" Yes, my man, here it is."

" It is most unfortunate that you did not bring me that key only one-quarter of an hour sooner," said the gate-keeper, with a sigh.

" And why that?" asked the other.

" Because I might have opened the gate to Mynheers De Witte; whereas, finding the gate locked, they were obliged to retrace their steps."

" Gate! gate!" cried a voice which seemed to be that of a man in a hurry.

The Prince, turning round, observed Captain Van Deken.

" Is that you, Captain?" he said. " You are not yet out of the Hague? This is executing my orders very slowly."

" Monseigneur," replied the Captain, " this is the third gate at which I have presented myself; the two others were closed."

" Well, this good man will open this one for you; do it, my friend."

The last words were addressed to the gatekeeper, who stood quite thunderstruck on hearing Captain Van Deken addressing by the title of Monsiegneur this pale young man, to whom he himself had spoken in such a familiar way.

As it were, to make up for his fault, he hastened to open the gate, which swung creaking on its hinges.

" Will Monseigneur avail himself of my horse?" asked the Captain.

" I thank you, Captain, I shall use my own steed, which is waiting for me close at hand."

And, taking from his pocket a golden whistle, such as was generally used at that time for summoning the servants, he sounded it with a shrill and prolonged call, on which an equerry on horseback speedily made his appearance, leading another horse by the bridle.

William, without touching the stirrup, vaulted into the saddle of the led horse, and, setting his spurs into its flanks, started off for the Leyden road.* Having reached it, he turned round and beckoned to the Captain, who was far behind, to ride by his side.

" Do you know," he then said, without stopping, " that those rascals have killed John De Witte as well as his brother?"

" Alas! Monseigneur," the Captain answered sadly. " I should like it much better if these two difficulties were still in your Highness's way of becoming *de facto* Stadtholder of Holland."

" Certainly, it would have been better," said William, " if what did happen had not happened. But it cannot be helped now, and we have had nothing to do with it. Let us push on, Captain, that we may arrive at Alphen before the message which the States-General are sure to send to me to the camp."

The Captain bowed, allowed the Prince to ride ahead, and, for the remainder of the journey, kept at the same respectful distance as he had done before His Highness called him to his side.

" How I should wish," William of Orange malignantly muttered to himself, with a dark frown and setting the spurs to his horse, " to see the figure which Louis will cut when he is apprised of the manner in which his dear friends De Witte have been served!"*

CHAPTER FIVE

The Tulip-Fancier and His Neighbour

WHILST THE burghers of the Hague were tearing in pieces the bodies of John and Cornelius De Witte, and whilst William of Orange, after having made sure that his two antagonists were really dead, was galloping on the Leyden road, followed by Captain Van Deken, whom he found a little too compassionate to honour him any longer with his confidence, Craeke, the faithful servant, mounted on a good horse, and little suspecting what terrible events had taken place since his departure, proceeded along the high road lined with trees, until he was clear of the town and the neighbouring villages.

Being once safe, he, with a view of avoiding suspicion, left his horse at a livery stable, and, quietly continuing his journey on the canal-boats to Dort,* soon descried that cheerful city, at the foot of a hill dotted with windmills. He saw the fine red brick houses, mortared in white lines, standing on the edge of the water, and their balconies, open towards the river, decked out with silk tapestry, embroidered with gold flowers, the wonderful manufacture of India and China; and near these brilliant stuffs, large lines set to catch the voracious eels, which are attracted towards the houses by the garbage thrown every day from the kitchens into the river.

Craeke, standing on the deck of the boat, saw across the moving sails of the windmills, on the slope of the hill, the red and pink house which was the goal of his errand. The outlines of its roof were merging in the yellow foliage of a curtain of poplar trees, the whole habitation having for background a dark grove of gigantic elms. The mansion was situated in such a way that the sun, falling on it as into a funnel, dried up, warmed, and fertilised the mist which the verdant screen could not prevent the river wind from carrying there every morning and evening.

Having disembarked unobserved among the usual bustle of the city, Craeke at once directed his steps towards the house which we have just described, and which—white, trim, and tidy, even more cleanly scoured and more carefully waxed in the hidden corners than in the places which were exposed to view—inclosed a truly happy mortal.

This happy mortal, *rara avis*,* was Doctor Van Baerle, the godson of Cornelius De Witt. He had inhabited the same house ever since his childhood; for it was the house in which his father and grandfather, old-established princely merchants of the princely city of Dort, were born.

Mynheer Van Baerle, the father, had amassed, in the Indian trade, three or four hundred thousand guilders, which Mynheer Van Baerle, the son, at the death of his dear and worthy parents, found still quite new, although one set of them bore the date of coinage of 1640, and the other that of 1610, a fact which proved that they were guilders of Van Baerle the father, and of Van Baerle the grandfather; but we will inform the reader at once, that these three or four hundred thousand guilders were only the pocket money, or a sort of purse,* for Cornelius Van Baerle, the hero of this story, as his landed property in the province yielded him an income of about ten thousand guilders a year.

When the worthy citizen, the father of Cornelius, passed from time into eternity, three months after having buried his wife, who seemed to have departed first to smooth for him the path of death as she had smoothed for him the path of life, he said to his son, as he embraced him for the last time—

" Eat, drink, and spend your money, if you wish to know what life really is; for as to toiling from morn to evening on a wooden stool, or a leathern chair, in a counting-house or a laboratory, that certainly is not living. Your time to die will also come; and if you are not then so fortunate as to have a son, you will let my name grow extinct, and my guilders, which no one has ever fingered but my father,

43

myself and the coiner, will have the surprise of passing to an unknown master. And least of all imitate the example of your godfather Cornelius De Witt, who has plunged into politics, the most ungrateful of all careers, and who will certainly come to an untimely end."

Having given utterance to this paternal advice, the worthy Mynheer Van Baerle died, to the intense grief of his son Cornelius, who cared very little for the guilders, and very much for his father.

Cornelius, then, remained alone in his large house. In vain his godfather offered to him a place in the public service; in vain did he try to give him a taste for glory. Cornelius Van Baerle, who was present in De Ruyter's flagship,* *The Seven Provinces*, at the battle of Southwold Bay, only calculated, after the fight was over, how much time a man, who likes to shut himself up within his own thoughts, is obliged to waste in closing his eyes and stopping his ears, whilst his fellow-creatures indulge in the pleasures of shooting at each other with cannon-balls. He therefore bade farewell to De Ruyter, to his godfather, and to glory; kissed the hands of the Grand Pensionary, for whom he felt a profound veneration, and retired to his house at Dort, where he possessed every element of what alone was happiness to him.

He studied plants and insects, collected and classified the flora of all the Dutch islands, arranged the whole entomology of the province, on which he wrote a treatise,* with plates drawn by his own hands; and at last, being at a loss what to do with his time, and especially with his money, which went on accumulating at a most alarming rate, he took it into his head to select for himself, from all the follies of his country and of his age, one of the most elegant and expensive—he became a tulip-fancier.

It was the time when the Dutch and the Portuguese, rivalling each other in this branch of horticulture, had begun to idolise and almost worship that flower, which originally had come from the East.*

Soon people from Dort to Mons began to talk of Mynheer Van Baerle's tulips; and his beds, pits, drying-rooms, and drawers of bulbs were visited, as the galleries and libraries of Alexandria* were by illustrious Roman travellers.

Van Baerle began by expending his yearly revenue in laying the ground-work of his collection, after which he broke in upon his new guilders to bring it to perfection. His exertions, indeed, were crowned with a most magnificent result: he produced three new tulips, which he called the "Jane," after his mother; the "Van Baerle," after his father; and the "Cornelius," after his godfather; the other names have escaped us, but the fanciers will be sure to find them in the catalogues of the times.*

In the beginning of the year 1672, Cornelius De Witte came to Dort for three months,* to live at his old family mansion; for not only was he born in that city, but his family had been resident there for centuries.

Cornelius, at that period, as William of Orange said, began to enjoy the most perfect unpopularity. To his fellow citizens, the good burghers of Dort, however, he did not appear in the light of a criminal who deserved to be hung.

It is true they did not particularly like his somewhat too austere republicanism, but they were proud of his valour; and when he made his entrance into their town, the cup of honour was offered to him, readily enough, in the name of the city.

After having thanked his fellow-citizens, Cornelius proceeded to his old paternal house, and gave directions for some repairs which he wished to have executed before the arrival of his wife and children; and thence he wended his way to the house of his godson, who, perhaps, was the only person in Dort as yet unacquainted with the presence of Cornelius in the town.

In the same degree as Cornelius De Witte had excited the hatred of the people by sowing those evil seeds which are called political passions, Van Baerle had gained the affections of his fellow-citizens by completely shunning the pursuit of politics, absorbed as he was in the peaceful pursuit of cultivating tulips.

Van Baerle was truly beloved by his servants and

labourers; nor had he any conception that there was in this world a man who wished ill to another.

And yet it must be said, to the disgrace of mankind, that Cornelius Van Baerle, without being aware of the fact, had a much more ferocious, fierce, and implacable enemy than the Grand Pensionary and his brother had among the Orange party.

At the time when Cornelius Van Baerle began to devote himself to tulip-growing, expending on this hobby his yearly revenue and the guilders of his father, there was at Dort, living next door to him, a citizen of the name of Isaac Boxtel,* who, from the age when he was able to think for himself, had indulged the same fancy, and who was in ecstasies at the mere mention of the word tulips.*

Boxtel had not the good fortune of being rich like Van Baerle. He had, therefore, with great care and patience, and by dint of strenuous exertions, laid out, near his house at Dort, a garden fit for the culture of his cherished flower; he had mixed the soil according to the most approved prescriptions, and given to his hotbeds just as much heat and fresh air as the strictest rules of horticulture exact.

Isaac knew the temperature of his frames to the twentieth part of a degree. He knew the strength of the current of air, and tempered it so as to adapt it to the wave of the stems of his flowers. His productions also began to meet with the favour of the public. They were beautiful; nay, distinguished. Several fanciers had come to see Boxtel's tulips. He had even started a tulip* which bore his name, and which, after having travelled all through France, had found its way into Spain, and penetrated as far as Portugal; and the king, Don Alphonso VI.,* who, being expelled from Lisbon, retired to the Island of Terceira, where he amused himself, not, like the great Condé, with watering his carnations, but with growing tulips, had, on seeing the Boxtel tulip, exclaimed, " Not so bad, by any means!"

All at once Cornelius Van Baerle, who, after all his learned pursuits, had been seized with the tulipomania, made some changes in his house at Dort, which, as we have stated, was next door to that of Boxtel. He raised a certain building in his courtyard by a storey, which, shutting out the sun, took half a degree of warmth from Boxtel's garden, and, on the other hand, added half a degree of cold in winter; not to mention that it cut the wind, and disturbed all the horticultural calculations and arrangements of his neighbour.

After all, this mishap appeared to Boxtel of no great consequence. Van Baerle was but a painter, a sort of fool who tried to reproduce, and disfigure on canvas, the wonders of nature. The painter, he thought, had raised his studio by a storey to get better light, and thus he had only been in the right. Mynheer Van Baerle was a painter, as Mynheer Boxtel was a tulip-grower; he wanted somewhat more sun for his paintings, and he took half a degree from his neighbour's tulips.

The law was for Van Baerle, and Boxtel had to abide by it.

Besides which, Isaac had made the discovery that too much sun was injurious to tulips, and that this flower grew quicker, and had a better colouring, with the temperature warmth of morning than with the powerful heat of the midday sun. He, therefore, felt amost grateful to Cornelius Van Baerle for having given him a screen gratis.

Maybe this was not quite in accordance with the true state of things in general, and of Isaac Boxtel's feelings in particular. It is certainly astonishing what rich comfort great minds, in the midst of momentous catastrophes, will derive from the consolations of philosophy.

But, alas! what was the agony of the unfortunate Boxtel on seeing the windows of the new storey set out with bulbs and seedlings of tulips for the border, and tulips in pots; in short, with everything pertaining to the pursuits of a tulip-fancier.

There were bundles of labels, cupboards, and drawers with compartments, and wire-guards for the cupboards, to allow free access to the air whilst keeping out slugs, mice, dormice, and rats, all of them very curious fanciers of tulips at two thousand francs a bulb.

Boxtel was quite amazed when he saw all this apparatus,

but he was not as yet aware of the full extent of his misfortune. Van Baerle was known to be fond of everything that pleases the eye. He studied nature in all her aspects for the benefit of his paintings, which were as minutely finished as those of Gerard Dow, his master, and of Mieris,* his friend. Was it not possible, that, having to paint the interior of a tulip-grower's, he had collected in his new studios all the accessories of decoration.

Yet, although thus consoling himself with illusory suppositions, Boxtel was not able to resist the burning curiosity which was devouring him. In the evening, therefore, he placed a ladder against the partition-wall between their gardens, and, looking into that of his neighbour Van Baerle, he convinced himself that the soil of a large square bed, which had formerly been occupied by different plants, was removed, and the ground disposed in beds of loam mixed with river mud (a combination which is particularly favourable to the tulip), and the whole surrounded by a border of turf to keep the soil in its place. Besides this, sufficient shade to temper the noon-day heat; aspect SSW.; water in abundant supply, and at hand; in short, every requirement to ensure not only success but also progress. There could not be a doubt but that Van Baerle had become a tulip-grower.

Boxtel at once pictured to himself this learned man, with a capital of four hundred thousand, and a yearly income of ten thousand guilders, devoting all his intellectual and financial resources to the cultivation of the tulip. He foresaw his neighbour's success, and he felt such a pang at the mere idea of this success, that his hands dropped powerless, his knees trembled, and he fell in despair from the ladder.

And thus it was not for the sake of painted tulips, but for real ones, that Van Baerle took from him half a degree of warmth. And thus Van Baerle was to have the most admirably fitted aspect, and, besides, a large, airy, and well-ventilated chamber, where to preserve his bulbs and seedlings; whilst he, Boxtel, had been obliged to give up for this purpose his bedroom, and, lest his sleeping in the same apartment might injure his bulbs and seedlings, had taken up his abode in a miserable garret.

Boxtel, then, was to have next door to him a rival and successful competitor; and his rival, instead of being some unknown, obscure gardener, was the godson of Mynheer Cornelius De Witte; that is to say, a celebrity.

Boxtel, as the reader may see, was not possessed of the spirit of Porus,* who, on being conquered by Alexander,* consoled himself with the celebrity of his conqueror.

And how if Van Baerle produced a new tulip, and named it the John De Witte, after having named one the Cornelius? It was indeed enough to choke honest Isaac with rage.

Thus Boxtel, with jealous foreboding, became the prophet of his own misfortune. And, after having made this melancholy discovery, he passed the most wretched night imaginable.

CHAPTER SIX

The Hatred of a Tulip-Fancier

FROM THAT moment Boxtel's interest in tulips was no longer a stimulus to his exertions, but a deadening anxiety. Henceforth all his thoughts ran only upon the injury which his neighbour would cause him, and thus his favourite occupation was changed into a constant source of misery to him.

Van Baerle, as may easily be imagined, had no sooner begun to apply his natural ingenuity to his new fancy than he succeeded in growing the finest tulips. Indeed, he knew better than anyone else at Haarlem* or Leyden—the two towns which boast the best soil and the most congenial climate—how to vary the colours, to modify the shape, and to produce new species.

Mynheer Van Baerle and his tulips, therefore, were in the mouth of everybody; so much so, that Boxtel's name disappeared for ever from the list of the notable tulip-growers in Holland, and those of Dort were now represented by Cornelius Van Baerle, the modest and inoffensive savant.

Engaging, heart and soul, in his pursuits of sowing, planting, and gathering, Van Baerle, caressed by the whole fraternity of tulip-growers in Europe, entertained not the least suspicion that there was at his very door a pretender whose throne he had usurped.

He went on in his career, and consequently in his triumphs; and, in the course of two years, he covered his borders with such marvellous productions, as no mortal man, following in the tracks of the Creator, except, perhaps, Shakespeare and Rubens, have equalled in point of numbers.

And also, if Dante had wished for a new type to be

added to his characters of the Inferno, he might have chosen Boxtel during the period of Van Baerle's successes. Whilst Cornelius was weeding, manuring, watering his beds, whilst, kneeling on the turf-border, he analysed every being of the flowering tulips, and meditated on the modifications which might be effected by crosses of colour or otherwise—Boxtel, concealed behind a small sycamore which he had trained at the top of the partition wall in the shape of a fan, watched, with his eyes starting from their sockets, and with foaming mouth, every step and every gesture of his neighbour; and, whenever he thought he saw him look happy, or descried a smile on his lips, or a flash of contentment glistening in his eyes, he poured out towards him such a volley of maledictions and furious threats as to make it indeed a matter of wonder that this venomous breath of envy and hatred did not carry a blight on the innocent flowers which had excited it.

When the evil spirit has once taken hold of the heart of man, it urges him on without letting him stop. Thus Boxtel soon was no longer content with seeing Van Baerle. He wanted to see his flowers too; he had the feelings of an artist; the masterpiece of a rival engrossed his interest.

He therefore bought a telescope, which enable him to watch, as accurately as did the owner himself, every progressive development of the flower, from the moment when in the first year, its pale seed-leaf begins to peep from under the ground, to that glorious one when, after five years, its petals at last reveal the hidden treasures of its chalice. How often had the miserable jealous man to observe, in Van Baerle's beds, tulips which dazzled him by their beauty, and almost choked him by their perfection.

And then, after the first blush of the admiration which he could not help feeling, he began to be tortured by the pangs of envy, by that slow fever which creeps over the heart and changes it into a nest of vipers, each devouring the other, and ever born anew. How often did Boxtel, in the midst of tortures which no pen is able fully to describe —how often did he feel an inclination to jump down into

the garden, during the night, to destroy the plants, to tear
the bulbs with his teeth, and to sacrifice to his wrath the
owner himself, if he should venture to stand up for the
defence of his tulips.

But to kill a tulip was a horrible crime in the eyes of a
genuine tulip-fancier; as to killing a man, it would not
have mattered so very much.

Yet Van Baerle made such progress in the noble science
of growing tulips, which he seemed to master with the true
instinct of genius, that Boxtel at last was maddened to such
a degree as to think of throwing stones and sticks into the
flower-stands of his neighbour. But remembering that he
would be sure to be found out, and that he would not only
be punished by law, but also dishonoured for ever in the
face of all the tulip growers of Europe, he had recourse to
stratagem; and, to gratify his hatred, tried to devise a plan
by means of which he might gain his ends without being
compromised himself.

He considered a long time, and at last his meditations
were crowned with success.

One evening he tied two cats together by their hind-legs
with a string about six feet in length, and threw them from
the wall into the midst of that noble, that princely, that
royal bed, which contained not only the " Cornelius De
Witte," but, besides, the " Beauty of Brabant," milk-white,
edged with purple and pink; the " Marble of Rotterdam,"
colour of flax-blossom, feathered-red, and flesh-colour; and
the " Wonder of Haarlem," dark dove-colour, tinged with
a lighter shade of the same.*

The frightened cats, having alighted on the ground, first
tried to fly each in a different direction, until the string by
which they were tied together was tightly stretched across
the bed; then, however, feeling that they were not able
to get off, they began to pull to and fro, and to wheel
about with heart-rending caterwaulings, mowing down
with their string the flowers among which they were
disporting themselves, until, after a furious strife of about
a quarter of an hour, the string broke and the combatants
vanished.

Boxtel, hidden behind his sycamore, could not see any-thing, as it was pitch dark; but the piercing cries of the cats told the whole tale, and his heart, overflowing with gall, was now throbbing with triumphant joy.

Boxtel was so eager to ascertain the extent of the injury that he remained on his post until morning to feast his eyes at the sad state in which the two cats had placed the flower-beds of his neighbour. The mists of the morning chilled his frame, but he did not feel the cold, the hope of revenge keeping his blood at fever heat. The chagrin of his rival was to pay for all the inconvenience which he incurred himself.

At the earliest dawn the door of the white house opened, and Van Baerle made his appearance; approaching the flower-beds with the smile of a man who has passed the night comfortably in his bed, and has had happy dreams.

All at once he perceived furrows and little mounds of earth on the beds, which only the evening before had been as smooth as a mirror; all at once he perceived the sym-metrical rows of his tulips to be completely disordered, like the pikes of a battalion in the midst of which a shell has fallen.

He ran up to them with blanched cheeks.

Boxtel trembled with joy. Fifteen or twenty tulips, torn and crushed, were lying about, some of them bent, others completely broken and already withering; the sap was oozing from their bleeding bulbs: how gladly would Van Baerle have redeemed that precious sap with his own blood!

But what were his surprise and his delight! what was the disappointment of his rival! Not one of the four tulips which the latter had meant to destroy was injured at all. They raised proudly their noble heads above the corpses of their slain companions. This was enough to console Van Baerle, and enough to fan the rage of the horticultural murderer, who tore his hair at the sight of the effects of the crime which he had committed in vain.

Van Baerle could not imagine the cause of the mishap,

which, fortunately, was of far less consequence than it might have been. On making inquiries, he learned that the whole night had been disturbed by terrible caterwaulings. He, besides, found traces of the cats—their footmarks and hairs left behind on the battle-field; to guard, therefore, in future against a similar outrage, he gave orders that henceforth one of the under-gardners should sleep in the garden in a sentry-box near the flower-beds.

Boxtel heard him give the order, and saw the sentry-box put up that very day; but he deemed himself lucky in not having been suspected, and, being more than ever incensed against the successful horticulturalist, he resolved to abide his time.

Just then the Tulip Society of Haarlem* offered a prize for the production of the large black tulip without a spot of colour, a thing which had not yet been accomplished, and was considered impossible, as at that time there did not exist a flower of that species approaching even to dark nut-brown. It was, therefore, generally said that the founders of the prize might just as well have offered two millions as a hundred thousand guilders, since no one would be able to gain it.

The tulip-growing world, however, was thrown by it into a state of most active commotion. Some fanciers caught at the idea without believing it practicable; but such is the power of imagination amongst florists that, although considering the undertaking as certain to fail, all their thoughts were engrossed by that grand black tulip, which was looked upon as chimerical, as the black swan or the white raven were reputed to be in those days.*

Van Baerle was one of the tulip-growers who were struck with the idea; Boxtel thought of it in the light of a speculation. Van Baerle, as soon as the idea had once taken root in his clear and ingenious mind, began slowly the necessary sowings and operations to reduce the tulips, which he had grown already, from red to brown, and from brown to dark brown.*

By the next year he had obtained flowers of a perfect nut-brown, and Boxtel espied them in the border, whereas he had himself, as yet, only succeeded in producing the light brown.

Boxtel, once more worsted by the superiority of his hated rival, was now completely disgusted with tulip-growing, and, being driven half-mad, devoted himself entirely to observation.

The house of his rival was quite open to view: a garden exposed to the sun; cabinets with glass walls, shelves, cupboards, boxes and ticketed pigeon-holes, which could easily be surveyed by the telescope. Boxtel allowed his bulbs to rot in the pits, his seedlings to dry up in their cases, and his tulips to wither in the borders, and henceforward occupied himself with nothing else but the doings at Van Baerle's.

But the most curious part of the operations was not performed in the garden.

It might be one o'clock in the morning when Van Baerle went up to his laboratory, into the glazed cabinet whither Boxtel's telescope had such easy access; and here, as soon as the lamp illuminated the walls and windows, Boxtel saw the inventive genius of his rival at work.

He beheld him sifting his seeds, and soaking them in liquids which were destined to modify or to deepen their colours. He knew what Cornelius meant, when, heating certain grains, then moistening them, then combining them with others by a sort of grafting—a minute and marvellously delicate manipulation—he shut up in darkness those which were expected to furnish the black colour; exposed to the sun or to the lamp those which were to produce red; and place between the endless reflection of two water-mirrors those intended for white, the pure representation of the limpid element.

This innocent magic, the fruit at the same time of childlike musings and of manly genius—this patient untiring labour, of which Boxtel knew himself to be incapable—made him, gnawed as he was with envy, centre all his life, all his thoughts, and all his hopes, in his telescope.

For, strange to say, the love and interest of horticulture had not deadened in Isaac his fierce envy and thirst of revenge. Sometimes, whilst covering Van Baerle with his telescope he deluded himself into a belief that he was levelling a never-failing musket at him; and then he would seek with his finger for the trigger to fire the shot which was to have killed his neighbour. But it is time that we should connect with this epoch of the operations of the one, and the espionage of the other, the visit which Cornelius De Witte came to pay to his native town.

CHAPTER SEVEN

The Happy Man Makes Acquaintance with Misfortune

CORNELIUS DE WITTE, after having attended to his family affairs, reached the house of his godson Cornelius Van Baerle, one evening in the month of January, 1672.

De Witte, although being very little of a horticulturist or of an artist, went over the whole mansion from the studio to the greenhouse, inspecting everything from the pictures down to the tulips. He thanked his godson for having joined him on the deck of the Admiral's ship, *The Seven Provinces*, during the battle of Southwold Bay,* and for having given his name to a magnificent tulip; and whilst he thus, with the kindness and affability of a father to a son, visited Van Baerle's treasures, the crowd gathered with curiosity, and even respect, before the door of the happy man.

All this hubbub excited the attention of Boxtel, who was just taking his meal by his fireside. He inquired what it meant, and on being informed of the cause of all the stir, climbed up to his post of observation, where, in spite of the cold, he took his stand, with the telescope to his eye.

This telescope had not been of great service to him since the autumn of 1671. The tulips, like true daughters of the East, averse to cold, do not abide in the open ground in winter. They need the shelter of the house, the soft bed on the shelves, and the congenial warmth of the stove. Van Baerle, therefore, passed the whole winter in his laboratory, in the midst of his books and pictures. He went only rarely to the room where he kept his bulbs, unless it were to allow some occasional rays of the sun to enter, by opening one of the movable sashes of the glass front.

On the evening of which we are speaking, after two Corneliuses had visited together all the apartments of the

57

house, whilst a train of domestics followed their steps, De Witte said in a low voice to Van Baerle—

" My dear son, send these people away, and let us be alone for some minutes."

The young Cornelius bowing assent, said aloud—

" Would you now, sir, please to see my dry-room?"

The dry-room, this pantheon, this sanctum sanctorum of the tulip-fancier, was, as Delphi of old,* interdicted to the profane uninitiated.

Never had any of his servants been bold enough to set his foot there.* Cornelius admitted only the inoffensive broom of an old Frisian housekeeper, who had been his nurse, and who, from the time when he had devoted himself to the culture of tulips, ventured no longer to put onions in his stews, for fear of pulling to pieces and mincing the idol of her foster child.

At the mere mention of the *dry-room*, therefore, the servants, who were carrying the lights, respectfully fell back. Cornelius, taking the candlestick from the hands of the foremost, conducted his godfather into that room, which was no other than that very cabinet with a glass front,* into which Boxtel was continually prying with his telescope.

The envious spy was watching more intently than ever.

First of all he saw the walls and windows lit up.

Then two dark figures approached.

One of them tall, majestic, stern, sat down near the table on which Van Baerle had placed the taper.

In this figure Boxtel recognised the pale features of Cornelius De Witte, whose long hair, parted in front, fell over his shoulders.

De Witte, after having said some few words to Cornelius, the meaning of which the prying neighbour could not read in the movement of his lips, took from his breast pocket a white parcel, carefully sealed, which Boxtel, judging from the manner in which Cornelius received it, and placed it in one of the presses, supposed to contain papers of the greatest importance.

His first thought was that this precious deposit inclosed

some newly-imported bulbs from Bengal or Ceylon; but he soon reflected that Cornelius De Witte was very little addicted to tulip-growing, and that he only occupied himself with the affairs of man, a pursuit by far less peaceful and agreeable than that of the florist. He, therefore, came to the conclusion that the parcel contained simply some papers, and that these papers were relating to politics.

But why should papers of political import be entrusted to Van Baerle, who not only was, but also boasted of being, an entire stranger to the science of government, which, in his opinion, was more occult than alchemy itself?

It was undoubtedly a deposit which Cornelius De Witte, already threatened by the unpopularity with which his countrymen were going to honour him, was placing in the hands of his godson; a contrivance so much the more cleverly devised, as it certainly was not at all likely that it should be searched for at the house of one who had always stood aloof from every sort of intrigue.

And besides, if the parcel had been made up of bulbs, Boxtel knew his neighbour too well, not to expect that Van Baerle would not have lost one moment in satisfying his curiosity and feasting his eyes on the present which he had received.

But, on the contrary, Cornelius had received the parcel from the hands of his godfather with every mark of respect, and put it by with the same respectful manner in a drawer, stowing it away so that it should not take up too much of the room which was reserved to his bulbs.

The parcel thus being secreted, Cornelius De Witte got up, pressed the hand of his godson, and turned towards the door, Van Baerle seizing the candlestick, and lighting him on his way down to the street, which was still crowded with people who wished to see their great fellow-citizen getting into his coach.

Boxtel had not been mistaken in his supposition. The deposit entrusted to Van Baerle, and carefully locked up by him, was nothing more nor less than John De Witte's correspondence with the Marquise de Louvois,* the war-minister of the King of France; only the godfather forbore giving to his godson the least intimation concerning the political importance of the secret, merely desiring him not to deliver the parcel to anyone but to himself, or to whomsoever he would send to claim it in his name.

And Van Baerle, as we have seen, locked it up with his most precious bulbs, to think no more of it, after his godfather had left him; very unlike Boxtel, who looked upon this parcel as a clever pilot does on the distant and scarcely-perceptible cloud which is increasing on its way, and which is fraught with a storm.*

Little dreaming of the jealous hatred of his neighbour, Van Baerle had proceeded step by step towards gaining the prize offered by the Horticultural Society of Haarlem. He had progressed from hazel-nut shade to that of roasted coffee; and on the very day when the frightful events took place at the Hague, which we have related in the preceding chapters, we find him about one o'clock in the day, gathering from the border the young suckers, raised from tulips of the colour of roasted coffee; and which, being expected to flower for the first time in the spring of 1675,* would, undoubtedly, produce the large black tulip required by the Haarlem Society.

On the 20th of August, 1672, at one o'clock, Cornelius was, therefore, in his dry-room, with his feet resting on the foot-bar of the table, and his elbows on the cover, looking with intense delight on three suckers which he had just detached from the mother bulb, pure, perfect, and entire, and from which was to grow that wonderful produce of horticulture, which would render the name of Cornelius Van Baerle for ever illustrious.

" I shall find the black tulip," said Cornelius to himself, whilst detaching the suckers. " I shall obtain the hundred thousand guilders offered by the Society. I shall distribute them among the poor of Dort; and thus the hatred which every rich man has to encounter in times of civil wars will be soothed down, and I shall be able, without fearing any harm either from Republicans or Orangists, to keep as heretofore my borders in splendid condition. I need no more be afraid, lest on the day of a riot the shopkeepers of the town, and the sailors of the port, should come and tear out my bulbs, to boil them as onions for their families, as they have sometimes quietly threatened when they happened to remember my having paid two or three hundred guilders for one bulb. It is, therefore, settled I shall give the hundred thousand guilders of the prize Haarlem to the poor. And yet——"

Here Cornelius stopped, and heaved a sigh.

" And yet," he continued, " it would have been so very delightful to spend the hundred thousand guilders on the enlargement of my tulip-bed, or even on a journey to the East, the country of beautiful flowers. But, alas! these are no thoughts for the present times, when muskets, standards, proclamations, and beating of drums are the order of the day."

Van Baerle raised his eyes to Heaven, and sighed again. Then turning his glance towards his bulbs—objects of much greater importance to him than all those muskets, standards, drums, and proclamations, which he conceived only to be fit to disturb the minds of honest people, he said—

" These are, indeed, beautiful bulbs; how smooth they are—how well formed! There is that air of melancholy about them which promises to produce a flower of the colour of ebony. On their skin you cannot even distinguish the circulating veins with the naked eye. Certainly, certainly, not a light spot will disfigure the tulip which I have called into existence. And by what name shall we call this offspring of my sleepless nights, of my labour and my thought? *Tulipa nigra Barlaeensis*.

" Yes, *Barlaeensis*; a fine name. All the tulip-fanciers— that is to say, all the intelligent people of Europe—will feel a thrill of excitement when the rumour spreads to the four quarters of the globe: THE GRAND BLACK TULIP IS FOUND! ' How is it called?' the fanciers will ask—' *Tulipa nigra Barlaeensis!*' ' Why *Barlaeensis*?' ' After its grower, Van Baerle,' will be the answer. ' And who is this Van Baerle?' ' It is the same who has already produced five new tulips: The Jane, the John De Witte, the Cornelius De Witte, etc.' Well, this is what I call my ambition. It will cause tears to no one. And people will still talk of my *Tulipa nigra Barlaeensis*, when, perhaps, my godfather, this sublime politician, is only known from the tulip to which I have given his name.

" Oh! these darling bulbs!

" When my tulip has flowered," Baerle continued his soliloquy, " and when tranquillity is restored in Holland, I shall give to the poor only fifty thousand guilders, which, after all, is a goodly sum for a man who is under no obligation whatever. Then, with the remaining fifty thousand guilders, I shall make experiments. With them, I shall succeed in imparting scent to the tulip. Ah! if I succeeded in giving it the odour of the rose or the carnation, or, what would be still better, a completely new scent; if I restored to this queen of flowers its natural distinctive perfume which she has lost in passing from her Eastern to her European throne, and which she must have in the Indian Peninsula at Goa, Bombay, and Madras, and especially in that island which in olden times, as is asserted, was the terrestrial paradise, and which is called Ceylon*— oh, what glory! I must say, I would then rather be Cornelius Van Baerle than Alexander, Caesar, or Maximilian.*

" Oh, the admirable bulbs!"

Thus Cornelius indulged in the delights of contemplation, and was carried away by the sweetest dreams.

Suddenly the bell of his cabinet was rung much more violently than usual.

Cornelius, startled, laid his hands on his bulbs, and turned round.

" Who is here?" he asked. " Sir," answered the servant, " it is a messenger from the Hague."

" A messenger from the Hague! What does he want?"

" Sir, it is Craeke."

" Craeke! the confidential servant of Mynheer John De Witte? Good, let him wait."

" I cannot wait," said a voice in the lobby.

And at the same time forcing his way in, Craeke rushed into the dry-room.

This abrupt entrance was such an infringement on the established rules of the household of Cornelius Van Baerle, that the latter, at the sight of Craeke, almost convulsively moved his hand which covered the bulbs, so that two of them fell on the floor, one of them rolling under a small table, and the other into the fire-place.

"Zounds!" said Cornelius, eagerly picking up his precious bulbs, "what's the matter?"

"The matter, sir!" said Craeke, laying a paper on the large table, on which the third bulb was lying—" the matter is, that you are requested to read this paper without losing one moment."

And Craeke, who thought he had remarked in the streets of Dort symptoms of a tumult similar to that which he had witnessed before his departure from the Hague, ran off without even looking behind him.

"All right! all right! my dear Craeke," said Cornelius, stretching his arm under the table for the bulb; "your paper shall be read, indeed it shall."

Then, examining the bulb which he held in the hollow of his hand, he said, "Well, here is one of them uninjured. That confounded Craeke! thus to rush into my dry-room; let us now look after the other."

And, without laying down the bulb which he already held, Baerle went to the fire-place, knelt down, and stirred with the tip of his finger the ashes, which fortunately were quite cold. He at once felt the other bulb.

"Well, here it is," he said. And, looking at it with almost fatherly affection, he exclaimed, "Uninjured, as the first!"

At this very instant, and whilst Cornelius, still on his knees, was examining his pets, the door of the dry-room was so violently shaken, and opened in such a brusque manner, that Cornelius felt rising in his cheeks and his ears the glow of that evil counsellor which is called wrath.

"Now what is it again," he demanded; "are people going mad here?"

"Oh, sir! sir!" cried the servant, rushing into the dry-room, with a much paler face, and with much more frightened mien, than Craeke had shown.

" Well?" asked Cornelius, foreboding some mischief from this double breach of the strict rule of his house.

" Oh, sir, fly! fly quick!" cried the servant.

" Fly! and what for?"

" Sir, the house is full of the guards of the States."

" What do they want?"

" They want you."

" What for?"

" To arrest you."

" Arrest me? arrest me, do you say?"

" Yes, sir, and they are headed by a magistrate."

" What's the meaning of all this?" said Van Baerle, grasping in his hands the two bulbs, and directing his terrified glance towards the staircase.

" They are coming up! they are coming up!" cried the servant.

" Oh, my dear child, my worthy master!" cried the old housekeeper, who now likewise made her appearance in the dry-room, " take your gold, your jewellery, and fly, fly!"

" But how shall I make my escape, nurse?" said Van Baerle.

" Jump out of the window."

" Twenty-five feet from the ground!"

" But you will fall on six feet of soft soil."

" Yes, but I should fall on my tulips."

" Never mind, jump out."

Cornelius took the third bulb, approached the window, and opened it, but seeing what havoc he would necessarily cause in his borders, and, more than this, what a height he would have to jump, he called out, " Never!" and fell back a step.

In this moment they saw across the banister of the staircase the points of the halberds of the soldiers rising.

The housekeeper raised her hand to Heaven.

As to Cornelius Van Baerle, it must be stated to his honour, not as a man, but as a tulip-fancier, his only thought was for his inestimable bulbs.

Looking about for a paper in which to wrap them up, he

noticed the fly-leaf from the Bible which Craeke had laid upon the table, took it without, in his confusion, remembering whence it came, folded in it the three bulbs, secreted them in his bosom, and waited.

At this very moment the soldiers, preceded by a magistrate, entered the room.

" Are you Doctor Cornelius Van Baerle ? " demanded the magistrate (who, although knowing the young man very well, put his questions according to the forms of justice, which gave his proceedings a much more dignified air).

" I am that person, Master Van Spenne,"* answered Cornelius, politely bowing to his judge, " and you know it very well."

" Then give up to us the seditious papers which you secrete in your house."

" The seditious papers!" repeated Cornelius, quite dumbfounded at the imputation.

" Now don't look astonished, if you please."

" I vow to you, Master Van Spenne," Cornelius replied, " that I am completely at a loss to understand what you want."

" Then I shall put you in the way, doctor," said the judge; " give up to us the paper which the traitor Cornelius De Witt deposited with you, in the month of January last."

A sudden light came into the mind of Cornelius.

" Halloa!" said Van Spenne, " you begin now to remember, don't you?"

" Indeed I do; but you spoke of seditious papers, and I have none of that sort."

" You deny it then?"

" Certainly I do."

The magistrate turned round, and took a rapid survey of the whole cabinet.

" Where is the apartment you call your dry-room?" he asked.

" The very same where you now are, Master Van Spennen."

The magistrate cast a glance at a small note at the top of his papers.

" All right," he said, like a man who is sure of his ground.

Then, turning round towards Cornelius, he continued, " Will you give up those papers to me?"

" But I cannot, Master Van Spennen; those papers do not belong to me; they have been deposited with me as a trust, and a trust is sacred."

" Doctor Cornelius," said the judge, " in the name of the State, I order you to open this drawer, and to give up to me the papers it contains."

Saying this, the judge pointed with his finger to the third drawer of the press, near the fire-place.

In this very drawer, indeed, the papers deposited by the Warden of the Dykes with his godson were lying; a proof that the police had received very exact information.

" Ah! you will not," said Van Spennen, when he saw Cornelius standing immovable and bewildered; " then I shall open the drawer myself."

And, pulling out the drawer to its full length, the magistrate at first alighted on about twenty bulbs, carefully arranged and ticketed, and then on the paper parcel, which had remained in exactly the same state as it was when delivered by the unfortunate Cornelius De Witte to his godson.

The magistrate broke the seals, tore off the envelope, cast an eager glance on the first leaves which met his eye, and then exclaimed with a terrible voice:

" Well, justice has been rightly informed after all!"

" How," said Cornelius, " how is this?"

" Don't pretend to be ignorant, Mynheer Van Baerle," answered the magistrate, " follow me."

" How's that, follow you?" cried the Doctor.

" Yes, sir, for in the name of the States I arrest you."

Arrests were not as yet made in the name of William of Orange—he had not been Stadtholder long enough for that.*

" Arrest me?" cried Cornelius, " but what have I done?"

" That's no affair of mine, Doctor; you will explain all that before your judges."

66

" Where?"

" At the Hague."

Cornelius, in mute stupefaction, embraced his old nurse, who was in a swoon; shook hands with his servants, who were bathed in tears; and followed the magistrate, who put him in a coach, as a prisoner of State, and had him driven at full gallop to the Hague.

CHAPTER EIGHT

An Invasion

THE INCIDENT just related was, as the reader has guessed before this, the mischievous work of Mynheer Isaac Boxtel.

It will be remembered that, with the help of his telescope, not even the least detail of the private meeting between Cornelius De Witte and Van Baerle had escaped him. He had, indeed, heard nothing; but he had seen everything, and had rightly concluded that the papers entrusted by the Warden to the Doctor must have been of great importance, as he saw Van Baerle so carefully secreting the parcel in the drawer where he used to keep his most precious bulbs.

The upshot of all this was that when Boxtel, who watched the course of political events much more attentively than his neighbour Cornelius was used to do, heard the news of the brothers De Witte being arrested*on a charge of high treason against the States, he thought within his heart that very likely he, Boxtel, needed only to say one word, and the godson would be arrested as well as the godfather.

Yet, full of hatred as was Boxtel's heart, he at first shrank with horror from the idea of informing against a man whom this information might lead to the scaffold.

But there is this terrible in evil thoughts, that evil minds grow soon familiar with them.

Besides this, Mynheer Isaac Boxtel encouraged himself with the following sophism:

" Cornelius De Witte is a bad citizen, as he is charged with high treason, and arrested.

" I, on the contrary, am a good citizen, as I am not charged with anything in the world, and as I am as free as the air of heaven.

" If, therefore, Cornelius De Witte is a bad citizen—of

which there can be no doubt, as he is charged with high treason and arrested—his accomplice, Cornelius Van Baerle is no less a bad citizen than himself.

" And as I am a good citizen, and as it is the duty of every good citizen to inform against the bad ones, it is my duty to inform against Cornelius Van Baerle."

Specious as this mode of reasoning might sound, it would not, perhaps, have taken so complete a hold of Boxtel, nor would he, perhaps, have yielded to the mere desire of vengeance which was gnawing at his heart, had not the demon of envy been joined by that of cupidity.

Boxtel was quite aware of the progress which Van Baerle had made towards producing the grand black tulip.

Doctor Cornelius, notwithstanding all his modesty, had not been able to hide from his most intimate friends that he was all but certain to win, in the year of grace 1673, the prize of a hundred thousand guilders offered by the Horticultural Society of Haarlem.

Just this certainty of Cornelius Van Baerle caused the fever which raged in the heart of Isaac Boxtel.

If Cornelius should be arrested, there would necessarily be a great upset in his house, and, during the night after his arrest, no one would think of keeping watch over the tulips in his garden.

Now, in that night, Boxtel would climb over the wall, and, as he knew the place of the bulb which was to produce the grand black tulip, he would filch it; and instead of flowering for Cornelius, it would flower for him, Isaac; he also, instead of Van Baerle, would have the prize of a hundred thousand guilders, not to speak of the sublime honour of calling the new flower *Tulipa nigra Boxtellensis*—a result which would satisfy not only his vengeance, but also his cupidity and his ambition.

Awake, he thought of nothing but the grand black tulip; asleep, he dreamed of it.

At last, on the 19th of August, about two o'clock in the afternoon, the temptation grew so strong, that Mynheer Isaac was no longer able to resist it.

Accordingly he wrote an anonymous information, the

minute exactness of which made up for its want of authenticity; and posted his letter.

Never did a venomous paper, slipped into the jaws of the bronze lions at Venice,* produce a more prompt and terrible effect.

On the same evening the letter reached the principal magistrate, who, without a moment's delay, convoked his colleagues early for the next morning. On the following morning, therefore, they assembled, and decided on Van Baerle's arrest, placing the order for its execution in the hands of Master Van Spennen, who, as we have seen, performed his duty like a true Hollander, and who arrested the doctor at the very hour when the Orange party at the Hague were roasting the bleeding shreds of flesh torn from the corpses of Cornelius and John De Witte.

But, whether from a feeling of shame, or from craven weakness, Isaac Boxtel did not venture that day to point his telescope either at the garden, or at the laboratory, or at the dry-room.

He knew too well what was about to happen in the house of the poor doctor, as that he should have felt a desire to look into it. He did not even get up when his only servant —who envied the lot of the servants of Cornelius just as bitterly as Boxtel did that of their master—entered his bedroom. He said to the man—

" I shall not get up to-day; I am ill."

About nine o'clock he heard a great noise in the street, which made him tremble; at this moment he was paler than a real invalid, and shook more violently than a man in the height of fever.

His servant entered the room; Boxtel hid himself under the counterpane.

" Oh, sir!" cried the servant, not without some inkling that, whilst deploring the mishap which had befallen Van Baerle, he was announcing agreeable news to his master— " oh, sir! you do not know, then, what is happening at this moment?"

" How can I know it?" answered Boxtel, with an almost unintelligible voice.

" Well, Mynheer Boxtel, at this moment your neighbour Cornelius Van Baerle is arrested for high treason."

" Nonsense!" Boxtel muttered, with a faltering voice; " the thing is impossible."

" Faith! sir, at any rate that's what people say; and, besides, I have seen Judge Van Spennen with the archers entering the house."

" Well, if you have seen it with your own eyes, that's a different case altogether."

" At all events," said the servant, " I shall go and inquire once more; be you quiet, sir, I shall let you know all about it."

Boxtel contented himself with signifying his approval of the zeal of his servant by dumb-show.

The man went out, and returned in half an hour.

" Oh, sir! all that I told you is indeed quite true."

" How so?"

" Mynheer Van Baele is arrested, and has been put into a carriage, and they are driving him to the Hague."

" To the Hague?"

" Yes, to the Hague; and if what people say is true, it won't do him much good."

" And what do they say?" Boxtel asked.

" Faith, sir, they say—but it is not quite sure—that by this hour the burghers must be murdering Mynheer Cor-neilus and Mynheer John De Witte."

" Oh!" muttered, or rather growled, Boxtel, closing his eyes from the dreadful picture which presented itself to his imagination.

" Why, to be sure," said the servant to himself, whilst leaving the room, " Mynheer Isaac Boxtel must be very sick not to have jumped from his bed on hearing such good news."

And, in reality, Isaac Boxtel was very sick, like a man who has murdered another.

But he had murdered his man with a double object; the first was attained, the second was still to be attained.

Night closed in. It was the night which Boxtel had looked forward to.

71

As soon as it was dark he got up.

He then climbed into his sycamore.

He had correctly calculated; no one thought of keeping watch over the garden; the house and the servants were all in the utmost confusion.

He heard the clock strike ten, eleven, twelve.

At midnight, with a beating heart, trembling hands, and a livid countenance, he descended from the tree, took a ladder, leaned it against the wall, mounted it to the last step but one, and listened. All was perfectly quiet; not a sound broke the silence of the night; one solitary light, that of the housekeeper, was burning in the house.

This silence and this darkness emboldened Boxtel; he got astride on the wall, stopped for an instant, and, after having ascertained that there was nothing to fear, he put his ladder from his own garden into that of Cornelius, and descended.

After this, knowing to an inch where the bulbs which were to produce the black tulip were planted, he ran towards the spot, following, however, the crisp gravelled walks in order not to be betrayed by his footprints, and on arriving at the precise spot, he rushed, with the eagerness of a tiger, to plunge his hand into the soft ground.

He found nothing, and thought he was mistaken.

In the meanwhile the cold sweat stood on his brow.

He rummaged close by it—nothing.

He rummaged on the right, and on the left—nothing.

He rummaged in front, and at the back—nothing.

He was nearly mad, when at last he satisfied himself that on that very morning the earth had been turned.

In fact, whilst Boxtel was lying in bed, Cornelius had gone down to his garden, had taken up the mother-bulb, and, as we have seen, divided it into three.

Boxtel could not bring himself to leave the place. He dug with his hands more than ten square feet of ground.

At last no doubt remained of his misfortune.

Mad with rage he returned to his ladder, mounted the wall, drew up the ladder, flung it into his own garden, and jumped after it.

All at once a last ray of hope presented itself to his mind: the seedling bulbs might be in the dry-room; it was therefor only requisite to make his entry there as he had done into the garden.

There he would find them; and, moreover, it was not at all difficult, as the sashes of the dry-room might be raised like those of a green-house. Cornelius had opened them on that morning, and no one had thought of closing them again.

Everything, therefore, depended upon whether he could procure a ladder of sufficient length—one of twenty-five feet, instead of ten.

Boxtel had noticed in the street where he lived a house which was being repaired, and against which a very tall ladder was placed.

This ladder would do admirably, unless the workmen had taken it away.

He ran to the house—the ladder was there. Boxtel took it, carried it with great exertion to his garden, and with even greater difficulty raised it against the wall of Van Baerle's house, where it just reached to the window.

Boxtel put a lighted dark lantern into his pocket, mounted the ladder, and slipped into the dry-room.

On reaching this sanctuary of the florist he stopped, supporting himself against the table; his legs failed him—his heart beat as if it would choke him. Here it was even worse than in the garden: there Boxtel was only a trespasser, here he was a thief.

However, he took courage again: he had not gone so far to turn back with empty hands.

But it was of no use to search the whole room, to open and shut all the drawers, even that privileged one where the parcel which had been so fatal to Cornelius had been deposited; he found ticketed, as in a botanical garden, the " Jane," the " John De Witte," the hazel-nut, and the roasted-coffee-coloured tulip; but of the black tulip, or rather of the seedling bulbs within which it was still sleeping, not a trace was to be found.

And yet, on looking over the register of seeds and bulbs

which Van Baerle kept, if possible, even with greater exactitude and care than the first commercial houses of Amsterdam their ledgers, Boxtel read the following entry:

"To-day, 20th of August, 1672, I have taken up the mother-bulb of the grand black tulip, which I have divided into three perfect suckers."

"Oh, these suckers, these suckers!" howled Boxtel, turning over everything in the dry-room. "Where could he have concealed them?"

Then, suddenly striking his forehead in his frenzy, he called out, "Oh, wretch that I am! Would anyone be separated from his suckers? Would one leave them at Dort when one goes to the Hague? Could one live far from one's bulbs, when they enclose the grand black tulip? He had time to get hold of them, the scoundrel; he has them about him; he has taken them to the Hague!"

It was like a flash of lightning which showed to Boxtel the abyss of a uselessly-committed crime.

Boxtel sank quite paralysed on that very table, and on that very spot where, some hours before, the unfortunate Van Baerle had so leisurely, and with such intense delight, contemplated his darling bulbs.

"Well, then, after all," said the envious Boxtel, raising his livid face from his hands in which it had been buried, "if he has them, he can keep them only as long as he lives, and——"

The rest of this detestable thought merged in a hideous smile.

"The suckers are at the Hague," he said, "therefore, I can no longer live at Dort: away, then, for them, to the Hague! to the Hague!"

And Boxtel, without taking any notice of the treasures about him, so entirely were his thoughts absorbed by another inestimable treasure, let himself out by the window, glided down the ladder, carried it back to the place whence he had taken it, and, like a beast of prey, returned growling to his house.

CHAPTER NINE

The Family Cell

IT WAS about midnight when poor Van Baerle was locked up in the prison of the Buitenhof.

What Rosa foresaw had come to pass. On finding the cell of Cornelius De Witte empty, the wrath of the people ran very high, and had Gryphus fallen into the hands of those madmen, he would certainly have had to pay with his life for the prisoner.

But this fury had vented itself most amply on the two brothers when they were overtaken by the murderers, thanks to the precaution which William—the man of precautions—had taken in having the gates of the city closed.

A momentary lull had therefore set in, whilst the prison was empty, and Rosa availed herself of this favourable moment to come forth from her hiding-place, which she also induced her father to leave.

The prison was therefore completely deserted. Why should people remain in the jail whilst murder was going on at the Tol-Hek?*

Gryphus came forth trembling behind the courageous Rosa. They went to close the great gate, at least as well as it would close, considering that it was half-demolished. It was easy to see that a hurricane of mighty fury had passed here.

About four o'clock a return of the noise was heard, but of no threatening character to Gryphus and his daughter. The people were only dragging in the two corpses, which they came back to gibbet at the usual place of execution.

Rosa hid herself this time also, but only that she might not see the ghastly spectacle.

At midnight people again knocked at the gate of the jail, or rather at the barricade which served in its stead: it was Cornelius Van Baerle whom they were bringing.

75

When the jailer received this new inmate, and saw from the warrant the name and station of his prisoner, he muttered with his turnkey smile—

"Godson of Cornelius De Witte! Well, young man, we have just here the family cell, and we shall give it to you."

And quite enchanted with his joke, the ferocious Orangeman took his cresset*and his keys to conduct Cornelius to the cell, which, on that very morning, Cornelius De Witte had left to go into exile, or what, in revolutionary times, is meant instead by those sublime philosophers who lay it down as an axiom of high policy, "It is the dead only who do not return."

On the way which the despairing florist had to traverse to reach that cell, he heard nothing but the barking of a dog, and saw nothing but the face of a young girl.

The dog rushed forth from a niche in the wall, shaking his heavy chain, and sniffing all round Cornelius in order so much the better to recognise him, in case he should be ordered to pounce upon him.

The young girl, whilst the prisoner was mounting the staircase, appeared at the narrow door of her chamber, which opened on that very flight of steps; and, holding the lamp in her right hand, she at the same time lit up her pretty blooming face, surrounded by a profusion of rich wavy golden locks, whilst with her left she held her white night dress closely over her breast, having been roused from her first slumber by the unexpected arrival of Van Baerle.

It would have made a fine picture, worthy of Rembrandt, the gloomy winding stairs illuminated by the reddish glare of the cresset of Gryphus, with his scowling jailer's countenance at the top, the melancholy figure of Cornelius bending over the banister, to look down upon the sweet face of Rosa, standing, as it were, in the bright frame of the door of her chamber, with flurried mien at being thus seen by a stranger.

And at the bottom, quite in the shade, where the details are absorbed in the obscurity, the mastiff, with his eyes glistening like carbuncles, and shaking his chain, on which the double light from the lamp of Rosa and cresset of Gryphus threw a brilliant glitter.

The sublime master would, however, have been altogether unable to render the sorrow expressed in the face of Rosa, when she saw this pale, handsome young man slowly climbing the stairs, and thought of the full import of the words, which her father had just spoken, " *You will have the family cell.*" This vision lasted but a moment—much less time than we have taken to describe it. Gryphus then proceeded on his way, Cornelius was forced to follow him, and five minutes after he entered his prison, of which it is unnecessary to say more, as the reader is already acquainted with it.

Gryphus pointed with his finger to the bed on which the martyr had suffered so much, who on that day had rendered his soul to God. Then, taking up his cresset, he quitted the cell.

Thus left alone Cornelius threw himself on his bed, but he slept not; he kept his eye fixed on the narrow window, barred with iron, which looked on the Buitenhof; and in this way saw from behind the trees that first pale beam of light which morning sheds on the earth, as a white mantle.

Now and then during the night, horses had galloped at a smart pace over the Buitenhof, the heavy tramp of the patrols had resounded from the pavement, and the slow matches of the arquebuses,* flaring in the east wind, had thrown up at intervals a sudden glare as far as to the panes of his window.

But when the rising sun began to gild the coping stones at the gable ends of the houses, Cornelius, eager to know whether there was any living creature about him, approached the window, and cast a sad look round the circular yard before him.

At the end of the yard a dark mass, tinted with a dingy blue by the morning dawn, rose before him, its dark outlines standing out in contrast to the houses already illuminated by the pale light of early morning.

Cornelius recognised the gibbet.

On it were suspended two shapeless trunks, which indeed were no more than bleeding skeletons.

The good people of the Hague had chopped off the flesh of its victims, but faithfully carried the remainder to the gibbet, to have a pretext for a double inscription, written on a huge placard,* on which Cornelius, with the keen sight of a young man of twenty-eight, was able to read the following lines, daubed by the coarse brush of a sign-painter:

" Here are hanging the great rogue of the name of John De Witte, and the little rogue Cornelius De Witte, his brother, two enemies of the people, but great friends of the king of France."

Cornelius uttered a cry of horror, and in the agony of his frantic terror, knocked with his hands and feet at his door so violently and continuously that Gryphus, with his huge bunch of keys in his hand, ran furiously up to him.

The jailer opened the door, with terrible imprecations against the prisoner, who disturbed him at an hour at which Master Gryphus was not accustomed to be aroused.

" Well, now, I declare, he is mad, this new De Witte," he cried; " but all those De Wittes have the devil in them."

" Master, master," cried Cornelius, seizing the jailer by the arm and dragging him towards the window; " master, what have I read down there?"

" Where, down there?"

" On that placard."

And trembling, pale and gasping for breath, he pointed to the gibbet at the other side of the yard, with the cynic inscription surmounting it.

Gryphus broke out in a laugh.

" Eh! Eh!" he answered, " so you have read it. Well, my good sir, that's what people will get for corresponding with the enemies of His Highness the Prince of Orange."

" The brothers De Witte are murdered!" Cornelius muttered, with the cold sweat on his brown, and sank on his bed, his arms hanging by his side, and his eyes closed.

" The brothers De Witte have been judged by the people," said Gryphus; " you call that murdered, do you? Well, I call it executed."

And seeing that the prisoner was not only quiet, but entirely prostrate and senseless, he rushed from the cell, violently slamming the door, and noisily drawing the bolts.

Recovering his consciousness, Cornelius found himself alone, and recognised the room where he was—" the family cell," as Gryphus had called it—as the fatal passage leading to ignominious death.

And as he was a philosopher, and, more than that, as he was a Christian, he began to pray for the soul of his god-father, then for that of the Grand Pensionary, and at last submitted with resignation to all the sufferings which God might ordain for him.

Then turning again to the concerns of earth, and having satisfied himself that he was alone in his dungeon, he drew from his breast the three bulbs of the black tulip, and concealed them behind a block of stone, on which the traditional water-jug of the prison was standing, in the darkest corner of his cell.

Useless labour of so many years! such sweet hopes crushed; his discovery was, after all, to lead to nought, just as his own career was to be cut short. Here, in his prison, there was not a trace of vegetation, not an atom of soil, not a ray of sunshine.

At this thought Cornelius fell into a gloomy despair, from which he was only roused by an extraordinary circumstance.

What was this circumstance?

We shall inform the reader in the next chapter.

CHAPTER TEN

The Jailer's Daughter

O<small>N THE</small> same evening Gryphus, as he brought the prisoner his mess, slipped on the damp flags whilst opening the door of the cell, and fell in the attempt to steady himself on his hand, but as it was turned the wrong way he broke his arm just above the wrist.

Cornelius rushed forward towards the jailer, but Gryphus, who was not yet aware of the serious nature of his injury, called out to him:

" It is nothing, don't you stir."

He then tried to support himself on his arm, but the bone gave way; then only he felt the pain, and uttered a cry.

When he became aware that his arm was broken, this man, so harsh to others, fell swooning on the threshold, where he remained motionless and cold as if dead.

During all this time the door of the cell stood open, and Cornelius found himself almost free. But the thought never entered his mind of profiting by this accident; he had seen from the manner in which the arm was bent, and from the noise it made in bending, that the bone was fractured, and that the patient must be in great pain; and now he thought of nothing else but of administering relief to the sufferer, however little benevolent the man had shown himself during their short interview.

At the noise of Gryphus's fall, and at the cry which escaped him, a hasty step was heard on the staircase, and immediately after a lovely apparition presented itself to the eyes of Cornelius.

It was the beautiful young Frisian, who, seeing her father stretched on the ground, and the prisoner bending over him, uttered a faint cry, as, in the first fright, she thought Gryphus, whose brutality she well knew, had fallen in consequence of a struggle between him and the prisoner.

Cornelius understood what was passing in the mind of the girl, at the very moment when the suspicion arose in her heart.

But one moment told her the true state of the case, and, ashamed of her first thoughts, she cast her beautiful eyes, wet with tears, on the young man, and said to him—

" I beg your pardon, and thank you, sir; the first for what I have thought, and the second for what you are doing."

Cornelius blushed, and said, " I am but doing my duty as a Christian, in helping my neighbour."

" Yes, and affording him your help this evening, you have forgotten the abuse which he heaped on you this morning. Oh, sir! this is more than humanity—this is indeed Christian charity."

Cornelius cast his eyes on the beautiful girl, quite astonished to hear from the mouth of one so humble such a noble and feeling speech.

But he had no time to express his surprise. Gryphus recovered from his swoon, opened his eyes, and as his brutality was returning with his senses, he growled, " That's it, a fellow is in a hurry to bring to a prisoner his supper, and falls and breaks his arm, and is left lying on the ground."

" Hush, my father," said Rosa, " you are unjust to this gentleman, whom I found endeavouring to give you his aid."

" His aid?" Gryphus replied, with a doubtful air.

" It is quite true, master; I am quite ready to help you still more."

" You!" said Gryphus, " are you a medical man?"

" It was formerly my profession."

" And so you would be able to set my arm?"

" Perfectly."

" And what would you need to do it; let us hear?"

" Two splinters of wood, and some linen for a bandage."

" Do you hear, Rosa?" said Gryphus, " the prisoner is going to set my arm, that's a saving; come, assist me to get up, I feel as heavy as lead."

Rosa lent the sufferer her shoulder; he put his unhurt arm round her neck, and making an effort, got on his legs, whilst Cornelius, to save him a walk, pushed a chair towards him.

Gryphus sat down; then, turning towards his daughter, he said—

" Well, didn't you hear, go and fetch what is wanted."

Rosa went down, and immediately after returned with two staves of a small barrel and a large roll of linen bandage.

Cornelius had made use of the intervening moments to take off the man's coat, and to tuck up his shirt sleeve.

" Is this what you require, sir?" asked Rosa.

" Yes, miss," answered Cornelius, looking at the things which she had brought, " yes, that's right. Now push this table, whilst I support the arm of your father."

Rosa pushed the table, Cornelius placed the broken arm on it, so as to make it flat, and with perfect skill set the bone, adjusted the splinter, and fastened the bandages.

At the last touch the jailer fainted a second time.

" Go and fetch vinegar, miss," said Cornelius; " we will bathe his temples, and he will recover."

But, instead of acting up to the doctor's prescription, Rosa, after having assured herself that her father was still unconscious, approached Cornelius and said—

" Service for service, sir."

" What do you mean, my dear?" said Cornelius.

" I mean to say, sir, that the judge who is to examine you to-morrow has inquired to-day for the room in which you are confined, and, on being told that you were occupying the cell of Mynheer Cornelius De Witte, laughed in a very strange and disagreeable manner, which makes me fear that no good awaits you."

" But," asked Cornelius, " what harm can they do to me?"

" Look at that gibbet!"

" But I am not guilty," said Cornelius.

" Were they guilty whom you see down there? gibbeted, mangled, and torn to pieces?"

" That's true," said Cornelius gravely.

" And besides," continued Rosa, " the people want to find you guilty. But whether innocent or guilty, your trial begins to-morrow, and the day after you will be condemned. Matters are settled very quickly in these times."

" Well, and what do you conclude from all this?"

" I conclude that I am alone, that I am weak, that my father is lying in a swoon, that the dog is muzzled, and that consequently there is nothing to prevent your making your escape. Fly, then, that's what I mean."

" What do you say?"

" I say that I was not able to save Mynheer Cornelius or Mynheer John De Witte, and that I should like to save you. Only be quick; there, my father is regaining his breath; one minute more, and he will open his eyes, and it will be too late. Do you hesitate?"

In fact, Cornelius stood immovable, looking at Rosa, yet looking at her as if he did not hear her.

" Don't you understand me?" said the young girl, with some impatience.

" Yes, I do," said Cornelius; " but——"

" But?"

" I will not; they would accuse you."

" Never mind," said Rosa, blushing, " never mind that."

" You are very good, my dear child," replied Cornelius, " but I stay."

" You stay, oh, sir! oh, sir! don't you understand that you will be condemned to death, executed on the scaffold, perhaps assassinated and torn to pieces, just like Mynheer John and Mynheer Cornelius. For Heaven's sake, don't think of me, but fly from this place. Take care; it bears ill luck to the De Wittes!"

" Halloa!" cried the jailer, recovering his senses, " who is talking of those rogues, those wretches, those villains, the De Wittes?"

" Don't be angry, my good man," said Cornelius, with his good-tempered smile, " the worst thing for a fracture is excitement, by which the blood is heated."

Thereupon, he said in an undertone to Rosa, " My child,

I am innocent, and I shall await my trial with tranquillity and an easy mind."

" Hush," said Rosa.

" Why hush?"

" My father must not suppose that we have been talking to each other."

" What harm would that do?"

" What harm? He would never allow me to come here any more," said Rosa.

Cornelius received this innocent confidence with a smile; he felt as if a ray of good fortune was shining on his path.

" Now, then, what are you chattering there together about?" said Gryphus, rising and supporting his right arm with his left.

" Nothing," said Rosa; " the doctor is explaining to me what diet you are to keep."

" Diet, diet for me? Well, my fine girl, I shall put you on diet too."

" On what diet, my father?"

" Never to go to the cells of the prisoners, and if ever you should happen to, to leave them as soon as possible. Come, off with me; lead the way, and be quick."

Rosa and Cornelius exchanged glances.

That of Rosa tried to express:

" There, you see?"

That of Cornelius said:

" Let it be as the Lord will."

CHAPTER ELEVEN

Cornelius van Baerle's Will

ROSA HAD not been mistaken; the judges came on the following day to the Buitenhof, and proceeded with the trial of Cornelius Van Baerle. The examination, however, did not last long, it having appeared on evidence that Cornelius had kept at his house that fatal correspondence of the brothers De Witte with France.

He did not deny it.

The only point about which there seemed any difficulty was, whether this correspondence had been entrusted to him by his godfather Cornelius De Witte.

But as, since the death of those two martyrs, Van Baerle had no longer any reason for withholding the truth, he not only did not deny that the parcel had been delivered to him by Cornelius De Witte himself, but he also stated all the circumstances under which it was done.

This confession involved the godson in the crime of the godfather; manifest complicity being considered to exist between Cornelius De Witte and Cornelius Van Baerle.

The honest doctor did not confine himself to this avowal, but told the whole truth with regard to his own tastes, habits, and daily life. He described his indifference to politics, his love of study, of the fine arts, of science, and of flowers. He explained that, since the day when Cornelius De Witte handed to him the parcel at Dort, he himself had never touched, nor even noticed it.

To this it was objected, that in this respect he could not possibly be speaking the truth, since the papers had been deposited in a press, in which both his hands and his eyes must have been engaged every day.

Cornelius answered that it was indeed so; that, however, he never put his hand into the press but to ascertain whether

85

his bulbs were dry, and that he never looked into it but to see if they were beginning to sprout.

To this again it was objected, that his pretended indifference respecting this deposit was not to be reasonably entertained, as he could not have received such papers from the hand of his godfather without being made acquainted with their important character.

He replied that his godfather Cornelius loved him too well, and, above all, that he was too considerate a man to have communicated to him anything of the contents of the parcel, well knowing that such a confidence would only have caused anxiety to him who received it.

To this it was objected, that if De Witte had wished to act in such a way, he would have added to the parcel, in case of accidents, a certificate, setting forth that his godson was an entire stranger to the nature of this correspondence, or at least he would, during his trial, have written a letter to him, which might be produced as his justification.

Cornelius replied that undoubtedly his godfather could not have thought that there was any risk for the safety of his deposit, hidden as it was in a press which was looked upon as sacred as the tabernacle by the whole household of Van Baerle; and that, consequently, he had considered the certificate as useless. As to a letter, he certainly had some remembrance that some moments previous to his arrest, whilst he was absorbed in the contemplation of one of the rarest of his bulbs, John De Witte's servant entered his dry-room, and handed to him a paper, but the whole was to him only like a vague dream; the servant had disappeared, and as to the paper, perhaps it might be found, if a proper search were made.

As far as Craeke was concerned, it was impossible to find him, as he had left Holland.

The paper also was not very likely to be found, and no one gave himself the trouble to look for it.

Cornelius himself did not much press this point, since, even supposing that the paper should turn up, it could not have any direct connection with the correspondence which constituted the crime.

The judges wished to make it appear as though they wanted to urge Cornelius to make a better defence; they displayed that benevolent patience which is generally a sign of the magistrates being interested for the prisoner; or of a man's having so completely got the better of his adversary, that he needs no longer any oppressive means to ruin him.

Cornelius did not accept of this hypocritical protection, and in a last answer, which he set forth with the noble bearing of a martyr and the calm serenity of a righteous man, he said—

" You ask me things, gentlemen, to which I can answer only the exact truth. Hear it. The parcel was put into my hands in the way I have described; I vow before God that I was, and am still, ignorant of its contents, and that it was not until my arrest that I learned that this deposit was the correspondence of the Grand Pensionary with the Marquis of Louvois. And, lastly, I vow and protest, that I do not understand how any one should have known that this parcel was in my house; and, above all, how I can be deemed criminal for having received what my illustrious and unfortunate godfather brought to my house."

This was Van Baerle's whole defence, after which the judges began to deliberate on the verdict.

They considered that every offshoot of civil discord is mischievous, because it revives the contest which it is the interest of all to put down.

One of them, who bore the character of a profound observer, laid down as his opinion that this young man, so phlegmatic in appearance, must in reality be very dangerous, as, under his icy exterior, he was sure to conceal an ardent desire to revenge his friends the De Wittes.

Another observed that the love of tulips agreed perfectly well with that of politics, and that it was proved in history that many very dangerous men were engaged in gardening, just as if it had been their profession, whilst really they occupied themselves with perfectly different concerns; witness Tarquin the Elder,* who grew poppies at Gabii, and the Great Condé, who watered his carnations at the dungeon of Vincennes, at the very moment when the former meditated his return to Rome, and the latter his escape from prison.

The judge summed up with the following dilemma:

" Either Cornelius Van Baerle is a great lover of tulips, or a great lover of politics; in either case he has told us a falsehood, first, because his having occupied himself with politics is proved by his letters which were found at his house; and secondly, because his having occupied himself with tulips is proved by the bulbs, which leave no doubt of the fact—and herein lies the enormity of the case—as Cornelius Van Baerle was concerned in the growing of tulips, and in the pursuit of politics at one and the same time, the prisoner is of a hybrid character, of an amphibious organisation, working with equal ardour at politics and at tulips, which proves him to belong to the class of men most dangerous to public tranquillity, and shows a certain, or rather a complete, analogy between his character and that of those masterminds of which just now Tarquin the Elder and the Great Condé have been felicitously quoted as examples."

The upshot of all these reasonings was, that His Highness, the Prince Stadtholder of Holland, would feel infinitely obliged to the magistracy of the Hague if they simplified for him the government of the Seven Provinces by destroying even the least germ of conspiracy against his authority.

This argument capped all the others, and in order so much the more effectually to destroy the germ of conspiracy, sentence of death was unanimously pronounced against Cornelius Van Baerle, as being arraigned, and convicted, for having, under the innocent appearance of a tulip-fancier, participated in the detestable intrigues and abominable plots of the brothers De Witte against Dutch nationality, and in their secret relations with their French enemy.

A supplementary clause was tacked to the sentence to the effect that " the aforesaid Cornelius Van Baerle should be led from the prison of the Buitenhof to the scaffold in the yard of the same name, where the public executioner would cut off his head."

As this deliberation was a most serious affair, it lasted a full half-hour, during which the prisoner was remanded to his cell.

There the Recorder of the States came to read the sentence to him.

Master Gryphus was detained in bed by the fever caused by the fracture of his arm. His keys had passed into the hands of one of his assistants. Behind this turnkey, who introduced the Recorder, Rosa, the fair Frisian maid, had slipped into the recess of the door, with a handkerchief to her mouth to stifle her sobs.

Cornelius listened to the sentence with an expression rather of surprise than sadness.

After the sentence was read, the Recorder asked him whether he had anything to answer.

" Indeed, I have not," he replied. " Only I confess that among all the causes of death, against which a cautious man may guard, I should never have supposed this to be comprised."

On this answer, the Recorder saluted Van Baerle, with all that consideration which such functionaries generally bestow upon great criminals of every sort.

But whilst he was about to withdraw, Cornelius asked, " By the bye, Mr. Recorder, what day is the thing—you know what I mean—to take place?"

" Well, to-day," answered the Recorder, a little surprised by the self-possession of the condemned man.

A sob was heard behind the door, and Cornelius turned round to look from whom it came; but Rosa, who had foreseen this movement, had fallen back.

" And," continued Cornelius, " what hour is appointed?"

" Twelve o'clock, sir."

" Indeed," said Cornelius. " I think I heard the clock strike ten about twenty minutes ago: I have not much time to spare."

" Indeed you have not, if you wish to make your peace with God," said the Recorder, bowing to the ground. " You may ask for any clergyman you please."

Saying these words he went out backwards, and the

assistant turnkey was going to follow him, and to lock the door of Cornelius's cell, when a white and trembling arm interposed between him and the heavy door.

Cornelius saw nothing but the golden brocade cap, tipped with lace, such as the Frisian girls wore; he heard nothing, but someone whispering into the ear of the turnkey. But the latter put his heavy keys into the white hand which was stretched out to receive them, and, descending some steps, sat down on the staircase, which thus was guarded above by himself and below by the dog. The head-dress turned round, and Cornelius beheld the face of Rosa, blanched with grief, and her beautiful eyes streaming with tears.

She went up to Cornelius, crossing her arms on her heaving breast.

" Oh, sir, sir!" she said, but sobs choked her utterance.

" My good girl," Cornelius replied with emotion, " what do you wish? I may tell you that my time on earth is short."

" I come to ask a favour of you," said Rosa, extending her arms partly towards him and partly towards Heaven.

" Don't weep so, Rosa," said the prisoner, " for your tears go much more to my heart than my approaching fate, and you know, the less guilty a prisoner is, the more it is his duty to die calmly, and even joyfully, as he dies a martyr. Come, there's a dear, don't cry any more, and tell me what you want, my pretty Rosa."

She fell on her knees. " Forgive my father," she said.

" Your father, your father!" said Cornelius, astonished.

" Yes, he has been so harsh to you, but it is his nature; he is so to everyone, and you are not the only one whom he has bullied."

" He is punished, my dear Rosa, more than punished, by the accident that has befallen him, and I forgive him."

" I thank you, sir," said Rosa. " And now tell me—oh, tell me—can I do anything for you?"

" You can dry your beautiful eyes, my dear child." answered Cornelius, with a good-tempered smile.

" But what can I do for you; for you, I mean?"

" A man who has only one hour longer to live must be a great Sybarite*still to want anything, my dear Rosa."

" The clergyman whom they have proposed to you?"

" I have worshipped God all my life; I have worshipped Him in His works, and praised Him in His decrees. I am at peace with Him, and do not wish for a clergyman. The last thought which occupies my mind, however, has reference to the glory of the Almighty, and indeed, my dear, I should ask you to help me in carrying out this last thought."

" Oh, Mynheer Cornelius, speak, speak!" exclaimed Rosa, still bathed in tears.

" Give me your hand, and promise me not to laugh, my dear child."

" Laugh," exclaimed Rosa, frantic with grief; " laugh, at this moment! but do you not see my tears?"

" Rosa, you are no stranger to me. I have not seen much of you, but that little is enough to make me appreciate your character. I have never seen a woman more fair or more pure than you are, and if from this moment I take no more notice of you, forgive me; it is only because, on leaving this world, I do not wish to have any further regret."

Rosa felt a shudder creeping over her frame, for, whilst the prisoner pronounced these words, the belfry clock of the Buitenhof struck eleven.

Cornelius understood her. " Yes, yes, let us make haste," he said; " you are right, Rosa."

Then, taking the paper with the three suckers from his breast, where he had again put it, since he had no longer any fear of being searched, he said, " My dear girl, I have been very fond of flowers. That was at a time when I did not know that there was any thing else to be loved. Don't blush, Rosa, nor turn away; and even if I were making you a declaration of love, alas! poor dear, it would be of no more consequence. Down there in the yard there is an instrument of steel, which in sixty minutes will put an end to my boldness. Well, Rosa, I loved flowers dearly, and I have found, or at least I believe so, the secret of the grand black tulip, which it has been considered impossible to grow, and for which, as you know, or may not know, a prize of a hundred thousand guilders has been offered by the Horticultural Society of Haarlem. These hundred thousand guilders—and, Heaven knows, I do not regret them—these hundred thousand guilders I have here in this paper; for they are won by the three bulbs wrapped up in it, which you may take, Rosa, as I make you a present of them."

" Mynheer Cornelius !"

" Yes, yes, Rosa, you may take them; you are not wronging anyone, my child. I am alone in this world; my parents are dead; I never had a sister or a brother. I have never had a thought of loving anyone with what is called love, and if anyone has loved me I have not known it. However, you see well, Rosa, that I am abandoned by everybody, as in this sad hour you alone are with me in my prison, consoling and assisting me."

" But, sir, a hundred thousand guilders !"

" Well, let us talk seriously, my dear child: those hundred thousand guilders will be a nice marriage portion, with your pretty face; you shall have them for I am quite sure of my bulb. You shall have them, Rosa, dear Rosa, and I ask nothing in return but your promise that you will marry a fine young man whom you love, and who will love you, as dearly as I loved my flowers. Don't interrupt me, Rosa dear, I have only a few minutes more."

The poor girl was nearly choking with her sobs.

Cornelius took her by the hand.

" Listen to me," he continued: " I'll teach you how to manage it. Go to Dort and ask Butruysheim, my gardener, for soil from my border number six, fill a deep box with it, and plant in it these three bulbs. They will flower next May—that is to say, in seven months;* and when you see the flower forming on the stem, be careful at night to protect them from the wind, and by day to screen them from the sun. They will flower black; I am quite sure of it. You are then to apprise the president of the Haarlem Society. He will cause the colour of the flower to be proved before the committee, and those hundred thousand guilders will be paid to you."

Rosa heaved a deep sign. " And now," continued Cornelius, wiping away a tear which was glistening in his eye, and which was shed much more for that marvellous black tulip which he was not to see, than for the life which he was about to lose, " I have no wish left except that the tulip should be called ' *Rosa Barlaeensis*,' that is to say, that its name should combine yours and mine; and as, of course, you do not understand Latin, and might therefore forget this name, try to get for me pencil and paper, that I may write it down for you."

Rosa sobbed afresh, and handed to him a book, bound in shagreen, which bore the initials C. W.

" What is this?" asked the prisoner.

" Alas!" replied Rosa, " it is the Bible of your poor godfather Cornelius De Witte. From it he derived strength to endure the torture, and to hear his sentence without flinching. I found it in this cell, after the death of the martyr, and have preserved it as a relic. To-day I brought it to you, for it seemed to me that this book must possess in itself a power which is quite heavenly. Write in it what you have to write, Mynheer Cornelius; and though, unfortunately, I am not able to read, I will take care that what you write shall be accomplished." Cornelius took the Bible, and kissed it reverently.

" With what shall I write?" asked Cornelius.

" There is a pencil in the Bible," said Rosa.

This was the pencil which John De Witte had lent to his brother, and which he had forgotten to take away with him.

Cornelius took it, and, on the last fly-leaf (for it will be remembered that the first was torn out), drawing near his end like his godfather, he wrote, with a no less firm hand:

" On this day, the 23rd of August, 1672, being on the point of rendering, although innocent, my soul to God on the scaffold, I bequeath to Rosa Gryphus, the only worldly good which has remained to me of all that I have possessed in this world, the rest having been confiscated; I bequeath, I say, to Rosa Gryphus, three bulbs, which I am convinced must produce, in the next May, the Grand Black Tulip, for which a prize of a hundred thousand guilders has been offered by the Haarlem Society, requesting that she may be paid the same sum in my stead, as my sole heiress, under the only condition of her marrying a respectable young man of about my age, who loves her, and whom she loves, and of her giving the grand black tulip, which will constitute a new species, the name of ' *Rosa Barlaeensis*,' that is to say, hers and mine combined.

" So may God grant me mercy; and to her health and long life!

" CORNELIUS VAN BAERLE."

The prisoner, then giving the Bible to Rosa, said—
" Read."

" Alas!" she answered, " I have already told you I cannot read."

Cornelius then read to Rosa the testament that he had just made.

The agony of the poor girl almost overpowered her.

" Do you accept my conditions?" asked the prisoner, with a melancholy smile, kissing the trembling hands of the afflicted girl.

" Oh, I don't know, sir," she stammered.

" You don't know, child; and why not?"

" Because there is one condition which I am afraid I cannot keep."

" Which? I should have thought that all was settled between us."

" You give me the hundred thousand guilders as a marriage-portion, don't you?"

" Yes."

" And under the condition of my marrying a man whom I love?"

" Certainly."

" Well, then, sir, this money cannot belong to me. I shall never love anyone; neither shall I marry."

And, after having with difficulty uttered these words, Rosa almost swooned away in the violence of her grief.

Cornelius, frightened at seeing her so pale and sinking, was going to take her in his arms, when a heavy step, followed by other dismal sounds, was heard on the staircase, amidst the continued barking of the dog.

" They are coming to fetch you. O God! O God!" cried Rosa, wringing her hands. " And have you nothing more to tell me?"

She fell on her knees, with her face buried in her hands, and became almost senseless.

" I have only to say that I wish you to preserve these bulbs as the most precious treasure, and carefully to treat them according to the directions I have given you! Do it for my sake; and now farewell, Rosa."

" Yes, yes," she said, without raising her head; " I will do anything you bid me, except marrying," she added, in a low voice, " for that, oh! that is impossible for me."

She then put that cherished treasure next her beating heart.

The noise on the staircase which Cornelius and Rosa had heard was caused by the Recorder, who was coming for the prisoner.

He was followed by the executioner, by the soldiers who were to form the guard round the scaffold, and by some curious hangers-on of the prison.

Cornelius, without showing any weakness, but likewise without any bravado, received them rather as friends than as persecutors, and quietly submitted to all those preparations which these men were obliged to make in performance of their duty.

Then, casting a glance into the yard through the narrow iron-barred window of his cell, he perceived the scaffold, and, at twenty paces distant from it, the gibbet, from which, by order of the Stadtholder, the outraged remains of the two brothers De Witte had been taken down.*

When the moment came to descend, in order to follow the guards, Cornelius sought with his eyes the angelic look of Rosa; but he saw, behind the swords and halberds, only a form lying outstretched near a wooden bench, and a death-like face, half-covered with long golden locks.

But, whilst falling down senseless, Rosa, still obeying her friend, had pressed her hand on her velvet bodice, and, forgetting everything in the world besides, instinctively grasped the precious deposit which Cornelius had entrusted to her care.

Leaving the cell the young man could still see, in the convulsively-clenched fingers of Rosa, the yellowish leaf from that Bible on which Cornelius De Witte had with such difficulty and pain written those few lines, which, if Van Baerle had read them, would undoubtedly have been the saving of a man and a tulip.

CHAPTER TWELVE

The Execution

CORNELIUS HAD not three hundred paces to walk outside the prison to reach the foot of the scaffold. At the bottom of the staircase the dog quietly looked at him whilst he was passing: Cornelius even fancied he saw in the eyes of the monster a certain expression, as it were, of compassion.

The dog, perhaps, knew the condemned prisoners, and only bit those who left as free men.

The shorter the way from the door of the prison to the foot of the scaffold, the more fully, of course, it was crowded with curious people.

These were the same who, not satisfied with the blood which they had shed three days before, were now craving for a new victim.

And scarcely had Cornelius made his appearance, than a fierce groan ran through the whole street, spreading all over the yard, and re-echoing from the streets which led to the scaffold, and which were likewise crowded with spectators.

The scaffold indeed looked like an islet at the confluence of several rivers.

In the midst of these threats, groans, and yells, Cornelius, very likely in order not to hear them, had buried himself in his own thoughts.

And what did he think of, in his last melancholy journey?

Neither of his enemies, nor of his judges, not of his executioners.

He thought of the beautiful tulips which he would see from heaven above, at Ceylon, or Bengal, or elsewhere, when he would be able to look with pity on this earth, where John and Cornelius De Witte had been murdered, for having thought too much of politics, and where Cornelius Van Baerle was about to be murdered for having thought too much of tulips.

" It is only one stroke of the axe," said the philosopher to himself, " and my beautiful dream will begin to be realised."

Only there was still a chance, just as it had happened before to M. De Chalais, to M. De Thou,* and other slovenly-executed people, that the headsman might inflict more than one stroke; that is to say, more than one martyrdom, on the poor tulip-fancier.

Yet, notwithstanding all this, Van Baerle mounted the scaffold not the less resolutely, proud of having been the friend of that illustrious John, and godson of that noble Cornelius De Witte, whom the ruffians, who were now crowding to witness his own doom, had torn to pieces and burnt three days before.

He knelt down, said his prayers, and observed, not without a feeling of sincere joy, that laying his head on the block, and keeping his eyes open, he would be able, to his last moment, to see the grated window of the Buitenhof.

At length the fatal moment arrived, and Cornelius placed his chin on the cold, damp block. But in this moment his eyes closed involuntarily, to receive more resolutely the terrible avalanche which was about to fall on his head, and to engulf his life.

A gleam, like that of lightning, passed over the scaffold: it was the executioner raising his sword.

Van Baerle bade farewell to the grand black tulip, certain of awakening in another world full of light and glorious tints.

Three times he felt, with a shudder, the cold stream of air from the knife coming near his neck, but, what a surprise! he felt neither pain nor shock.

He saw no change in the colour of the sky, and of the world around him.

Then suddenly, Van Baerle felt gentle hands raising him, and soon stood on his feet again, although trembling a little.

He looked around him. There was someone by his side,

reading a large parchment, sealed with a huge seal of red wax.

And the same sun, yellow and pale, as it behoves a Dutch sun to be, was shining in the skies; and the same grated window looked down upon him from the Buitenhof.

And the same rabble, no longer yelling, but completely thunderstruck, was staring at him from the streets below.

Van Baerle began to be sensible to what was going on around him.

High Highness, William, Prince of Orange, very likely afraid that Van Baerle's blood would turn the scale of judgment against him, had compassionately taken into consideration his good character, and the apparent proofs of his innocence.

His Highness, accordingly, had granted him his life.*

Cornelius at first hoped that the pardon would be complete, and that he would be restored to his full liberty and to his flower-borders at Dort.

But Cornelius was mistaken. To use an expression of Madame de Sevigné,* who wrote about the same time, " there was a postscript to the letter "; and the most important point of the letter was contained in the postscript.

In this postscript, William of Orange, Stadtholder of Holland, condemned Cornelius Van Baerle to imprisonment for life. He was not sufficiently guilty to suffer death, but he was too much so to be set at liberty.

Cornelius heard this clause; but, the first feeling of vexation and disappointment over, he said to himself—

" Never mind, all is not lost yet; there is some good in this perpetual imprisonment; Rosa will be there, and also my three bulbs of the black tulip are there."

But Cornelius forgot that the Seven Provinces had seven prisons, one for each; and that the board of the prisoner is anywhere else less expensive than at the Hague, which is a capital.

High Highness, who, as it seems, did not possess the means to feed Van Baerle at the Hague, sent him to undergo his perpetual imprisonment at the fortress of Loevestein,* very near Dort, but, alas! also very far from it; for Loevestein, as the geographers tell us, is situated at the point of the islet which is formed by the confluence of the Waal and the Meuse, opposite Gorcum.

Van Baerle was sufficiently versed in the history of his country to know that the celebrated Grotius was confined in that castle, after the death of Barneveldte;* and that the States, in their generosity to the illustrious publicist, jurist, historian, poet, and divine, had granted to him for his daily maintenance the sum of twenty-four stivers.*

" I," said Baerle to himself—" I am worth much less than Grotius: they will hardly give me twelve stivers, and I shall live miserably; but, never mind, at all events, I shall live."

Then, suddenly, a terrible thought struck him.

" Ah!" he exclaimed, " how damp and misty that part of the country is; and the soil so bad for the tulips; and then Rosa will not be at Loevestein!"

CHAPTER THIRTEEN

What Was Going On all this Time in the Mind of One of the Spectators

WHILST CORNELIUS was engaged with his own thoughts, a coach had driven up to the scaffold. This vehicle was for the prisoner. He was invited to enter it, and he obeyed.

His last look was toward the Buitenhof. He hoped to see at the window the face of Rosa, brightening up again. But the coach was drawn by good horses, who soon carried Van Baerle away from among the shouts, which the rabble roared in honour of the most magnanimous Stadtholder, mixing with it a spice of abuse against the brothers De Witte and the godson of Cornelius, who had just now been saved from death.

This reprieve suggested to the worthy spectators remarks such as the following:

" It's very fortunate that we used such speed in having justice done to that great villain John, and to that little rogue Cornelius, otherwise His Highness might have snatched them from us, just as he has done this fellow."

Among all the spectators whom Van Baerle's execution had attracted to the Buitenhof, and whom the sudden turn iif affairs had disagreeably surprised, undoubtedly the one most disappointed was a certain respectably-dressed burgher, who, from early morning, had made such a good use of his feet and elbows that he at last was separated from the scaffold only by the file of soldiers which surrounded it.

Many had shown themselves eager to see the perfidious blood of the guilty Cornelius flow, but not one had shown such a keen anxiety as the individual just alluded to.

The most furious had come to the Buitenhof at daybreak.

to secure a better place; but he, outdoing even them, had passed the night at the threshold of the prison, from whence, as we have already said, he had advanced to the very foremost rank, *unguibus et rostro;** that is to say, coaxing some, and kicking the others.

And when the executioner had brought the prisoner to scaffold, the burgher who had mounted on the stone of the pump, the better to see and be seen, made to the executioner a sign, which meant—

" It's a bargain, isn't it?"

The executioner answered by another sign, which was meant to say:

" Be quiet, it's all right."

This burgher was no other than Mynheer Isaac Boxtel, who, since the arrest of Cornelius, had come to the Hague, to try if he could not get hold of the three suckers of the black tulip.

Boxtel had at first tried to bring over Gryphus to his interest, but the jailer had not only the snarling fierceness, but likewise the fidelity of a dog. He had therefore bristled up at Boxtel's hatred, whom he suspected to be a warm friend of the prisoner, making trifling inquiries, to contrive, with the more certainty, some means of escape for him.

Thus to the very first proposals which Boxtel made to Gryphus to filch the bulbs, which Cornelius Van Baerle must be supposed to conceal, if not in his breast, at least in some corner of his cell, the surly jailer had only answered by kicking Mynheer Isaac out, and setting the dog at him.

The piece which the mastiff had torn from his hose did not discourage Boxtel. He came back to the charge, but this time Gryphus was in his bed, feverish, and with a broken arm. He, therefore, was not able to admit the petitioner, who then addressed himself to Rosa, offering to buy for her a head-dress of pure gold if she would but get the bulbs for him. On this the generous girl, although not yet knowing the value of the object of the robbery, which was to be so well remunerated, had directed the tempter to the executioner, as the heir of the prisoner.

In the meanwhile the sentence had been pronounced. Thus Isaac had no more time to bribe anyone. He therefore clung to the idea which Rosa had suggested: he went to the executioner.

Isaac had not the least doubt but that Cornelius would die with his bulbs on his heart.

But there were two things which Boxtel did not calculate upon.

Rosa, that is to say—love.

William of Orange, that is to say—clemency.

But for Rosa and William, the calculations of the envious neighbour would have been correct.

But for William, Cornelius would have died.

But for Rosa, Cornelius would have died with his bulbs on his heart.

Mynheer Boxtel went to the headsman, to whom he gave himself out as a great friend of the condemned man and from whom he bought all the clothes of the dead man that was to be, for one hundred guilders, rather an exorbitant sum, as he engaged to leave all the trinkets of gold and silver to the executioner.

But what was the sum of a hundred guilders to a man who was all but sure to buy with it the prize of the Haarlem Society?

It was money lent at a thousand per cent., which, as nobody will deny, was a very handsome investment.

The headsman, on the other hand, had scarcely anything to do to earn his hundred guilders. He needed only, as soon as the execution was over, to allow Mynheer Boxtel to ascend the scaffold with his servants, to remove the inanimate remains of his friend.

The thing was, moreover, quite customary among the "faithful brethren," when one of their masters died a public death in the yard of the Buitenhof.

A fanatic like Cornelius might very easily have found another fanatic who gave a hundred guilders for his remains.

The executioner also readily acquiesced in the proposal, making only one condition—that of being paid in advance.

Boxtel, like the people who enter a show at a fair, might not be pleased, and refuse to pay on going out.

Boxtel paid in advance, and waited.

After this the reader may imagine how excited Boxtel was; with what anxiety he watched the guards, the Recorder, and the executioner; and with what intense interest he surveyed the movements of Van Baerle. How would he place himself on the block? how would he fall? and would he not, in falling, crush those inestimable bulbs? had not he at least taken care to enclose them in a golden box? as gold is the hardest of all metals.*

Every trifling delay irritated him. Why did that stupid executioner thus lose his time in brandishing his sword over the head of Cornelius, instead of cutting that head off?

But when he saw the Recorder take the hand of the condemned, and raise him, whilst drawing forth the parchment from his pocket; when he heard the pardon of the Stadtholder publicly read out—then Boxtel was no more like a human being; the rage and malice of the tiger, of the hyena, and of the serpent glistened in his eyes, and vented itself in his yell and his movements. Had he been able to get at Van Baerle he would have pounced upon him and strangled him.

And so, then, Cornelius was to live, and was to go to Loevestein, and thither to his prison he would take with him his bulbs; and perhaps he would even find a garden where the black tulip would flower for him.*

Boxtel, quite overcome by his frenzy, fell from the stone on some Orangemen, who, like him, were sorely vexed at the turn which affairs had taken. They, mistaking the frantic cries of Mynheer Isaac for demonstrations of joy, began to belabour him with kicks and cuffs, such as could not have been administered in better style by any prize-fighter on the other side of the Channel.*

Blows were, however, nothing to him. He wanted to run after the coach which was carrying away Cornelius with his bulbs. But in his hurry he overlooked a paving-stone in his way, stumbled, lost his centre of gravity, rolled over to a distance of some yards, and only rose again, bruised and begrimed, after the whole rabble of the Hague with their muddy feet had passed over him.

One would think that this was enough for one day, but Mynheer Boxtel did not seem to think so, as in addition to having his clothes torn, his back bruised, and his hands scratched, he inflicted upon himself the further punishment of tearing out his hair by handfuls as an offering to that goddess of envy, who, as mythology teaches us, has for her head-dress only a set of serpents.*

CHAPTER FOURTEEN

The Pigeons of Dort

IT WAS, indeed, in itself a great honour for Cornelius Van
Baerle to be confined in the same prison which had once
received the learned master Grotius.

But, on arriving at the prison, he met with an honour
even greater. As chance would have it, the cell formerly
inhabited by the illustrious Barneveldte happened to be
vacant, when the clemency of the Prince of Orange sent
the tulip-fancier Van Baerle there.

The cell had a very bad character at the castle, since the
time when Grotius, by means of the device of his wife, made
escape from thence in that famous book-chest, which the
jailers forgot to examine.

On the other hand, it seemed to Van Baerle an auspicious
omen that this very cell was assigned to him; for, according
to his ideas, a jailer ought never to have given to a second
pigeon the cage from which the first had so easily flown.

The cell has an historical character. We will only state
here that, with the exception of an alcove, which was contrived there for the use of Madame Grotius, it differed in
no respect from the other cells of the prison; only, perhaps,
it was a little higher, and had a splendid view from the
grated window.

Cornelius himself felt perfectly indifferent as to the place
where he had to lead an existence which was little more
than vegetation. There were only two things now for which
he cared, and the possession of which was a happiness
enjoyed only in imagination.

A flower and a woman, both of them, as he conceived,
lost to him for ever.*

Fortunately the good doctor was mistaken. In his prison-
cell the most adventurous life which ever fell to the lot of
any tulip-fancier was reserved for him.

One morning, whilst at his window, inhaling the fresh air which came from the river, and casting a longing look to the windmills of his dear old city, Dort, which were looming in the distance behind a forest of chimneys, he saw flocks of pigeons coming from that quarter, to perch fluttering on the pointed gable ends of Loevestein.

These pigeons, Van Baerle said to himself, are coming from Dort, and consequently may return there. By fastening a little note to the wing of one of these pigeons, one might have a chance to send a message there. Then, after a few moments' consideration, he exclaimed—

" I will do it."

A man grows very patient who is twenty-eight years of age, and condemned to a prison for life—that is to say, to something like twenty-two or twenty-three thousand days of captivity.

Van Baerle, from whose thoughts the three bulbs were never absent, made a snare for catching the pigeons, baiting the birds with all the resources of his kitchen, such as it was, for eight stivers (sixpence, English) a day; and, after a month of unsuccessful attempts, he at last caught a female bird.

It cost him two more months to catch a male bird; he then shut them up together, and having about the beginning of the year 1673 obtained some eggs from them, he released the female, which, leaving the male behind to hatch the eggs in her stead, flew joyously to Dort, with the note under her wing.

She returned in the evening. She had preserved the note.

Thus it went on for fifteen days, at first to the disappointment, and then to the great relief of Van Baerle.

On the sixteenth day, at last, she came back without it.

Van Baerle had addressed it to his nurse, the old Frisian woman; and implored any charitable soul who might find it to convey it to her as safely and speedily as possible.

In this letter there was a little note enclosed for Rosa.

Van Baerle's nurse had received the letter in the following way.

Leaving Dort, Mynheer Isaac Boxtel had abandoned not

only his house, his servant, his observatory, and his telescope, but also his pigeons.

The servant, having been left without wages, first lived on his little savings, and then on his master's pigeons.

Seeing this, the pigeons emigrated from the roof of Isaac Boxtel to that of Cornelius Van Baerle.

The nurse was a kind-hearted woman, who could not live without having something to love. She conceived an affection for the pigeons which had thrown themselves on her hospitality; and when Boxtel's servant reclaimed them with culinary intentions, having eaten the first fifteen already, and now wishing to eat the other fifteen, she offered to buy them from him for a consideration of six stivers per head.

This being just double their value, the man was very glad to close the bargain, and the nurse found herself in undisputed possession of the pigeons of her master's envious neighbour.*

The note, as we have said, had reached Van Baerle's nurse.

And also, it came to pass, that one evening in the beginning of February, just when the stars were beginning to twinkle, Cornelius heard on the staircase of the little turret a voice, which thrilled through him.

He put his hand on his heart, and listened.

It was the sweet harmonious voice of Rosa.

Let us confess it, Cornelius was not so stupefied with surprise, or so beyond himself with joy, as he would have been, but for the pigeon, which, in answer to his letter, had brought back hope to him, under her empty wing; and, knowing Rosa, he expected, if the note had ever reached her, to hear of her whom he loved, and also of his three darling bulbs.

He rose, listened once more, and bent forward towards the door.

Yes, they were indeed the accents which had fallen so sweetly on his heart at the Hague.

The question now was whether Rosa, who had made the journey from the Hague to Loevestein, and who—Cornelius did not understand how—had succeeded even in penetrating into the prison, would also be fortunate enough in penetrating to the prisoner himself.

Whilst Cornelius, debating this point within himself, was building all sorts of castles in the air, and was struggling between hope and fear, the shutter of the grating in the door opened, and Rosa, beaming with joy, and beautiful in her pretty national costume, but still more beautiful from the grief which for the last five months had blanched her cheeks, pressed her little face against the wire-grating of the window, saying to him—

" Oh! sir, sir, here I am!"

Cornelius stretched out his arms, and, looking to Heaven, uttered a cry of joy—

" Oh, Rosa, Rosa!"

" Hush! let us speak low; my father follows on my heels," said the girl.

" Your father?"

" Yes, he is in the courtyard at the bottom of the staircase, receiving the instructions of the Governor; he will presently come up."

" The instructions of the Governor?"

" Listen to me; I'll try to tell you all in a few words. The Stadtholder has a country-house, one league distant from Leyden, properly speaking a kind of large dairy, and my aunt, who was his nurse, has the management of it. As soon as I received your letter, which, alas! I could not read myself, but which your housekeeper read to me, I hastened to my aunt; there I remained until the Prince should come to the dairy; and when he came I asked him, as a favour, to allow my father to exchange his post at the prison of the Hague with the jailer of the fortress of Loevestein. The Prince could not have suspected my object; had he known it, he would have refused my request; but, as it is, he granted it."

" And so you are here?"

" As you see."

" And thus I shall see you every day?"

" As often as I can manage it."

" Oh, Rosa, my beautiful Rosa, do you love me a little?"

" A little?" she said; " you make no great pretensions, Mynheer Cornelius."

Cornelius tenderly stretched out his hands towards her, but they were only able to touch each other with the tips of their fingers through the wire grating.

" Here is my father," said she.

Rosa then abruptly drew back from the door, and ran to meet old Gryphus, who made his appearance at the top of the staircase.

CHAPTER FIFTEEN

The Little Grated Window

GRYPHUS WAS followed by the mastiff. The turnkey took the animal round the jail, so that, if needs be, he might recognise the prisoners.

" Father," said Rosa, " here is the famous prison from which Mynheer Grotius escaped. You know Mynheer Grotius?"

" Oh, yes, that rogue Grotius; a friend of that villain Barneveldte, whom I saw executed when I was a child. Ah! so Grotius; and that's the chamber from which he escaped. Well, I'll answer for it that no one shall escape after him in my time."

And thus opening the door, he began in the dark to talk to the prisoner.

The dog, on his part, went up to the prisoner, and growling, smelled about his legs, just as though to ask him what right he had still to be alive, after having left the prison in the company of the Recorder and the executioner.

But the fair Rosa called him to her side.

" Well, my master," said Gryphus, holding up his lantern to throw a little light around, " you see in me your new jailer. I am head turnkey, and have all the cells under my care. I'm not vicious, but I'm not to be trifled with, as far as discipline goes."

" My good master Gryphus, I know you perfectly well," said the prisoner, approaching to within the circle of light cast around by the lantern.

" Halloa! that's you, Mynheer Van Baerle," said Gryphus. " That's you; well, I declare, it's astonishing how people do meet."

" Oh, yes, and it's really a great pleasure to me, good Master Gryphus, to see that your arm is doing well, as you are able to hold your lantern with it."

Gryphus knitted his brow. " Now, that's just it," he said; " people always make blunders in politics. His Highness has granted you your life; I'm sure I should never have done so."

" Don't say so," replied Cornelius; " why not?"

" Because you are the very man to conspire again. You learned people have dealings with the devil."

" Nonsense, Master Gryphus. Are you dissatisfied with the manner in which I have set your arm, or with the price that I asked you?" said Cornelius laughing.

" On the contrary," growled the jailer, " you have set it only too well. There is some witchcraft in this. After six weeks I was able to use it as if nothing had happened; so much so that the doctor of the Buitenhof, who knows his trade well, wanted to break it again, to set it in the regular way, and promised me that I should have my blessed three months for my money before I should be able to move it."

" And you did not want that?"

" I said, ' Nay, as long as I can make the sign of the cross with that arm ' (Gryphus was a Roman Catholic), ' I laugh at the devil.' "

" But if you laugh at the devil, Master Gryphus, you ought with so much more reason to laugh at learned people."

" Ah, learned people, learned people. Why I would rather have to guard ten soldiers than one scholar. The soldiers smoke, guzzle, and get drunk; they are as gentle as lambs, if you only give them brandy or Moselle; but scholars, and drink, smoke, and fuddle—ah, that's altogether different. They keep sober, spend nothing, and have their heads always clear to make conspiracies. But I tell you, at the very outset, it won't be such an easy matter for you to conspire. First of all, you will have no books, no paper, and no conjuring book. It's books that helped Mynheer Grotius to get off."

" I assure you, Master Gryphus," replied Van Baerle, " that if I have entertained the idea of escaping, I most decidedly have it no longer."

" Well, well," said Gryphus, " just look sharp; that's

what I shall do also. But, for all that, I say His Highness has made a great mistake."

"Not to have cut off my head? Thank you, Master Gryphus."

"Just so, look whether the Mynheers de Witte don't keep very quiet now."

"That's very shocking what you say now, Master Gryphus," cried Van Baerle, turning away his head to conceal his disgust. "You forget that one of those unfortunate gentlemen was my friend, and the other my second father."

"Yes, but I also remember that the one, as well as the other, is a conspirator. And, moreover, I am speaking from Christian charity."

"Oh, indeed; explain that a little to me, my good Master Gryphus. I do not quite understand it."

"Well, then, if you had remained on the block of Master Harbruck——"*

"What?"

"You would not suffer any longer; whereas, I will not disguise it from you, I shall lead you a sad life of it."

"Thank you for the promise, Master Gryphus."

And whilst the prisoner smiled ironically at the old jailer, Rosa, from the outside, answered by a bright smile, which carried sweet consolation to the heart of Van Baerle.

Gryphus stepped towards the window.

It was still light enough to see, although indistinctly, through the gray haze of the evening, the vast expanse of the horizon.

"What view has one from here?" asked Gryphus.

"Why, a very fine and pleasant one," said Cornelius, looking at Rosa.

"Yes, yes; too much of a view—too much."

And at this moment the two pigeons, scared by the sight, and especially by the voice of the stranger, left their nest, and disappeared, quite frightened, in the evening mist.

"Halloa! what's this?" cried Gryphus.

"My pigeons," answered Cornelius.

"Your pigeons," cried the jailer, "your pigeons! Has a prisoner anything of his own?"

"Why, then," said Cornelius, "the pigeons which a merciful Father in Heaven has lent to me."

"So, here we have a breach of the rules already," replied Gryphus. "Pigeons! ah, young man, young man; I'll tell you one thing, that before to-morrow is over, your pigeons will boil in my pot."

"First of all you should catch them, Master Gryphus. You won't allow these pigeons to be mine. Well, I vow they are even less yours than mine."

"Omittance is no acquittance," growled the jailer, "and I shall certainly wring their necks before twenty-four hours are over; you may be sure of that."

Whilst giving utterance to this ill-natured promise, Gryphus put his head out of the window to examine the nest. This gave Van Baerle time to run to the door, and squeeze the hand of Rosa, who whispered to him—

"At nine o'clock this evening."

Gryphus, quite taken up with the desire of catching the pigeons next day, as he had promised he would do, saw and heard nothing of this short interlude; and, after having closed the window, he took the arm of his daughter, left the cell, turned the key twice, drew the bolts, and went off to make the same kind promises to the other prisoners.

He had scarcely withdrawn, when Cornelius went to the door to listen to the sound of his footsteps, and, as soon as they had died away, he ran to the window, and completely demolished the nest of the pigeons.

Rather than expose them to the tender mercies of his bullying jailer, he drove away for ever those gentle messengers, to whom he owed the happiness of having seen Rosa again.

This visit of the jailer, his brutal threats, and the gloomy prospect of the harshness with which, as he had before experienced, Gryphus watched his prisoners—all this was unable to extinguish in Cornelius the sweet thoughts, and especially the sweet hope, which the presence of Rosa had re-awakened in his heart.

He waited eagerly to hear the clock of the tower of Lœvestein strike nine.

The last chime was till vibrating through the air, when Cornelius heard on the staircase the light step, and the rustle of the flowing dress of the fair Frisian maid, and, soon after, a light appeared at the little grated window in the door, on which the prisoner fixed his earnest gaze.

The shutter opened on the outside.

" Here I am," said Rosa, out of breath from running up the stairs; " here I am."

" Oh, my good Rosa!"

" You are then glad to see me?"

" Can you ask? But how did you contrive to get here? Tell me."

" Now, listen to me. My father falls asleep every evening almost immediately after his supper; I then make him lie down, a little stupefied with his gin. Don't say anything about it, because, thanks to this nap, I shall be able to come every evening and chat for an hour with you."

" Oh, I thank you Rosa, dear Rosa."

Saying these words, Cornelius put his face so near the little window that Rosa withdrew hers.

" I have brought back to you your bulbs."*

Cornelius's heart leaped with joy. He had not yet dared to ask Rosa what she had done with the precious treasure which he had entrusted to her.

" Oh! you have preserved them, then?"

" Did you not give them to me as a thing which was dear to you?"

" Yes, but as I have given them to you, it seems to me that they belong to you."

" They would have belonged to me after your death, but, fortunately, you are alive now. Oh! how I blessed His Highness in my heart. If God grants to him all the happiness that I have wished him, certainly Prince William will be the happiest man on earth. When I looked at the Bible of your godfather Cornelius, I was resolved to bring back to you your bulbs, only I did not know how to accomplish it. I had, however, already formed the plan of going to the Stadtholder to ask from him, for my father, the appointment of jailer at Lœvestein when your housekeeper brought me your letter. Oh, how we wept together. But your letter only confirmed me the more in my resolution. I then left for Leyden, and the rest you know."

" What! my dear Rosa, you thought, even before receiving my letter, of coming to meet me again?"

" If I thought of it?" said Rosa, allowing her love to get the better of her bashfulness, " I thought of nothing else."

And, saying these words, Rosa looked so exceedingly pretty, that for the second time Cornelius placed his forehead and lips against the wire-grating; of course, we must presume with the laudable desire to thank the young lady.

Rosa, however, drew back as before.

" In truth," she said, with that coquetry which somehow or other is in the heart of every young girl, " I have often been sorry that I am not able to read, but never so much so, as when your housekeeper brought me your letter. I kept the paper in my hands, which spoke to other people and which was dumb to poor stupid me."

" So you have often regretted not being able to read," said Cornelius. " I should just like to know on what occasions."

" Troth," said she, laughing, " to read all the letters which were written to me."

" Oh, you received letters, Rosa?"

" By hundreds!"

" But who wrote to you?"

" Who? Why, in the first place, all the students who passed over the Buitenhof, all the officers who went to parade, all the clerks and even the merchants who saw me at my little window."

" And what did you do with all these notes, my dear Rosa?"

" Formerly," she answered, " I got some friend to read them to me, which was capital fun; but since a certain time—well, what use is it to attend to all this nonsense? Since a certain time I have burnt them."

" Since a certain time!" exclaimed Cornelius, with a look beaming with love and joy.

Rosa cast down her eyes, blushing. In her sweet confusion, she did not observe the lips of Cornelius, which, alas! only met the cold wire-grating. Yet, in spite of this obstacle, they communicated to the lips of the young girl the glowing breath of the most tender kiss.

At this sudden outburst of tenderness, Rosa grew as pale, and perhaps paler, than she had been on the day of the execution. She uttered a plaintive sob, closed her fine eyes, and fled, trying in vain to still the beating of her heart.

And thus Cornelius was again alone.

Rosa had fled so precipitately that she completely forgot to return to Cornelius the three bulbs of the black tulip.

CHAPTER SIXTEEN

Master and Pupil

THE WORTHY Master Gryphus, as the reader may have seen, was far from sharing the kindly feelings of his daughter for the godson of Cornelius De Witte.

There being only five prisoners at Lœvestein, the post of turnkey was not a very onerous one, but rather a sort of sinecure, given after a long period of service.

But the worthy jailer, in his zeal, had magnified, with all the power of his imagination, the importance of his office.

To him Cornelius had swelled to the gigantic proportions of a criminal of the first order. He looked upon him, therefore, as the most dangerous of all his prisoners. He watched all his steps, and always spoke to him with an angry countenance; punishing him for what he called his dreadful rebellion against such a clement prince as the Stadtholder.

Three times a day he entered Van Baerle's cell, expecting to find him trespassing;* but Cornelius had ceased to correspond, since his correspondent was at hand. It is even probable that if Cornelius had obtained his full liberty, with permission to go wherever he liked, the prison, *with* Rosa, and his bulbs would have appeared to him preferable to any other habitation in the world without Rosa and his bulbs.

Rosa, in fact, had promised to come and see him every evening, and from the first evening she had kept her word.

On the following evening she went up as before, with the same mysteriousness and the same precaution. Only she had this time resolved within herself not to approach too near the grating. In order, however, to engage Van Baerle in a conversation from the very first, which would seriously occupy his attention, she tendered to him through the grating the three bulbs, which were still wrapped up in the same paper.

But to the great astonishment of Rosa, Van Baerle pushed back her white hand with the tips of his fingers.

The young man had been considering about the matter.

" Listen to me," he said. " I think we should risk too much by embarking our whole fortune in one ship. Only think, my dear Rosa, that the question is to carry out an enterprise, which until now has been considered impossible, namely, that of making the grand black tulip flower. Let us, therefore, take every possible precaution, so that, in case of a failure, we may not have anything to reproach ourselves with. I will now tell you the way I have traced out for us."

Rosa was all attention to what he would say, much more on account of the importance which the unfortunate tulip-fancier attached to it, than that she felt interested in the matter herself.

" I will explain to you, Rosa," he said. " I dare say you have in this fortress a small garden, or some courtyard, or, if not that, at least some terrace."

" We have a very fine garden," said Rosa; " it runs along the edge of the Waal, and is full of fine old trees."

" Could you bring me some soil from the garden, that I may judge?"

" I will do so to-morrow."

" Take some from a sunny spot, and some from a shady so that I may judge of its properties in a dry and in a moist state."

" Be assured I shall."

" After having chosen the soil, and, if it be necessary, modified it, we will divide our three suckers; you will take one and plant it, on the day that I will tell you, in the soil chosen by me. It is sure to flower, if you tend it according to my directions."

" I will not lose sight of it for a minute."

" You will give me another, which I will try to grow here in my cell, and which will help me to beguile those long weary hours when I cannot see you. I confess to you I have very little hope for the latter one, and I look before-hand on this unfortunate bulb as sacrificed to my selfishness. However, the sun sometimes visits me. I will, besides, try to convert everything into an artificial help, even the heat and the ashes of my pipe; and lastly, we, or rather you, will keep in reserve the third sucker as our last resource, in case our first two experiments should prove a failure. In this manner, my dear Rosa, it is impossible that we should not succeed in gaining the hundred thousand guilders for your marriage-portion; and how dearly shall we enjoy that supreme happiness of seeing our work brought to a successful issue!"

"I know it all now," said Rosa. "I will bring you the soil to-morrow, and you will choose it for your bulb and for mine. As to that in which yours is to grow, I shall have several journeys to convey it to you, as I cannot bring much at a time."

"There is no hurry for it, dear Rosa; our tulips need not be put into the ground for a month at least. So you see we have plenty of time before us. Only I hope that, in planting your bulb, you will strictly follow all my instructions."

"I promise you I will."

"And when you have once planted it, you will communicate to me all the circumstances which may interest our nursling; such as change of weather, footprints on the walks, or footprints in the borders. You will listen at night whether our garden is not resorted to by cats. A couple of those untoward animals laid waste two of my borders at Dort."

"I will listen."

"On moonlight nights—have you ever looked at your garden, my dear child?"

"The window of my sleeping-room overlooks it."

"Well, on moonlight nights you will observe whether any rats come out from the holes in the wall. The rats are most mischievous by their gnawing everything; and I have heard unfortunate tulip-growers complain most bitterly of Noah for having put a couple of rats in the ark."

"I will observe, and if there are cats or rats——"

"You will apprise me of it—that's right. And, moreover," Van Baerle, having become mistrustful in his captivity, continued, " there is an animal much more to be feared than even the cat or the rat."

" What animal?"

" Man. You comprehend, my dear Rosa, a man may steal a guilder, and risk the prison for such a trifle, and, consequently, it is much more likely that some one might steal a hundred thousand guilders."

" No one ever enters the garden but myself."

" Thank you, thank you, my dear Rosa. All the joy of my life has still to come from you."

And as the lips of Van Baerle approached the grating with the same ardour as the day before, and as, moreover, the hour for retiring had struck, Rosa drew back her head, and stretched out her hand.

In this pretty little hand, of which the coquettish damsel was particularly proud, was the bulb.

Cornelius kissed most tenderly the tips of her fingers. Did he do so because his hand kept one of the bulbs of the Grand Black Tulip, or because this hand was Rosa's? We shall leave this point to the decision of wiser heads than ours.

Rosa withdrew with the two other suckers, pressing them to her heart.

Did she press them to her heart because they were the bulbs of the Grand Black Tulip, or because she had them from Cornelius?

This point, we believe, might be more readily decided than the other.

However that may have been, from that moment life became sweet, and again full of interest to the prisoner.

Rosa, as we have seen, had returned to him one of the suckers.

Every evening she brought to him, handful by handful, a quantity of soil from that part of the garden which he had found to be the best, and which, indeed, was excellent.

A large jug, which Cornelius had skilfully broken, did service as a flower-pot. He half-filled it, and mixed the earth of the garden with a small portion of dried river-mud; a mixture which formed an excellent soil.

Then, at the beginning of April, he planted his first sucker in that jug.

Not a day passed on which Rosa did not come to have her chat with Cornelius.

The tulips, concerning whose cultivation Rosa was taught all the mysteries of the art, formed the principal topic of the conversation; but, interesting as the subject was, people cannot always talk about tulips.

They, therefore, began to chat also about other things, and the tulip-fancier found out, to his great astonishment, what a vast range of subjects a conversation may comprise.

Only Rosa had made it a habit to keep her pretty face invariably six inches distant from the grating, having, perhaps, become mistrustful of herself.*

There was one thing especially which gave Cornelius almost as much anxiety as his bulbs—a subject to which he always returned—the dependence of Rosa on her father.*

Indeed, Van Baerle's happiness depended on the whim of this man. He might one day find Lœvestein dull, or the air of the place unhealthy, or the gin bad, and leave the fortress, and take his daughter with him, when Cornelius and Rosa would again be separated.

" Of what use would the carrier-pigeons then be?" said Cornelius to Rosa, " as you, my dear girl, would not be able to read what I should write to you, nor to write to me your thoughts in return."

" Well," answered Rosa, who, in her heart, was as much afraid of a separation as Cornelius himself, " we have one hour every evening; let us make a good use of it."

" I don't think we make such a bad use of it as it is."

" Let us employ it even better," said Rosa, smiling. " Teach me to read and to write. I shall make the best of your lessons, believe me; and, in this way, we shall never be separated any more, except by our own will."

" Oh, then, we have eternity before us," said Cornelius.

Rosa smiled, and quietly shrugged her shoulders.

" Will you remain for ever in prison?" she said; " and, after having granted you your life, will not His Highness also grant you your liberty? And will you not then recover your fortune, and be a rich man; and then, when you are driving in your own coach, riding your own horse, will you still look at poor Rosa, the daughter of a jailer, scarcely better than a hangman?"

Cornelius tried to contradict her, and certainly he would have done so with all his heart, and with all the sincerity of a soul full of love. She, however, smilingly interrupted him, saying, " How is your tulip going on ? "

To speak to Cornelius of his tulip was an expedient resorted to by her to make him forget everything, even Rosa herself.

" Pretty well, indeed," he said; " the coat is growing black; the sprouting has commenced; the veins of the bulb are swelling; in eight days hence, and perhaps sooner, we may distinguish the first buds of the leaves protruding— and yours, Rosa?"

" Oh, I have done things on a large scale, and according to your directions."

" Now, let me hear, Rosa, what you have done," said Cornelius, with as tender an anxiety as he had lately shown to herself.

" Well," she said, smiling, for in her own heart she could not help studying this double love of the prisoner for herself and for the black tulip, " I have done things on a large scale; I have prepared a bed as you described it to me, on a clear spot, far from trees and walls, in a soil slightly mixed with sand, rather moist than dry, without a fragment of stone or pebble."

" Well done, Rosa, well done!"

" I am now only waiting for your further orders to put in the bulb; you know that I must be behindhand with you, as I have in my favour all the chances of good air, of the sun, and abundance of moisture."

" All true, all true," exclaimed Cornelius, clapping his hands with joy, " you are a good pupil, Rosa, and you are sure to gain your hundred thousand guilders."

" Don't forget," said Rosa, smiling, " that your pupil, as you call me, has still other things to learn beside the cultivation of tulips."

" Yes, yes; and I am as anxious as you are, Rosa, that you should learn to read."

" When shall we begin?"

" At once."

" No, to-morrow."

" Why to-morrow?"

" Because to-day our hour is expired, and I must leave you."

" Already? But what shall we read?"

" Oh!" said Rosa, " I have a book—a book which I hope will bring us luck."

" To-morrow, then."

" Yes, to-morrow."

On the following evening, Rosa returned with the Bible of Cornelius De Witte.

CHAPTER SEVENTEEN

The First Sucker

ON THE following evening, as we have said, Rosa returned with the Bible of Cornelius De Witte.

Then began between the master and the pupil one of those charming scenes which are the delight of the novelist who has to describe them.

The grated window, the only opening through which the two lovers were able to communicate, was too high for conveniently reading a book, although it had been quite sufficient for them to read each other's faces.

Rosa, therefore, had to press the open book against the grating edgeways, holding above it, in her right hand, the lamp, but Cornelius hit upon the lucky idea of fixing it to the bars, so as to afford her a little rest. Rosa was then enabled to follow with her finger the letters and syllables, which she was to spell for Cornelius, who with a straw pointed out the letters to his attentive pupil through the holes of the grating.

The light of the lamp illuminated the rich complexion of Rosa, her blue liquid eye and her golden hair under her head-dress of gold brocade; with her fingers held up, and showing in the blood, as it flowed downwards in the veins, that pale pink hue which shines before the light, owing to the living transparency of the flesh tint.

Rosa's intellect rapidly developed itself under the animating influence of the mind of Cornelius, and when the difficulties seemed too arduous, the sympathy of two loving hearts seemed to smooth them away.

And Rosa, after having returned to her room, repeated in her solitude the reading lessons, but, at the same time, recalled all the delight which she had felt whilst receiving them.

One evening she came half an hour later than usual. This was too extraordinary an incident not to call forth, at once, Cornelius's inquiries after its cause.

" Oh! do not be angry with me," she said, " it is not my fault. My father has renewed an acquaintance with an old crony who used to visit him at the Hague, and to ask him to let him see the prison. He is a good sort of fellow, fond of his bottle, tells funny stories, and, moreover, is very free with his money, so as always to be ready to stand a treat."

" You don't know anything further of him?" asked Cornelius, surprised.

" No," she answered, " it's only for about a fortnight that my father has taken such a fancy to this friend who is so assiduous in visiting him."

" Ah, so," said Cornelius, shaking his head uneasily, as every new incident seemed to him to forebode some catastrophe, " very likely some spy; one of those who are sent into jails to watch both prisoners and their keepers."

" I don't believe that," said Rosa, smiling; " if that worthy person is spying after any one, it is certainly not after my father."

" After whom, then?"

" Me, for instance."

" You?"

" Why not?" said Rosa, smiling.

" Ah, that's true," Cornelius observed with a sigh. " You will not always have suitors in vain. This man may become your husband."

" I don't say anything to the contrary."

" What cause have you to entertain such a happy prospect?"

" Rather say this fear, Mynheer Cornelius."

" Thank you, Rosa, you are right; well, I will say, then, this fear!"

" I have only this reason——"

" Tell me; I am anxious to hear."

" This man came several times before to the Buitenhof, at the Hague. I remember now, it was just about the time when you were confined there. When I left, he left too; when I came here, he came after me. At the Hague, his pretext was that he wanted to see you."

" See me?"

" Yes. It must have undoubtedly been only a pretext; for now, when he could plead the same reason, as you are my father's prisoner again, he does not care any longer for you; quite the contrary; I heard him say to my father only yesterday that he did not know you."

" Go on, Rosa, pray do, that I may guess who that man is, and what he wants."

" Are you quite sure, Mynheer Cornelius, that none of your friends can interest himself for you?"

" I have no friends, Rosa; I have only my old nurse, whom you know, and who knows you. Alas! poor Sue, she would come herself, and use no roundabout ways. She would at once say to your father or to you, ' My good sir, or my good miss, my child is here, see how grieved I am, let me see him only for one hour and I'll pray for you as long as I live.' No, no," continued Cornelius, " with the exception of my poor old Sue, I have no friends in this world."

" Then I come back to what I thought before; and the more so as last evening at sunset, whilst I was arranging the border where I am to plant your bulb, I saw a shadow gliding between the elder trees, and the aspens. I did not appear to see him, but it was this man. He concealed himself and saw me digging the ground, and certainly it was *me* whom he followed, and *me* whom he was spying after. I could not move my rake, or touch one atom of soil, without his noticing it."

" Oh! yes, yes, he is in love with you," said Cornelius. " Is he young? Is he handsome?"

Saying this, he looked anxiously at Rosa, eagerly waiting for her answer.

" Young? handsome?" cried Rosa, bursting into a laugh. " He is hideous to look at; crooked, nearly fifty years of age, and never dares to look me in the face, or to speak except in an undertone."

" And his name?"

" Jacob Gisels."

" I don't know him."

" Then you see that, at all events, he does not come after you."

" At any rate, if he loves you, Rosa, which is very likely, as to see you is to love you, at least you don't love him."

" To be sure I don't."

" Then you wish me to keep my mind easy?"

" I should certainly ask you to do so."

" Well, then, now as you begin to know how to read, you will read all that I write to you of the pangs of jealousy and of absence, won't you, Rosa?"

" I shall read it, if you write with good big letters."

Then, as the turn which the conversation took began to make Rosa uneasy, she asked—

" By the bye, how is your tulip going on?"

" Oh, Rosa, only imagine my joy; this morning I looked at it in the sun, and after having moved the soil aside which covers the bulb, I saw the first sprouting of the leaves. This small germ has caused me a much greater emotion than the order of His Highness which turned aside the sword, already raised, at the Buitenhof."

" You hope, then?" said Rosa, smiling.

" Yes, yes, I hope."

" And I, in my turn, when shall I plant my bulb?"

" Oh, the first favourable day I will tell you, but, whatever you do, let nobody help you, and don't confide your secret to any one in the world; do you see, a connoisseur, by merely looking at the bulb, would be able to distinguish its value; and so, my dearest Rosa, be careful in locking up the third sucker which remains to you."

" It is still wrapped up in the same paper in which you put it, and just as you gave it me. I have laid it at the bottom of my chest under my point lace, which keeps it dry without pressing upon it. But good night, my poor captive gentleman."

" How? already?"

" It must be, it must be."

" Coming so late, and going so soon."

" My father might grow impatient not seeing me return, and that precious lover might suspect a rival."

Here she listened uneasily.

" What is it?" asked Van Baerle.

" I thought I heard something."

" What, then?"

" Something like a step, creaking on the staircase."

" Surely," said the prisoner, " that cannot be Master Gryphus; he is always heard at a distance."

" No, it is not my father, I am quite sure, but——"

" But?"

" But it might be Mynheer Jacob."

Rosa rushed towards the staircase, and a door was really heard rapidly to close, before the young damsel had got down the first ten steps.

Cornelius was very uneasy about it, but it was, after all, only a prelude to greater anxieties.*

The following day passed without any remarkable incident. Gryphus made his three visits, and discovered nothing. He never came at the same hours, as he hoped thus to discover the secrets of the prisoner. Van Baerle, therefore, had devised a contrivance, a sort of pulley, by means of which he was able to lower or to raise his jug below the ledge of tiles and stone before his window. The strings by which this was effected he had found means to cover with that moss which generally grows on tiles, or in the crannies of the walls.

Gryphus suspected nothing, and the device succeeded for eight days. One morning, however, when Cornelius, absorbed in the contemplation of his bulb, from which a germ of vegetation was already peeping forth, had not heard old Gryphus coming upstairs, as a gale of wind was blowing which shook the whole tower, the door suddenly opened.

Gryphus, perceiving an unknown and consequently a forbidden object in the hands of his prisoner, pounced upon it with the same rapidity as the hawk on its prey.

As ill luck would have it, his coarse, hard hand, the same

which he had broken, and which Cornelius Van Baerle had set so well, grasped at once in the midst of the jug on the spot where the bulb was lying in the soil.

" What have you got here?" he roared. " Ah! have I caught you?" and with this he grubbed in the soil.

" I? nothing, nothing," cried Cornelius, trembling.

" Ah! have I caught you? A jug, and earth in it. There is some criminal secret at the bottom of all this."

" Oh, my good Master Gryphus," said Van Baerle imploringly and anxious, like the partridge robbed of her young by the reaper.

In fact, Gryphus was beginning to dig the soil with his crooked fingers.

" Take care, sir, take care," said Cornelius, growing quite pale.

" Care of what! zounds! of what?" roared the jailer.

" Take care, I say, you will crush it, Master Gryphus!"

And, with a rapid and almost frantic movement, he snatched the jug from the hands of Gryphus, and hid it like a treasure under his arms.

But Gryphus, obstinate, like an old man, and more and more convinced that he was discovering here a conspiracy against the Prince of Orange, rushed up to his prisoner, raising his stick; seeing, however, the impassible resolution of the captive to protect his flower-pot, he was convinced that Cornelius trembled much less for his head than for his jug.

He, therefore, tried to wrest it from him by force.

" Halloa!" said the jailer, furious, " here, you see, you are rebelling."

" Leave me my tulip," cried Van Baerle.

" Ah, yes, tulip," replied the old man, " we know well the shifts of prisoners."

" But I vow to you——"

" Let go," repeated Gryphus, stamping his foot, " let go, or I shall call the guard."

" Call whoever you like, but you shall not have this flower except with my life."

Gryphus, exasperated, plunged his finger a second time

into the soil, and now he drew out the bulb; which certainly looked quite black; and whilst Van Baerle, quite happy to have saved the vessel, did not suspect that the adversary had possessed himself of its precious contents, Gryphus hurled the softened bulb with all his force on the flags, where, almost immediately after, it was crushed to atoms under his heavy shoe.

Van Baerle saw the work of destruction, got a glimpse of the juicy remains of his darling bulb, and, guessing the cause of the ferocious joy of Gryphus, uttered a cry of agony, which would have melted the heart even of that ruthless jailer who some years before killed Pellisson's spider.*

The idea of striking down this spiteful bully passed like lightning through the brain of the tulip-fancier. The blood rushed to his brow, and seemed like fire in his eyes, which blinded him; and he raised in his two hands the heavy jug with all the now useless earth which remained in it. One instant more, and he would have flung it on the bald head of old Gryphus.

But a cry stopped him; a cry of agony, uttered by poor Rosa, who, trembling and pale, with her arms raised to Heaven, made her appearance behind the grated window, and thus interposed between her father and her friend.

Gryphus then understood the danger with which he had been threatened, and he broke out in a volley of the most terrible abuse.

" Indeed," said Cornelius to him, " you must be a very mean and spiteful fellow, to rob a poor prisoner of his only consolation, a tulip bulb."

" For shame, my father," Rosa chimed in, " it is indeed a crime you have committed here."

" Ah, is that you, my little chatterbox?" the old man cried, boiling with rage and turning towards her; " don't you meddle with what don't concern you, but go down as quickly as possible."

" Unfortunate me," continued Cornelius, overwhelmed with grief.

" After all, it is but a tulip," Gryphus resumed, as he

began to be a little ashamed of himself. "You may have as many tulips as you like; I have three hundred of them in my loft."

"To the devil with your tulips!" cried Cornelius; "you are worthy of each other: had I a hundred thousand millions of them, I would gladly give them for the one which you have just destroyed!"

"Ah! so," Gryphus said, in a tone of triumph; "now there we have it. It was not your tulip you cared for. There was in that false bulb some witchcraft, perhaps some means of correspondence with conspirators against His Highness who has granted you your life. I always said they were wrong in not cutting your head off."

"Father, father!" cried Rosa.

"Yes, yes! it is better as it is now," repeated Gryphus, growing warm; "I have destroyed it, and I'll do the same again, as often as you repeat the trick. Didn't I tell you, my fine fellow, that I would make your life a hard one?"

"A curse on you!" Cornelius exclaimed, quite beyond himself with despair, as he gathered, with his trembling fingers, the remnants of that bulb on which he had rested so many joys and so many hopes.

"We shall plant the other to-morrow, my dear Mynheer Cornelius," said Rosa, in a low voice, who understood the intense grief of the unfortunate tulip-fancier, and who, with the pure sacred love of her innocent heart, poured these kind words, like a drop of balm, on the bleeding wounds of Cornelius.

CHAPTER EIGHTEEN

Rosa's Lover

ROSA HAD scarcely pronounced these consolatory words, when a voice was heard from the staircase asking Gryphus how matters were going on.

" Do you hear, father?" said Rosa.

" What?"

" Master Jacob calls you; he is uneasy."

" There was such a noise," said Gryphus; " wouldn't you have thought he would murder me, this doctor? They are always very troublesome fellows, these scholars."

Then, pointing with his finger towards the staircase, he said to Rosa, " Just lead the way, miss."

After this, he locked the door and called out, " I shall be with you directly, friend Jacob."

Poor Cornelius, thus left alone with his bitter grief, muttered to himself—

" Ah! you old hangman, it is me you have trodden under foot; you have murdered me; I shall not survive it!"

And certainly the unfortunate prisoner would have fallen ill, but for the counterpoise which Providence had granted to his grief, and which was called Rosa.

In the evening she came back. Her first words announced to Cornelius that henceforth her father would no longer make any objection to his cultivating flowers.

" And how do you know that?" the prisoner asked, with a doleful look.

" I know it, because he has said so."

" To deceive me, perhaps."

" No, he repents."

" Ah! yes, but too late."

" This repentance is not of himself."

" And who put it into him?"

" If you only knew how his friend scolded him."

" Ah, Master Jacob; he does not leave you, then, that Master Jacob?"

" At any rate, he leaves us as little as he can help."

Saying this she smiled in such a way, that the little cloud of jealousy which had darkened the brown of Cornelius speedily vanished.

" How was it?" asked the prisoner.

" Well, being asked by his friend, my father told at supper the whole story of the tulip, or rather of the bulb, and of his own fine exploit of crushing it."

Cornelius heaved a sigh, which might have been called a groan.

" Had you only seen Master Jacob at that moment!" continued Rosa. " I really thought he would set fire to the castle; his eyes were like two flaming torches, his hair stood on end, and he clenched his fist for a moment; I thought he would have strangled my father."

" ' You have done that,' he cried, ' you have crushed the bulb?'

" ' Indeed I have.'

" ' It is infamous,' said Master Jacob, ' it is odious! You have committed a great crime.'

" My father was quite dumbfounded.

" ' Are you mad, too?' he asked his friend."

" Oh! what a worthy man is this Master Jacob," muttered Cornelius, " an honest soul, an excellent heart, that he is."

" The truth is, that it is impossible to treat a man more rudely than he did my father: he was really quite in despair, repeating, over and over again—

" ' Crushed, crushed the bulb; my God, my God! crushed!'

" Then, turning towards me, he asked, ' But it was not the only one that he had?' "

" Did he ask that?" inquired Cornelius, with some anxiety.

" ' You think it was not the only one?' said my father. ' Very well, we shall search for the others.'

" ' You will search for the others?' cried Jacob, taking my father by the collar; but he immediately loosed him. Then, turning towards me, he continued asking: ' And what did that poor young man say?'

" I did not know what to answer, as you had so strictly enjoined me never to allow any one to guess the interest which you are taking in the bulb. Fortunately, my father saved me from the difficulty, by chiming in—

" ' What did he say? Didn't he fume and fret?'

" I interrupted him, saying, ' Was it not natural that he should be furious; you were so unjust and brutal, father?'

" ' Well, now! are you mad?' cried my father; ' what immense misfortune is it to crush a tulip-bulb? You may buy a hundred of them in the market of Gorcum.'

" ' Perhaps some less precious one than that was!" I incautiously replied."

" And what did Jacob say or do at these words?" asked Cornelius.

" At these words, if I must say it, his eyes seemed to flash like lightning."

" But," said Cornelius, " that was not all; I am sure he said something in his turn."

" ' So then, my pretty Rosa,' he said, with a voice as sweet as honey, ' so you think that bulb to have been a precious one?'

" I saw that I had made a blunder.

" ' What do I know?' I said negligently; ' do I understand anything of tulips? I only know—as unfortunately it is our lot to live with prisoners—that for them any pastime is of value. This poor Mynheer Van Baerle amused himself with this bulb. Well, I think it is very cruel to take from him the only thing that he could have amused himself with.'

" ' But, first of all,' said my father, ' we ought to know how he has contrived to procure this bulb.'

" I turned my eyes away to avoid my father's look; but I met those of Jacob.

" It was as if he had tried to read my thoughts at the bottom of my heart.

" Some little show of anger sometimes saves an answer. I shrugged my shoulders, turned my back, and advanced towards the door.

" But I was kept by something which I heard, although it was uttered in a very low voice only.

" Jacob said to my father:

" ' It would not be so difficult to ascertain that.'

" ' How so?'

" ' You need only search his person; and if he has the other bulbs, we shall find them, as there usually are three suckers!' "

" Three suckers!" cried Cornelius. " Did he say that I have three?"

" The word certainly struck me just as much as it does you. I turned round. They were both of them so deeply engaged in their conversation, that they did not observe my movement.

" ' But,' said my father, ' perhaps he has not got his bulbs about him?'

" ' Then take him down, under some pretext or other, and I will search his cell in the meanwhile.' "

" Halloa, halloa!" said Cornelius. " But this Mr. Jacob of yours is a villain, it seems."

" I am afraid he is."

" Tell me, Rosa," continued Cornelius, with a pensive air.

" What?"

" Did not you tell me, that on the day when you prepared your border this man followed you?"

" So he did."

" That he glided like a shadow behind the elder-trees?"

" Certainly."

" That not one of your movements escaped him?"

" Not one, indeed."

" Rosa," said Cornelius, growing quite pale.

" Well?"

" It was not you he was after."

" Who else, then?"

" It is not you that he is in love with!"

" But with whom else?"

" He was after my bulb, and is in love with my tulip!"

" You don't say so—and yet it is very possible," said Rosa.

" Will you make sure of it?"

" In what manner?"

" Oh! it would be very easy."

" Tell me."

" Go to-morrow into the garden; manage matters so that Jacob may know, as he did the first time, that you are going there, and that he may follow you. Feign to put the bulb in the ground; leave the garden; but look through the keyhole of the door and watch him."

" Well, and what then?"

" What then? We shall do, as he does."

" Oh!" said Rosa, with a sign, " you are very fond of your bulbs."

" To tell the truth," said the prisoner, sighing likewise, " since your father crushed that unfortunate bulb, I feel as if part of my own self had been paralysed."

" Now just hear me," said Rosa; " will you try something else?"

" What?"

" Will you accept the proposition of my father?"

" Which proposition?"

" Did not he offer to you tulip-bulbs by hundreds?"

" Indeed he did."

" Accept two or three, and, along with them, you may grow the third sucker."

" Yes, that would do very well," said Cornelius, knitting his brow, " if your father were alone; but there is that Master Jacob, who watches all our ways."

" Well, that is true; but only think! you are depriving yourself, as I can easily see, of a very great pleasure."

She pronounced these words with a smile, which was not altogether without a tinge of irony.

Cornelius reflected for a moment; he evidently was struggling against some vehement desire.

" No!" he cried at last, with the stoicism of a Roman of

old; "no, it would be a weakness, it would be a folly, it would be a meanness! If I thus gave up the only and last resource which we possess, to the uncertain chances of the bad passions of anger and envy, I should never deserve to be forgiven. No, Rosa, no; to-morrow we shall come to a conclusion as to the spot to be chosen for your tulip; you will plant it according to my instructions; and as to the third sucker"—Cornelius here heaved a deep sign—"watch over it, as a miser over his first or last piece of gold; as the mother over her child; as the wounded over the last drop of blood in his veins—watch over it, Rosa! Some voice within me tells me that it will be our saving; that it will be a source of good to us."*

"Be easy, Mynheer Cornelius," said Rosa, with a sweet mixture of melancholy and gravity; "be easy, your wishes are commands to me."

"And even," continued Van Baerle, warming more and more with his subject, "if you should perceive that your steps are watched, and that your speech has excited the suspicion of your father and of that detestable Master Jacob: well, Rosa, don't hesitate for one moment to sacrifice me, who am only still living through you; me, who have no one in the world but you; sacrifice me—don't come to see me any more."

Rosa felt her heart sink within her, and her eyes were filling with tears.

"Alas!" she said.

"What is it?" asked Cornelius.

"I see one thing."

"What do you see?"

"I see," she said, bursting out in sobs, "I see that you love your tulips with such love as to have no more room in your heart left for other affections."

Saying this, she fled.

Cornelius, after this, passed one of the worst nights he ever had had in his life.

Rosa was vexed with him, and with good reason. Perhaps she would never return to see the prisoner, and then he would have no more news either of Rosa or of his tulips.

We have to confess, to the disgrace of our hero and of floriculture, that of his two affections he felt most strongly inclined to regret the loss of Rosa; and when, at about three in the morning, he fell asleep, overcome with fatigue, and harassed with remorse, the grand black tulip yielded precedence in his dreams to the sweet blue eyes of the fair maid of Friesland.

CHAPTER NINETEEN

The Maid and the Flower

BUT POOR Rosa, in her secluded chamber, could not have known of whom or of what Cornelius was dreaming.

From what he had said she was more ready to believe that he dreamed of the black tulip than of her; and yet Rosa was mistaken.

But as there was no one to tell her so, and as the words of Cornelius's thoughtless speech had fallen upon her heart like drops of poison, she did not dream, but she wept.*

During the whole of this terrible night the poor girl did not close an eye, and before she rose in the morning, she had come to the resolution of making her appearance at the grated window no more.

But as she knew with what ardent desire Cornelius looked forward to the news about his tulip; and as, notwithstanding her determination not to see any more a man, her pity for whose fate was fast growing into love; she did not, on the other hand, wish to drive him to despair; she resolved to continue by herself the reading and writing lessons; and, fortunately, she had made sufficient progress to dispense with the help of a master, when the master was not to be Cornelius.

Rosa, therefore, applied herself most diligently to reading poor Cornelius De Witte's Bible, on the second fly-leaf of which the last will of Cornelius Van Baerle was written.

" Alas!" she muttered, when perusing again this document, which she never finished without a tear, the pearl of love, rolling from her limpid eyes on her blanched cheeks; " alas! at that time, I thought for one moment he loved me."

Poor Rosa! she was mistaken. Never had the love of the prisoner been more sincere than at the time at which we are now arrived, when in the contest between the black tulip and Rosa, the tulip had had to yield to her the first and foremost place in Cornelius's heart.

But Rosa was not aware of it.

Having finished reading, she took her pen, and began with as laudable diligence the by far more difficult task of writing.

As, however, Rosa was already able to write a legible hand, when Cornelius so uncautiously opened his heart, she did not despair of progressing quickly enough to write after eight days at the latest to the prisoner an account of his tulip.

She had not forgotten one word of the directions given to her by Cornelius, whose speeches she treasured in her heart, even when they did not take the shape of directions.

He, on his part, awoke deeper in love than ever. The tulip, indeed, was still a luminous and prominent object in his mind; but he no longer looked upon it as a treasure to which he ought to sacrifice everything, and even Rosa; but as a marvellous combination of nature and art, with which he would have been happy to adorn the bosom of his beloved one.

Yet during the whole of that day he was haunted with a vague uneasiness,* at the bottom of which was the fear lest Rosa should not come in the evening to pay him her usual visit. This thought took more and more hold of him, until at the approach of evening his whole mind was absorbed in it.

How his heart beat when darkness closed in. The words which he had said to Rosa on the evening before, and which had so deeply afflicted her, came now back to his mind more vividly than ever; and he asked himself how he could have told his gentle comforter to sacrifice him to his tulip, that is to say, to give up, if needs be, seeing him, whereas to him the sight of Rosa had become a condition of life.

In Cornelius's cell one heard the chimes of the clock of the fortress. It struck seven, it struck eight, it struck nine. Never did the metal voice vibrate more forcibly through the heart of any man than did the last stroke, marking the ninth hour, through the heart of Cornelius.

All was then silent again. Cornelius put his hand on his heart to repress, as it were, its violent palpitation, and listened.

The noise of her footstep, the rustling of her gown on the staircase, were so familiar to his ear, that she had no sooner mounted one step than he used to say to himself—

" Here comes Rosa."

This evening none of those little noises broke the silence of the lobby; the clock struck nine and a quarter; the half-hour; then a quarter to ten; and at last its deep tone announced, not only to the inmates of the fortress, but also to all the inhabitants of Lœvestein, that it was ten.

This was the hour at which Rosa generally used to leave Cornelius. The hour had struck, but Rosa had not come.

Thus, then, his foreboding had not deceived him: Rosa, being vexed, shut herself up in her room and left him to himself.

" Alas!" he thought, " I have deserved all this. She will come no more, and she is right in staying away; in her place I should do just the same."

Yet, notwithstanding all this, Cornelius listened, waited, and hoped until midnight; then he threw himself, in his clothes, on his bed.

It was a long and sad night for him; and the day brought no hope to the prisoner.

At eight in the morning, the door of his cell opened; but Cornelius did not even turn his head; he had heard the heavy step of Gryphus in the lobby, but this step had perfectly satisfied the prisoner that his jailer was coming alone.

Thus Cornelius did not even look at Gryphus.

And yet he would have been so glad to draw him out, and to inquire about Rosa. He even very nearly made this inquiry, strange as it would needs have appeared to her father. To tell the truth, there was in all this some selfish hope, to hear from Gryphus that his daughter was ill.

Except on extraordinary occasions Rosa never came during the day. Cornelius, therefore, did not really expect her as long as the day lasted. Yet his sudden starts, his listening at the door, his rapid glances, at every little noise, towards the grated window, showed clearly that the prisoner entertained some latent hope that Rosa would, somehow or other, break her rule.

At the second visit of Gryphus, Cornelius, contrary to all his former habits, asked the old jailer, with the most winning voice, about her health; but Gryphus contented himself with giving the laconical answer:

" All's well."

At the third visit of the day, Cornelius changed his former inquiry.

" I hope nobody is ill at Lœvestein?"

" Nobody," replied, even more laconically, the jailer, shutting the door before the nose of the prisoner.

Gryphus, being little used to this sort of civility on the part of Cornelius, began to suspect that his prisoner was about to try and bribe him.

Cornelius now was alone once more; it was seven o'clock in the evening, and the anxiety of yesterday returned with increased intensity.

But another time the hours passed away without bringing the sweet vision, which lighted up through the grated window the cell of poor Cornelius; and which, in retiring, left light enough in his heart to last until it came back again.

Van Baerle passed the night in an agony of despair. On the following day, Gryphus appeared to him even more hideous, brutal, and hateful than usual: in his mind, or rather in his heart, there had been some hope that it was the old man who prevented his daughter from coming.

In his wrath he would have strangled Gryphus, but would not this have separated him for ever from Rosa?

The evening closing in, his despair changed into melancholy, which was the more gloomy as, involuntarily, Van Baerle mixed up with it the thought of his poor tulip. It was now just that week in April which the most experienced gardeners point out as the precise time when tulips ought to be planted. He had said to Rosa—

"I shall tell you the day when you are to put the bulb in the ground."

He had intended to fix, at the vainly hoped-for interview, the following day as the time for that momentous operation. The weather was propitious; the air, although still damp, began to be tempered by those pale rays of the April sun which, being the first, appear so congenial, although so pale. How, if Rosa allowed the right moment for planting the bulb to pass by? If, in addition to the grief of seeing her no more, he should have to deplore the misfortune of seeing his tulip fail on account of its having been planted too late, or of its not having been planted at all!

These two vexations, combined, might well make him leave off eating and drinking.

This was the case on the fourth day.

It was pitiful to see Cornelius, dumb with grief, and pale from utter prostration, stretch out his head through the iron bars of his window, at the risk of not being able to draw it back again, to try and get a glimpse of the garden on the left, spoken of by Rosa, who had told him that its parapet overlooked the river. He hoped, that perhaps he might see, in the light of the April sun, Rosa or the tulip, the two lost objects of his love.

In the evening, Gryphus took away the breakfast and dinner of Cornelius, who had scarcely touched them.

On the following day, he did not touch them at all, and Gryphus carried the dishes away just as he had brought them.

Cornelius had remained in bed the whole day.

"Well," said Gryphus, coming down from the last visit; "I think we shall soon get rid of our scholar."

Rosa was startled.

"Nonsense," said Jacob, "what do you mean?"

"He doesn't drink, he doesn't eat, he doesn't leave his bed. He will get out of it, like Mynheer Grotius, in a chest; only the chest will be a coffin."

Rosa grew as pale as death.

"Ah!" she said to herself, "he is uneasy about his tulip."

And rising with a heavy heart, she returned to her chamber, where she took a pen and paper, and, during the whole of that night, busied herself with tracing letters.

On the following morning, when Cornelius got up to drag himself to the window, he perceived a paper which had been slipped under the door.

He pounced upon it, opened it, and read the following words—in a handwriting which he could scarcely have recognised as that of Rosa, so much had she improved during her short absence of seven days:

" Be easy, your tulip is going on well."

Although these few words of Rosa's somewhat soothed the grief of Cornelius, yet he felt not the less the irony which was at the bottom of them. Rosa, then, was not ill, she was offended; she had not been forcibly prevented from coming, but had voluntarily stayed away. Thus Rosa, being at liberty, found in her own will the force not to come and see him, who was dying with grief at not having seen her.

Cornelius had paper and a pencil which Rosa had brought to him. He guessed that she expected an answer, but that she would not come before the evening to fetch it. He therefore wrote on a piece of paper, similar to that which he had received:

" It was not my anxiety about the tulip that has made me ill, but grief at not seeing you."

After Gryphus had made his last visit of the day, and darkness had set in, he slipped the paper under the door, and listened with the most intense attention; but he neither heard Rosa's footsteps, nor the rustling of her gown.

He only heard a voice as feeble as a breath, and gentle like a caress, which whispered through the grated little window in the door, the word—

" To-morrow."

Now to-morrow was the eighth day. For eight days Cornelius and Rosa had not seen each other.

CHAPTER TWENTY

The Events which Took Place during those Eight Days

ON THE following evening, at the usual hour, Van Baerle heard someone scratch at the grated little window, just as Rosa had been in the habit of doing in the hey-day of their friendship.

Cornelius being, as may easily be imagined, not far off from the door, perceived Rosa, who at last was waiting again for him with her lamp in her hand.

Seeing him so sad and pale, she was startled, and said—

" You are ill, Mynheer Cornelius?"

" Yes, I am," he answered, as indeed he was suffering in mind and in body.

" I saw that you did not eat," said Rosa; " my father told me that you remained in bed all day. I then wrote to you to calm your uneasiness concerning the fate of the most precious object of your anxiety."

" And I," said Cornelius, " I have answered. Seeing you return, my dear Rosa, I thought you had received my letter."

" It is true I have received it."

" You cannot this time excuse yourself with not being able to read. Not only do you read very fluently, but also you have made marvellous progress in writing."

" Indeed, I have not only received, but also read your note. Accordingly I am come to see whether there might not be some remedy to restore you to health."

" Restore me to health?" cried Cornelius; " but have you any good news to communicate to me?"

Saying this, the poor prisoner looked at Rosa, his eyes sparkling with hope.

Whether she did not, or would not, understand this look, Rosa answered gravely—

" I have only to speak to you about your tulip, which, as

I well know, is the object uppermost in your mind."

Rosa pronounced these few words in a freezing tone, which cut deeply into the heart of Cornelius. He did not suspect what lay hidden under this appearance of indifference, with which the poor girl affected to speak of her rival, the black tulip.

" Oh!" muttered Cornelius, " again! again! Have I not told you, Rosa, that I thought but of you; that it was you alone whom I regretted, you whom I missed, you whose absence I felt more than the loss of liberty and of life itself?"

Rosa smiled with a melancholy air.

" Ah!" she said, " your tulip has been in such danger."

Cornelius trembled involuntarily, and allowed himself to be caught in the trap, if ever the remark was meant as such.

" Danger!" he cried, quite alarmed, " what danger?"

Rosa looked at him with gentle compassion; she felt that what she wished was beyond the power of this man, and that he must be taken, as he was, with his little foible.

" Yes," she said, " you have guessed the truth, that suitor and amorous swain, Jacob, did not come on my account."

" And what did he come for?" Cornelius anxiously asked.

" He came for the sake of the tulip."

" Alas !" said Cornelius, growing even paler at this piece of information than he had been when Rosa, a fortnight before, had told him that Jacob was coming for her sake.

Rosa saw this alarm, and Cornelius guessed, from the expression of her face, in what direction her thoughts were running.

" Oh! pardon me, Rosa," he said, " I know you, and I am well aware of the kindness and sincerity of your heart. To you God has given the thought and strength for defending yourself, but to my poor tulip, when it is in danger, God has given nothing of the sort."

Rosa, without replying to this excuse of the prisoner, continued—

" From the moment when I first knew that you were

uneasy on account of the man who followed me, and in whom I had recognised Jacob, I was even more uneasy myself. On the day, therefore, after that on which I saw you last, and on which you said——"

Cornelius interrupted her.

"Once more, pardon me, Rosa!" he cried. "I was wrong in saying to you what I said. I have asked your pardon for that unfortunate speech before. I ask it again: shall I always ask it in vain?"

"On the following day," Rosa continued, "remembering what you had told me about the stratagem which I was to employ to ascertain whether that odious man was after the tulip, or after me——"

"Yes, yes, odious. Tell me," he said, "do you hate that man?"

"I do hate him," said Rosa, "as he is the cause of all the unhappiness I have suffered these eight days."

"You, too, have been unhappy, Rosa? I thank you a thousand times for this kind confession."

"Well, on the day after that unfortunate one, I went down into the garden, and proceeded towards the border where I was to plant your tulip, looking round all the while to see whether I was again followed as I was last time."

"And then?" Cornelius asked.

"And then the same shadow glided between the gate and the wall, and once more disappeared behind the elder-trees."

"You feigned not to see him, didn't you?" Cornelius asked, remembering all the details of the advice which he had given to Rosa.

"Yes, and I stooped over the border, in which I dug with a spade, as if I was going to put the bulb in."

"And he—what did he do during all this time?"

"I saw his eyes glisten through the branches of the tree, like those of a tiger!"

"There you see, there you see!" cried Cornelius.

"Then, after having finished my make-believe work, I retired."

"But only behind the garden-door, I dare say, so that

you might see through the keyhole what he was going to do when you had left?"

"He waited for a moment, very likely to make sure of my not coming back; after which he sneaked forth from his hiding-place, and approached the border by a long roundabout; at last, having reached his goal, that is to say: the spot where the ground was newly turned, he stopped with a careless air, looking about in all directions, and scanning every corner of the garden, every window of the neighbouring houses, and even the sky; after which, thinking himself quite alone, quite isolated, and out of everybody's sight, he pounced upon the border, plunged both his hands into the soft soil, took a handful of the mould, which he gently frittered between his fingers to see whether the bulb was in it, and repeated the same thing twice or three times, until at last he perceived that he was outwitted. Then, keeping down the agitation which was raging in his breast, he took up the rake, smoothed the ground, so as to leave it, on his retiring, in the same state as he had found it; and, quite abashed and rueful, walked back to the door, affecting the unconcerned air of an ordinary visitor of the garden."

"Oh! the wretch," muttered Cornelius, wiping the cold sweat from his brow. "Oh! the wretch. I guessed his intentions. But the sucker, Rosa; what have you done with it? It is already rather late to plant it."*

"The sucker? It has been in the ground for these six days."

"Where? and how?" cried Cornelius. "Good Heavens! what imprudence. Where is it? In what sort of soil is it? In what aspect? Good or bad? Is there no risk of having it filched by that detestable Jacob?"

"There is no danger of its being stolen," said Rosa, "unless Jacob will force the door of my chamber."

"Oh! then it is with you in your bedroom?" said Cornelius, somewhat relieved. "But in what soil? in what vessel? You don't let it grow, I hope, in water, like those good ladies of Haarlem and Dort,* who imagine that water could replace the earth?"

"You may make yourself comfortable on that score," said Rosa, smiling; "your sucker is not growing in water."

"I breathe again."

"It is in a good sound stone-pot, just about the size of the jug in which you had planted yours. The soil is composed of three parts of common mould, taken from the best spot of the garden, and one of the sweepings of the road. I have heard you and that detestable Jacob, as you call him, so often talk about what is the soil best fitted for growing tulips, that I know it as well as the first gardener of Haarlem."

"And now, what is the aspect, Rosa?"

"At present it has the sun all day long—that is to say, when the sun shines. But when it once peeps out of the ground, I shall do, as you have done here, dear Mynheer Cornelius, I shall put it out in my window, on the eastern side, from eight in the morning until eleven, and in my window, towards the west, from three to five in the afternoon."

"That's it, that's it," cried Cornelius: "and you are a perfect gardener, my pretty Rosa. But I am afraid the nursing of my tulip will take up all your time."

"Yes, it will," said Rosa, "but never mind. Your tulip is my daughter. I shall devote to it the same time as I should to a child of mine, if I were a mother. Only by becoming its mother," Rosa added, smilingly, "can I cease to be its rival."

"My kind and pretty Rosa!" muttered Cornelius, casting on her a glance, in which there was much more of the lover than of the gardener, and which afforded Rosa some consolation.

Then, after a silence of some moments, during which Cornelius had grasped through the openings of the grating for the receding hand of Rosa, he said—

"Do you mean to say that the bulb has now been in the ground for six days?"

"Yes, six days, Mynheer Cornelius," she answered.

"And it does not yet show leaf?"

" No; but I think it will to-morrow."

" Well, then, to-morrow you will bring me news about it, and about yourself, won't you, Rosa? I care very much for the daughter, as you called it just now, but I care even much more for the mother."

" To-morrow?" said Rosa, looking at Cornelius askance, " I don't know whether I shall be able to-morrow."

" Good Heavens!" said Cornelius, " why can't you come to-morrow?"

" Mynheer Cornelius, I have lots of things to do."

" And I have only one," muttered Cornelius.

" Yes," said Rosa, " to love your tulip."

" To love you, Rosa."

Rosa shook her head, after which followed a pause.

" Well " (Cornelius at last broke the silence), " well, Rosa, everything changes in the realm of nature; the flowers of spring are succeeded by other flowers; and the bees, which so tenderly caressed the violets and the wall-flowers, will flutter with just as much love about the honey-suckles, the rose, the jessamine, and the carnation."

" What does all this mean?" asked Rosa.

" You have abandoned me, Miss Rosa, to seek your pleasure elsewhere. You have done well, and I will not complain. What claim have I to your fidelity?"

" My fidelity!" Rosa exclaimed, with her eyes full of tears, and without caring any longer to hide from Cornelius this dew of pearls dropping on her cheeks, " my fidelity! have I not been faithful to you?"

" Do you call it faithful to desert me, and to leave me here to die?"

" But, Mynheer Cornelius," said Rosa, " am I not doing everything for you that could give you pleasure? have I not devoted myself to your tulip?"

" You are bitter, Rosa; you reproach me with the only unalloyed pleasure which I have had in this world."

" I reproach you with nothing, Mynheer Cornelius, except, perhaps, with the intense grief which I felt when people came to tell me at the Buitenhof that you were about to be put to death."

" You are displeased, Rosa, my sweet girl, with my loving flowers."

" I am not displeased with your loving them, Mynheer Cornelius, only it makes me sad to think that you love them better than you do me."

" Oh! my dear, dear Rosa, look how my hands tremble; look at my pale cheek; hear how my heart beats.* It is for you, my love, not for the black tulip. Destroy the bulb, destroy the germ of that flower, extinguish the gentle light of that innocent and delightful dream, to which I have accustomed myself; but love me, Rosa, love me; for I feel deeply that I love but you."

" Yes, after the black tulip," sighed Rosa, who at last no longer coyly withdrew her warm hands from the grating, as Cornelius most affectionately kissed them.

" Above and before everything in this world, Rosa."

" May I believe you?"

" As you believe in your own existence."

" Well, then, be it so; but loving me does not bind you to much."

" Unfortunately it does not bind me more than I am bound, but it binds you, Rosa—you."

" To what?"

" First of all, not to marry."

She smiled.

" That's your way," she said; " you are tyrants, all of you. You worship a certain beauty; you think of nothing but her. Then you are condemned to death; and, whilst walking to the scaffold, you devote to her your last sigh; and now you expect poor me to sacrifice to you all my dreams and my happiness."

" But who is the beauty you are talking of, Rosa?" said Cornelius, trying in vain to remember a woman to whom Rosa might possibly be alluding.

" The dark beauty, with a slender waist, small feet, and a noble head; in short, I am speaking of your flower."

Cornelius smiled.

" That is an imaginary lady-love, at all events; whereas, without counting that amorous Master Jacob—you, by your own account, are surrounded with all sorts of swains eager to make love to you. Do you remember, Rosa, what you told me of the students, officers, and clerks of the Hague ? Are there no clerks, officers, or students at Lœvestein ? "

" Indeed there are, and lots of them."

" Who write letters?"

" They do write."

" And now, as you know how to read——?"

Here Cornelius heaved a sigh at the thought, that, poor captive as he was, to him alone Rosa owed the faculty of reading the love-letters which she received.

" As to that," said Rosa, " I think that in reading the notes addressed to me, and passing the different swains in review who send them to me, I am only following your instructions."

" How so? My instructions?"

" Indeed, your instructions, sir," said Rosa, sighing in her turn; " have you forgotten the will written by your hand on the Bible of Cornelius De Witte? I have not forgotten it; for now, as I know how to read, I read it every day over and over again. In that will you bid me to love and marry a handsome young man of twenty-six or eight years. I am on the look-out for that young man, and as the whole of my day is taken up with your tulip, you must needs leave me the evenings to find him."

" But, Rosa, the will was made in the expectation of death, and, thanks to Heaven, I am still alive."

" Well, then, I shall not be after the handsome young man, and I shall come and see you."

" That's it, Rosa; come! come!"

" Under one condition."

" Granted beforehand!"

" That the black tulip shall not be mentioned for the next three days."

" It shall never be mentioned any more, if you wish it, Rosa."

" No, no," the damsel said, laughing, " I will not ask for impossibilities."

And, saying this, she brought her fresh cheek, as if unconsciously, so near the iron grating that Cornelius was able to touch it with his lips.

Rosa uttered a little scream, which, however, was full of love, and disappeared.

CHAPTER TWENTY-ONE

The Second Sucker

THE NIGHT was a happy one, and the whole of the next day happier still.

During the last few days, the prison had been heavy, dark, and lowering, as it were, with all its weight on the unfortunate captive. Its walls were black, its air chilling, the iron bars seemed to exclude every ray of light.

But when Cornelius awoke next morning, a beam of the morning sun was playing about those iron bars; pigeons were hovering about with outspread wings, whilst others were lovingly cooing on the roof or near the still closed window.

Cornelius ran to that window and opened it; it seemed to him as if new life, and joy, and liberty itself were entering, with this sunbeam, into his cell, which, so dreary of late, was now cheered and irradiated by the light of love.*

When Gryphus, therefore, came to see his prisoner in the morning, he no longer found him morose and lying in bed, but standing at the window, and singing a little ditty.

" Halloa !" exclaimed the jailer.

" How are you this morning?" asked Cornelius.

Gryphus looked at him with a scowl.

" And how is the dog, and Master Jacob, and our pretty Rosa?"

Gryphus ground his teeth, saying—

" Here is your breakfast."

" Thank you, friend Cerberus,"*said the prisoner; " you are just in time, I am very hungry."

" Oh! you are hungry, are you?" said Gryphus.

" And why not?" asked Van Baerle.

" The conspiracy seems to thrive," remarked **Gryphus**.

" What conspiracy?"

155

" Very well; I know what I know, Master Scholar; just be quiet, we shall be on our guard."

" Be on your guard, friend Gryphus; be on your guard, as long as you please; my conspiracy as well as my person is entirely at your service."

" We'll see that at noon."

Saying this, Gryphus went out.

" At noon?" repeated Cornelius; " what does that mean? Well, let us wait until the clock strikes twelve, and we shall see."

It was very easy for Cornelius to wait for twelve at mid-day, as he was already waiting for nine at night.

It struck twelve, and there was heard on the staircase not only the steps of Gryphus, but also those of three or four soldiers who were coming up with him.

The door opened, Gryphus entered, led his men in, and shut the door after them.

" There, now search!"

They searched not only the pockets of Cornelius, but even his person; yet they found nothing.

They then searched the sheets, the mattress and the straw-mattress of his bed; and again they found nothing.

Now, Cornelius rejoiced that he had not taken the third sucker under his own care. Gryphus would have been sure to ferret it out in the search, and would then have treated it as he did the first.

And, certainly, never did prisoner look with greater complacency at a search made in his cell than Cornelius.

Gryphus retired with the pencil and the two or three leaves of white paper which Rosa had given to Van Baerle; this was the only trophy brought back from the expedition.

At six Gryphus came again, but alone; Cornelius tried to propitiate him, but Gryphus growled, showed a large tooth like a tusk, which he had in the corner of his mouth, and went out backwards like a man who is afraid of being attacked from behind.

Cornelius burst out laughing, to which Gryphus answered through the grating:

" Let him laugh that wins."

The winner that day was Cornelius—Rosa came at nine.

She was without a lantern. She needed no longer a light as she could now read. Moreover, the light might betray her, as Jacob was dogging her steps more than ever. And lastly, the light would have shown her blushes.

Of what did the young people speak that evening? Of those matters of which lovers speak at the house-doors in France, or from a balcony into the street in Spain; or down from a terrace into a garden in the East?

They spoke of those things which give wings to the hours; they spoke of everything except the black tulip.

At last, when the clock struck ten, they parted as usual.

Cornelius was happy, as thoroughly happy as a tulip-fancier would be, to whom one has not spoken about his tulip.

He found Rosa pretty, good, graceful, and charming.

But why did Rosa object to the tulip being spoken of?

This was indeed a great defect in Rosa.

Cornelius confessed to himself, sighing, that woman was not perfect.

Part of the night he thought of this imperfection; that is to say, as long as he was awake he thought of Rosa.

After having fallen asleep he dreamed of her.

But the Rosa of his dreams was by far more perfect than the Rosa of real life. Not only did the Rosa of his dreams speak of the tulip, but also brought to him a black one in a china vase.

Cornelius then awoke, trembling with joy and muttering—

" Rosa, Rosa, I love you."

And as it was already day he thought it right not to fall asleep again, and he continued following up the line of thought in which his mind was engaged when he awoke.

Ah! if Rosa had only conversed about the tulip, Cornelius would have preferred her to Queen Semiramis, to Queen Cleopatra, to Queen Elizabeth, to Queen Anne of Austria; that is to say, to the greatest or most beautiful queens whom the world has seen.*

There was one consolation—of the seventy-two hours during which Rosa would not allow the tulip to be mentioned, thirty-six had passed already; and the remaining thirty-six would pass quickly enough, eighteen with waiting for the evening's interview, and eighteen with rejoicing in its remembrance.

Rosa came at the same hour, and Cornelius submitted most heroically to the pangs which the compulsory silence concerning the tulip gave him.

His fair visitor, however, was well aware, that to command on the one hand people must yield on another; she, therefore, no longer drew back her hands from the grating, and even allowed Cornelius tenderly to kiss her beautiful golden tresses.

Poor girl! she had no idea that these playful little lovers' tricks were much more dangerous than speaking of the tulip was; but she became aware of the fact as she returned with a beating heart, with glowing cheeks, dry lips, and moist eyes.

And on the following evening, after the first exchange of salutations, she retired a step, looking at him with a glance, the expression of which would have rejoiced his heart could he but have seen it.

" Well," she said, " she is up."

" She is up! Who? What?" asked Cornelius, who did not venture on a belief that Rosa would, of her own accord, have abridged the term of his probation.

" She? Well! my daughter, the tulip," said Rosa.

" What!" cried Cornelius, " you give me permission, then?"

" I do," said Rosa, with the tone of an affectionate mother who grants a pleasure to her child.

" Ah, Rosa!" said Cornelius, putting his lips to the grating, with the hope of touching a cheek, a hand, a forehead—anything, in short.

He touched something much better—two warm and half-open lips.

Rosa uttered a slight scream.

Cornelius understood that he must make haste to continue the conversation. He guessed that this unexpected kiss had frightened Rosa.

" Is it growing up straight?" he asked.

" Straight as a rocket," said Rosa.

" How high?"

" At least two inches."

" Oh, Rosa, take good care of it, and we shall soon see it grow quickly."

" Can I take more care of it?" said she; " indeed, I think of nothing else but the tulip."

" Of nothing else, Rosa? Why now, I shall grow jealous in my turn."

" Oh, you know that to think of the tulip is to think of you; I never lose sight of it. I see it from my bed; on my awaking, it is the first object that meets my eyes; and on falling asleep, the last on which they rest. During the day I sit and work by its side, for I have never left my chamber since I put it there."

" You are right, Rosa; it is your dowry, you know."

" Yes, and with it I may marry a young man of twenty-six or twenty-eight years, whom I shall be in love with."

" Don't talk in that way, you naughty girl."

That evening Cornelius was one of the happiest of men. Rosa allowed him to press her hand in his, and to keep it as long as he would, besides which he might talk of his tulip as much as he liked.

From that hour, every day marked some progress in the growth of the tulip and in the affection of the two young people.

At one time it was that the leaves had expanded, and at another that the flower itself had formed.

Great was the joy of Cornelius at this news, and his questions succeeded each other with a rapidity which gave proof of their importance.

" Formed!" exclaimed Cornelius, " is it really formed?"

" It is," repeated Rosa.

Cornelius trembled with joy, so much so that he was obliged to hold by the grating.

"Good Heavens!" he exclaimed.

Then turning again to Rosa, he continued his questions.

"Is the oval regular? the cylinder full? and are the points very green?"

"The oval is almost one inch long, and tapers like a needle, the cylinder swells at the sides, and the points are ready to open."

Two days after Rosa announced that they were open.

"Open, Rosa?" cried Cornelius. "Is the involucrum open? but then one may see, and already distinguish——"

Here the prisoner paused, anxiously taking breath.

"Yes," answered Rosa, "one may already distinguish a thread of different colour, as thin as a hair."

"And its colour?" asked Cornelius, trembling.

"Oh!" answered Rosa, "it is very dark."

"Brown?"

"Darker than that."

"Darker, my good Rosa, darker? Thank you. Dark like——"

"Dark, like the ink with which I wrote to you."

Cornelius uttered a cry of mad joy.

Then suddenly stopping, and clasping his hands, he said:

"Oh, there is not an angel in Heaven that may be compared to you, Rosa!"

"Indeed!" said Rosa, smiling at his enthusiasm.

"Rosa, you have worked with such ardour; you have done so much for me. Rosa, my tulip is about to flower, and it will flower black. Rosa! Rosa! you are the most perfect being on earth."

"After the tulip, though."

"Ah! be quiet, you malicious little creature, be quiet; for shame do not spoil my pleasure! But tell me, Rosa; as the tulip is so far advanced, it will flower in two or three days at the latest?"

"To-morrow, or the day after?"

"Ah! and I shall not see it," cried Cornelius, starting back, "I shall not kiss it, as a wonderful work of the Almighty, as I kiss your hand and your cheek, Rosa, when by chance they are near the grating."

Rosa drew near, not by accident, but intentionally, and Cornelius kissed her tenderly.

"Faith, I shall cull it, if you wish it."

"Oh, no, no, Rosa; when it is open, place it carefully in the shade, and immediately send a message to Haarlem, to the President of the Horticultural Society, that the grand black tulip is in flower. I know well it is far to Haarlem, but with money you will find a messenger; have you any money, Rosa?"

Rosa smiled.

"Oh! yes," she said.

"Enough?" asked Cornelius.

"I have three hundred guilders."

"Oh! if you have three hundred guilders, you must not send a messenger, Rosa, but you must go to Haarlem yourself."

"But what, in the meanwhile, is to become of the flower?"

"Oh, the flower? You must take it with you. You understand that you must not separate from it for an instant."

"But whilst I am not separating from it, I am separating from you, Mynheer Cornelius."

"Ah! that's true, my sweet Rosa. Oh! good Heavens! how wicked men are! What have I done to offend them, and why have they deprived me of my liberty? You are right, Rosa, I cannot live without you. Well, you will send someone to Haarlem—that's settled; really, the matter is wonderful enough for the President to put himself to some trouble. He will come himself to Loevestein to see the tulip."

Then, suddenly checking himself, he said with a faltering voice—

"Rosa, Rosa, if after all it should not flower black!"

"Oh, surely, surely you will know to-morrow, or the day after."

"And to wait until evening to know it, Rosa! I shall die with impatience. Could we not agree about a signal?"

"I shall do better than that."

" What will you do?"

" If it opens at night, I shall come and tell you myself. If it is day, I shall pass your door, and slip you a note either under the door or through the grating, during the time between my father's first and second inspection."

" Yes, Rosa, let it be so. One word of yours, announcing this news to me, will be a double happiness."

" There, ten o'clock strikes," said Rosa, " I must now leave you."

" Yes, yes," said Cornelius; " go, Rosa, go."

Rosa withdrew, almost melancholy, for Cornelius had all but sent her away.

It is true that he did so, in order that she might watch over his black tulip.

CHAPTER TWENTY-TWO

Joy

THE NIGHT passed away very sweetly for Cornelius, although in great agitation. Every instant he fancied he heard the gentle voice of Rosa calling him. He then started up, went to the door, and looked through the grating, but no one was behind it, and the lobby was empty.

Rosa, no doubt, would be watching too, but, happier than he, she watched over the tulip; she had before her eyes that noble flower, that wonder of wonders, which not only was unknown, but was not even thought possible until then.

What would the world say when it heard that the black tulip was found, that it existed, and that it was the prisoner Van Baerle who had found it?

How Cornelius would have spurned the offer of his liberty in exchange for his tulip!

Day came, without any news; the tulip was not yet in flower.

The day passed as the night. Night came, and with it Rosa, joyous and cheerful as a bird.

" Well?" asked Cornelius.

" Well, all is going on prosperously. This night, without any doubt, our tulip will be in flower."

" And will it flower black?"

" Black as jet."

" Without a speck of any other colour?"

" Without one speck."

" Good Heavens! my dear Rosa, I have been dreaming all night, in the first place of you " (Rosa made a sign of incredulity), " and then of what we must do."

" Well?"

" Well, and I will tell you now what I have decided on. The tulip once being in flower, and it being quite certain that it is perfectly black, you must find a messenger."

" If it is no more than that, I have a messenger quite ready."

" Is he safe?"

" One for whom I will answer—he is one of my lovers."

" I hope not Jacob."

" No, be quiet; it is the ferryman of Lœvestein, a smart young man of twenty-five."

" By Jove!"

" Be quiet," said Rosa, smiling, " he is still under age, as you yourself have fixed it at from twenty-six to twenty-eight."

" In fine, do you think you may rely on this young man?"

" As on myself; he would throw himself into the Waal or the Meuse if I bade him."

" Well, Rosa, this lad may be at Haarlem in ten hours; you will give me paper and pencil, and, perhaps better still, pen and ink, and I will write, or rather, on second thoughts, you will, for if I did it, being a poor prisoner, people might, like your father, see a conspiracy in it. You will write to the President of the Horticultural Society, and I am sure he will come."

" But if he tarries?"

" Well, let us suppose that he tarries one day, or even two; but it is impossible. A tulip-fancier like him will not tarry one hour, not one minute, not one second, to set out to see the eighth wonder of the world. But as I said, if he tarried one or even two days, the tulip will still be in its full splendour. The flower once being seen by the President, and the protocol being drawn up, all is in order; you will only keep a duplicate of the protocol, and entrust the tulip to him. Ah! if we had been able to carry it ourselves, Rosa, it would never have left my hands but to pass into yours; but this is a dream, which we must not entertain," continued Cornelius, with a sigh, " the eyes of strangers will see it flower to the last. And above all, Rosa, before the President has seen it, let it not be seen by anyone. Alas! if anyone saw the black tulip, it would be stolen."

" Oh!"

" Did you not tell me yourself what you apprehend from your lover Jacob? People will steal one guilder, why not a hundred thousand?"

" I shall watch; be quiet."

" But if it opened whilst you are here?"

" The whimsical little thing would indeed be quite capable of playing such a trick," said Rosa.

" And if on your return you find it open?"

" Well?"

" Oh, Rosa, whenever it opens, remember that not a moment must be lost in apprising the President."

" And in apprising you. Yes, I understand."

Rosa sighed, yet without any bitter feeling, but rather like a woman who begins to understand a foible, and to accustom herself to it.

" I return to your tulip, Mynheer Van Baerle, and as soon as it opens I will give you news, which being done the messenger will set out immediately."

" Rosa, Rosa, I don't know to what wonder under the sun I shall compare you."

" Compare me to the black tulip, and I promise you I shall feel very much flattered. Good night, then, till we meet again, Mynheer Cornelius."

" Oh, say good night, *my friend*."

" Good night, my friend," said Rosa, a little consoled.

" Say, my very dear friend."

" Oh, my friend."

" Very dear friend, I entreat you, say, very dear, Rosa; very dear."

" Very dear, yes, very dear," said Rosa, with a beating heart, beyond herself with happiness.*

During part of the night Cornelius, with his heart full of joy and delight, remained at his window, gazing at the stars, and listening for every sound.

Then, casting a glance from time to time towards the lobby—

" Down there," he said, " is Rosa, watching like myself, and waiting from minute to minute; down there, under Rosa's eyes, is the mysterious flower, which lives, which expands, which opens; perhaps Rosa holds in this moment the stem of the tulip between her delicate fingers. Touch it gently, Rosa. Perhaps she touches with her lips its expanding chalice. Touch it cautiously, Rosa, your lips are burning. Yes, perhaps at this moment, the two objects of my dearest love caress each other under the eye of Heaven."

At this moment a star blazed in the southern sky, and shot through the whole horizon, falling down, as it were, on the fortress of Lœvestein.

Cornelius felt a thrill run through his frame.

" Ah!" he said, " here is Heaven sending a soul to my flower."

And as if he had guessed correctly, nearly at that very moment the prisoner heard in the lobby a step light as that of a sylph, and the rustling of a gown, and a well-known voice, which said to him—

" Cornelius, my friend, my very dear friend, and very happy friend, come, come quickly."

Cornelius darted with one spring from the window to the door, his lips met those of Rosa's, who told him, with a kiss:

" It is open; it is black! Here it is."

" How, here it is!" exclaimed Cornelius.

" Yes, yes, we ought, indeed, to run some little risk to give a great joy; here it is; take it."

And with one hand she raised to the level of the grating a dark lantern, which she had lit in the meanwhile, whilst with the other she held to the same height the miraculous tulip.

Cornelius uttered a cry, and was nearly fainting.

" Oh!" muttered he, " my God, my God, thou dost reward me for my innocence and my captivity, as thou hast allowed two such flowers to grow at the grated window of my prison."

The tulip was beautiful, splendid, magnificent; its stem was more than eighteen inches high, it rose from out of four green leaves, which were as smooth and straight as iron lance-heads; the whole of the flower was as black and shining as jet.

"Rosa," said Cornelius, almost gasping, "Rosa, there is not one moment to lose in writing the letter."

"It is written, my dearest Cornelius," said Rosa.

"Is it indeed?"

"Whilst the tulip opened I wrote it myself, for I did not wish to lose a moment. Here is the letter, and tell me whether you approve of it."

Cornelius took the letter, and read, in a handwriting which was much improved even since the last little note he had received from Rosa, as follows:

"MYNHEER PRESIDENT—The black tulip is about to open, perhaps in ten minutes. As soon as it is open I shall send a messenger to you, with the request that you will come and fetch it in person from the fortress at Lœvestein. I am the daughter of the jailer, Gryphus, almost as much a captive as the prisoners of my father. I cannot, therefore, bring to you this wonderful flower. This is the reason why I beg you to come and fetch it yourself.

"It is my wish that it should be called *Rosa Barlaeensis*.

"It has opened; it is perfectly black; come, Mynheer President, come.

"I have the honour to be, your humble servant,
                                        "ROSA GRYPHUS."

"That's it, dear Rosa, that's it. Your letter is admirable! I could not have written it with such beautiful simplicity. You will give to the committee all the information that will be asked of you. They will then know how the tulip has been grown, how much care and anxiety, and how many sleepless nights it has cost. But, for the present, not a minute must be lost, for the messenger—the messenger."

"What's the name of the President?"

"Give me the letter; I will direct it. Oh, he is very well known. It is Mynheer Van Herysen,* the burgomaster of Haarlem; give it me, Rosa, give it me."

And with a trembling hand Cornelius wrote the address "To Mynheer Peter Van Herysen, Burgomaster, and President of the Horticultural Society of Haarlem."

"And now, Rosa, go, go," said Cornelius, "and let us implore the protection of God, who has so kindly watched over us until now."

CHAPTER TWENTY-THREE

The Rival

Aᴺᴰ ɪɴ fact the poor young people were in great need of protection.

They had never been so near the destruction of their hopes as at this moment, when they thought themselves certain of their fulfilment.

The reader cannot but have recognised in Jacob our old friend, or rather enemy, Isaac Boxtel, and has guessed, no doubt, that this worthy had followed, from the Buitenhof to Lœvestein, the object of his love and the object of his hatred —the black tulip and Cornelius Van Baerle.

What no one but a tulip-fancier, and an envious tulip-fancier could have discovered—the existence of the suckers and the endeavours of the prisoner, jealousy had enabled Boxtel if not to discover, at least to guess.

We have seen him, more successful under the name of Jacob than under that of Isaac, gain the friendship of Gryphus, which for several months he cultivated by means of the best Genièvre* ever distilled from the Texel to Antwerp, and he lulled the suspicion of the jealous turnkey by holding out to him the flattering prospect of his designing to marry Rosa.

Beside thus offering a bait to the ambition of the father, he managed, at the same time, to interest his zeal as a jailer, picturing to him in the blackest colours the learned prisoner whom Gryphus had in his keeping, and who, as the sham Jacob had it, was in league with Satan, to the detriment of His Highness the Prince of Orange.

At first he had also made some way with Rosa; not, indeed, in her affections, but inasmuch as, by talking to her of marriage and of love, he had evaded all the suspicions which he might otherwise have excited.

We have seen how his imprudence in following Rosa into the garden had unmasked him in the eyes of the young damsel, and how the instinctive fears of Cornelius had put the two lovers on their guard against him.

The reader will remember that the first cause for uneasiness was given to the prisoner by the rage of Jacob when Gryphus crushed the first sucker. In that moment Boxtel's exasperation was the more fierce, as, though suspecting that Cornelius possessed a second sucker, he by no means felt sure of it.

From that moment he began to dodge the steps of Rosa, not only following her to the garden, but also to the lobbies.

Only as at this time he followed her in the night, and barefooted, he was neither seen nor heard, except once, when Rosa thought she saw something like a shadow on the staircase.

Her discovery, however, was made too late, as Boxtel had heard from the mouth of the prisoner himself that a second sucker existed.

Taken in by the stratagem of Rosa, who had feigned to put it in the ground, and entertaining no doubt but that this little farce had been played in order to force him to betray himself, he redoubled his precaution, and employed every means suggested by his crafty nature to watch the others without being watched himself.

He saw Rosa conveying a large flower-pot of white earthenware from her father's kitchen to her bedroom. He saw Rosa washing in pails of water her pretty little hands, begrimed as they were with the mould which she had handled, to give her tulip the best soil possible.

And at last he hired, just opposite Rosa's window, a little attic, distant enough not to allow him to be recognised with the naked eye, but sufficiently near to enable him, with the help of his telescope, to watch everything that was going on at Lœvestein in Rosa's room, just as at Dort he had watched the dry-room of Cornelius.

He had not been installed more than three days in his attic before all his doubts were removed.

From morning to sunset the flower-pot was in the window, and like those charming female figures of Mieris and Metzys,* Rosa appeared at that window as in a frame, formed by the first budding sprays of the wild vine and the honeysuckle encircling her window.

Rosa watched the flower-pot with an interest which betrayed to Boxtel the real value of the object enclosed in it.

This object could not be anything else but the second sucker, that is to say, the quintessence of all the hopes of the prisoner.

When the nights threatened to be too cold, Rosa took in the flower-pot.

Well, it was then quite evident she was following the instructions of Cornelius, who was afraid of the bulb being killed by frost.

When the sun became too hot, Rosa likewise took in the pot from eleven in the morning until two in the afternoon.

Another proof: Cornelius was afraid lest the soil should become too dry.

But when the first leaves peeped out of the earth, Boxtel was fully convinced, and his telescope left him no longer in any uncertainty, before they had grown one inch in height.

Cornelius possessed two suckers, and the second was entrusted to the love and care of Rosa.

For it may well be imagined that the tender secret of the two lovers had not escaped the prying curiosity of Boxtel.

The question, therefore, was how to wrest the second sucker from the care of Rosa.

Certainly this was no easy task.

Rosa watched over the tulip as a mother over her child, or a dove over her eggs.

Rosa never left her room during the day, and, more than that, strange to say, she never left it in the evening.

For seven days Boxtel in vain watched Rosa; she was always at her post.

This happened during those seven days which made Cornelius so unhappy, depriving him at the same time of all news of Rosa and of his tulip.

Would the coolness between Rosa and Cornelius last for ever?

This would have made the theft much more difficult than Mynheer Isaac had at first expected.

We say the theft, for Isaac had simply made up his mind to steal the tulip; and as it grew in the most profound secrecy, and as, moreover, his word, being that of a renowned tulip-grower,* would any day be taken against that of an unknown girl without any knowledge of horticulture, or against that of a prisoner convicted of high treason, he confidently hoped that, having once got possession of the bulb, he would be certain to obtain the prize; and then the tulip, instead of being called *Tulipa nigra Barlaeensis*, would go down to posterity under the name of *Tulipa nigra Boxtellensis* or *Boxtellea*.

Mynheer Isaac had not yet quite decided which of these two names he would give to the tulip, but as both meant the same thing, this was, after all, not the question.

The question was, to steal the tulip. But in order that Boxtel might steal the tulip, it was necessary that Rosa should leave her room.

Great, therefore, was his joy when he saw the usual evening meetings of the lovers resumed.

He, first of all, took advantage of Rosa's absence to make himself fully acquainted with all the peculiarities of the door of her chamber. The lock was a double one, and in good order, but Rosa always took the key with her.

Boxtel at first entertained an idea of stealing the key, but it soon occurred to him that not only would it be exceedingly difficult to abstract it from her pocket, but also that, when she perceived her loss, she would not leave her room until the lock was changed, and then Boxtel's first theft would be useless.

He thought it, therefore, better to employ a different expedient. He collected as many keys as he could, and tried all of them during one of those delightful hours which Rosa and Cornelius passed together at the grating of the cell.

Two of the keys entered the lock, and one of them turned round once, but not the second time.

There was therefore only a little to be done to this key.

Boxtel covered it with a slight coat of wax, and when he thus renewed the experiment, the obstacle which prevented the key from being turned a second time left its impression on the wax.

It cost Boxtel two days more to bring his key to perfection, with the aid of a small file.

Rosa's door thus opened without noise and without difficulty, and Boxtel found himself in her room along with the tulip.

The first guilty act of Boxtel had been to climb over a wall in order to dig up the tulip; the second, to introduce himself into the dry-room of Cornelius, through an open window; and the third, to enter Rosa's room by means of a false key.

Thus envy urged Boxtel on with rapid steps in the career of crime.

Boxtel, as we have said, was alone with the tulip.

A common thief would have taken the pot under his arm, and carried it off.

But Boxtel was not a common thief, and he reflected.

It was not yet certain, although very probable, that the tulip would flower black; if, therefore, he stole it now, he not only might be committing a useless crime, but also the theft might be discovered in the time which must elapse until the flower should open.

He, therefore—as, being in possession of the key, he might enter Rosa's chamber whenever he liked—thought it better to wait and to take it either an hour before or after opening, and to start on the instant to Haarlem, where the tulip would be before the judges of the committee before any one else could put in a reclamation.*

Should any one then reclaim it, Boxtel would, in his turn, charge him or her with theft.

This was a deep-laid scheme, and quite worthy of its author.

Thus, every evening, during that delightful hour which the two lovers passed together at the grated window, Boxtel entered Rosa's chamber to watch the progress which the black tulip had made towards flowering.

On the evening at which we have arrived, he was going to enter according to custom; but the two lovers, as we have seen, only exchanged a few words before Cornelius sent Rosa back to watch over the tulip.

Seeing Rosa enter her room ten minutes after she had left it, Boxtel guessed that the tulip had opened, or was about to open.

During that night, therefore, the great blow was to be struck. Boxtel presented himself before Gryphus with a double supply of Genièvre, that is to say, with a bottle in each pocket.

Gryphus being once fuddled, Boxtel was very nearly master of the house.

At eleven o'clock Gryphus was dead drunk. At two in the morning Boxtel saw Rosa leaving the chamber; but evidently she held in her arms something which she carried with great care.

He did not doubt but that this was the black tulip which was in flower.

But what was she going to do with it? Would she set out that instant to Haarlem with it?

It was not possible that a young girl should undertake such a journey alone during the night.

Was she only going to show the tulip to Cornelius? This was more likely.

He followed Rosa, in his stocking feet, walking on tip-toe.

He saw her approach the grated window. He heard her calling Cornelius. By the light of the dark-lantern he saw the tulip, open, and black as the night in which he was hidden.

He heard the plan concerted between Cornelius and Rosa to send a messenger to Haarlem. He saw the lips of the lovers meet, and then heard Cornelius send Rosa away.

He saw Rosa extinguish the light, and return to her chamber. Ten minutes after, he saw her leave the room again, and lock it twice.

Boxtel, who saw all this whilst hiding himself on the landing-place of the staircase above, descended step by step from his storey, as Rosa descended from hers; so that when she touched with her light foot the lowest step of the staircase, Boxtel touched, with a still lighter hand, the lock of Rosa's chamber.

And in that hand, it must be understood, he held the false key which opened Rosa's door, as easily as did the real one.

And this is why, in the beginning of the chapter, we said that the poor young people were in great need of the protection of God.

CHAPTER TWENTY-FOUR

The Black Tulip Changes Masters

CORNELIUS REMAINED standing on the spot where Rosa had left him. He was quite overpowered with the weight of his twofold happiness.

Half an hour passed away. Already did the first rays of the sun enter through the iron grating of the prison, when Cornelius was suddenly startled at the noise of steps which came up the staircase, and of cries which approached nearer and nearer.

Almost at the same instant he saw before him the pale and distracted face of Rosa.

He started, and turned pale with fright.

" Cornelius, Cornelius!" she screamed, gasping for breath.

" Good Heavens! what is it?" asked the prisoner.

" Cornelius, the tulip."

" Well?"

" How shall I tell you?"

" Speak, speak, Rosa!"

" Someone has taken—stolen it from us."

" Stolen—taken?" said Cornelius.

" Yes," said Rosa, leaning against the door to support herself; " yes, taken, stolen."

And saying this, she felt her limbs failing her, and she fell on her knees.

" But how? Tell me, explain to me."

" Oh, it is not my fault, my friend."

Poor Rosa! she no longer dared to call him " My beloved one."

" You have then left it alone," said Cornelius ruefully.

" One minute only, to instruct our messenger, who lives scarcely fifty yards off, on the banks of the Waal."

176

"And during that time, notwithstanding all my injunctions, you left the key behind—unfortunate child!"

"No, no, no! that is what I cannot understand. The key was never out of my hands; I clenched it as if I were afraid it would take wings."

"But how did it happen, then?"

"That's what I cannot make out. I had given the letter to my messenger; he started before I left his house; I came home, and my door was locked; everything in my room was as I had left it, except the tulip—that was gone. Someone must have had a key for my room or have got a false one made on purpose."

She was nearly choking with sobs, and was unable to continue.

Cornelius, immovable and full of consternation, heard almost without understanding, and only muttered—

"Stolen, stolen, stolen; I am lost!"

"Oh, Cornelius, forgive me, forgive me; it will kill me!"

Seeing Rosa's distress, Cornelius seized the iron bars of the grating, and furiously shaking them, called out—

"Rosa, Rosa, we have been robbed, it is true, but shall we allow ourselves to be dejected for all that? No, no; the misfortune is great, but it may perhaps be remedied; Rosa, we know the thief!"

"Alas! what can I say about it?"

"But I say that it is no one else but that infamous Jacob. Shall we allow him to carry to Haarlem the fruit of our labour, the fruit of our sleepless nights, the child of our love? Rosa, we must pursue, we must overtake him!"

"But how can we do all this, my friend, without letting my father know that we were in communication with each other? How should I, a poor girl with so little knowledge of the world and its ways, be able to attain this end, which, perhaps, you could not attain yourself?"

"Rosa, Rosa, open this door to me, and you will see whether I will not find the thief—whether I will not make him confess his crime and beg for mercy."

"Alas!" cried Rosa, sobbing, "can I open the door for

you? have I the keys? If I had had them, would not you have been free long ago?"

"Your father has them—your wicked father, who has already crushed the first sucker of my tulip. Oh, the wretch, the wretch, he is an accomplice of Jacob!"

"Don't speak so loud, for Heaven's sake."

"Oh, Rosa, if you don't open the door to me," Cornelius cried in his rage, "I shall force these bars, and kill everything I find in the prison!"

"Be merciful, be merciful, my friend."

"I tell you, Rosa, that I shall demolish this prison, stone for stone;" and the unfortunate man, whose strength was increased tenfold by his rage, began to shake the door with a great noise, little heeding that the thunder of his voice was re-echoing through the spiral staircase.

Rosa, in her fright, made vain attempts to check this furious outbreak.

"I tell you that I shall kill that infamous Gryphus!" roared Cornelius, "I tell you I shall shed his blood, as he did that of my black tulip!"

The wretched prisoner began really to rave.

"Well, then, yes," said Rosa, all in a tremble, "yes, yes, only be quiet. Yes, I will take his keys, I will open the door for you—yes, only be quiet, my own dear Cornelius."

She did not finish her speech, as a growl by her side interrupted her.

"My father!" cried Rosa.

"Gryphus!" roared Van Baerle. "Oh, you villain."

Old Gryphus, in the midst of all the noise, had ascended the staircase without being heard.

He rudely seized his daughter by the wrist.

"So you will take my keys?" he said, in a voice choked with rage; "ah! this dastardly fellow, this monster, this gallows-bird of a conspirator is your own dear Cornelius, is he? Ah! Missy has communications with prisoners of State. Ah! won't I teach you, won't I?"

Rosa clasped her hands in despair.

"Ah!" Gryphus continued, passing from the madness of anger to the cool irony of a man who has got the better of his enemy, " ah! you innocent tulip-fancier, you gentle scholar; you will kill me, and drink my blood! Very well! very well! And you have my daughter for an accomplice. Am I, forsooth, in a den of thieves—in a cave of brigands? Yes; but the Governor shall know all to-morrow, and His Highness the Stadtholder the day after. We know the law; we shall give a second edition of the Buitenhof, Master Scholar, and a good one this time. Yes, yes; just gnaw your paws like a bear in his cage, and you, my fine little lady, devour your dear Cornelius with your eyes. I tell you, my lambkins, you shall not much longer have the felicity of conspiring together. Away with you! unnatural daughter! And as to you, Master Scholar, we shall see each other again. Just be quiet—we shall."

Rosa, beyond herself with terror and despair, kissed her hands to her friend; then, suddenly struck with a bright thought, she rushed towards the staircase, saying—

" All is not yet lost, Cornelius. Rely on me, my Cornelius."

Her father followed her, growling.

As to poor Cornelius, he gradually loosened his hold of the bars, which his fingers still grasped convulsively. His head was heavy, his eyes almost started from their sockets, and he fell heavily on the floor of his cell, muttering—

" Stolen; it has been stolen from me!"

During this time Boxtel had left the fortress, by the door which Rosa herself had opened. He carried the black tulip wrapped up in a cloak, and, throwing himself into a coach, which was waiting for him at Gorcum, he drove off, without, as may well be imagined, having informed his friend Gryphus of his sudden departure.

And now, as we have seen him enter his coach, we shall, with the consent of the reader, follow him to the end of his journey.

He proceeded but slowly, as a black tulip could not bear travelling post haste.

But Boxtel, fearing that he might not arrive early enough, procured at Delft*a box, lined all round with fresh moss, in which he packed the tulip. The flower was so lightly pressed upon all sides, with a supply of air from above, that the coach could now travel full speed without any possibility of injury to the tulip.

He arrived next morning at Haarlem, fatigued but triumphant; and, to do away with every trace of the theft, he transplanted the tulip, and, breaking the original flower-pot, threw the pieces into the canal. After which he wrote the President of the Horticultural Society a letter, in which he announced to him that he had just arrived at Haarlem with a perfectly black tulip; and, with his flower all safe, took up his quarters at a good hotel in the town, and there he waited.

CHAPTER TWENTY-FIVE

The President Van Herysen

Rosa, on leaving Cornelius, had fixed on her plan, which was no other than to restore to Cornelius the stolen tulip, or never to see him again.

She had seen the despair of the prisoner, and she knew that it was derived from a double source, and that it was incurable.

On the one hand, separation became inevitable; Gryphus having, at the same time, surprised the secret of their love and of their secret meetings.

On the other hand, all the hopes, on the fulfilment of which Cornelius Van Baerle had rested his ambition for the last seven years, were now crushed.

Rosa was one of those women who are dejected by trifles; but who, in great emergencies, are supplied by the misfortune itself with the energy for combating, or with the resources for remedying it.

She went to her room, and cast a last glance about her, to see whether she had not been mistaken, and whether the tulip was not stowed away in some corner, where it had escaped her notice. But she sought in vain; the tulip was still wanting; the tulip was indeed stolen.

Rosa made up a little parcel of things indispensable for a journey; took her three hundred guilders, that is to say, all her fortune; fetched the third sucker from among her lace, where she had laid it up, and carefully hid it in her bosom; after which she locked her door twice, to disguise her flight as long as possible; and, leaving the prison by the same door which an hour before had let out Boxtel, she went to a stable-keeper to hire a carriage.

The man had only a two-wheel chaise, and this was the vehicle which Boxtel had hired since last evening, and in which he was now driving along the road to Delft; for the road from Lœvestein to Haarlem, owing to the many canals, rivers, and rivulets intersecting the country, is exceedingly circuitous.*

Not being able to procure a vehicle, Rosa was obliged to take a horse, with which the stable-keeper readily entrusted her, knowing her to be the daughter of the jailer of the fortress.

Rosa hoped to overtake her messenger, a kind-hearted and honest lad, whom she would take with her, and who might, at the same time, serve her as a guide and a protector.

And, in fact, she had not proceeded more than a league before she saw him hastening along one of the side paths of a very pretty road by the river. Setting her horse off at a canter, she soon came up with him.

The honest lad was not aware of the important character of his message; nevertheless, he used as much speed as if he had known it; and, in less than an hour, he had already gone a league and a half.

Rosa took from him the note, which had now become useless, and explained to him what she wanted him to do for her. The boatman placed himself entirely at her disposal, promising to keep pace with the horse, if Rosa would allow him to take hold of either the croup, or the bridle of her horse. The two travellers had been on their way for five hours, and made more than eight leagues, and yet Gryphus had not the least suspicion of his daughter having left the fortress.

The jailer, who was of a very spiteful and cruel disposition, chuckled within himself at the idea of having struck such terror into his daughter's heart.

But whilst he was congratulating himself on having such a nice story to tell to his boon companion, Jacob, that worthy was on his road to Delft; and, thanks to the swiftness of the horse, had already the start of Rosa and her companion by four leagues.

And whilst the affectionate father was rejoicing at the thought of his daughter weeping in her room Rosa was making the best of her way towards Haarlem.

Thus, the prisoner alone was where Gryphus thought him to be.

Rosa was so little with her father since she took care of the tulip, that at his dinner hour, that is to say, at twelve o'clock, he was reminded, for the first time, by his appetite, that his daughter was fretting rather too long.

He sent one of the under-turnkeys to call her; and, when the man came back to tell him that he had called and sought her in vain, he resolved to go and call her himself.

He first went to her room, but, loud as he knocked, Rosa answered not. The locksmith of the fortress was sent for; he opened the door, but Gryphus no more found Rosa than she had found the tulip.

At that very moment she entered Rotterdam.

Gryphus, therefore, had just as little chance of finding her in the kitchen as in her room, and just as little in the garden as in the kitchen.

The reader may imagine the anger of the jailer, when, after having made inquiries about the neighbourhood, he heard that his daughter had hired a horse, and, like an adventuress, set out on a journey, without saying where she was going.

Gryphus again went up in his fury to Van Baerle, abused him, threatened him, knocked all the miserable furniture of his cell about, and promised him all sorts of misery, even starvation and flogging.

Cornelius, without even hearing what his jailer said, allowed himself to be ill-treated, abused, and threatened, remaining all the while sullen, immovable, dead to every emotion and fear.

After having sought for Rosa in every direction, Gryphus looked out for Jacob, and, as he could not find him either, he began to suspect from that moment that Jacob had run away with her.

The damsel, in the meanwhile, after having stopped for two hours at Rotterdam, had started again on her journey. On that evening she slept at Delft; and, on the following morning she reached Haarlem, four hours after Boxtel had arrived there.

Rosa, first of all, caused herself to be led before Mynheer Van Herysen, the President of the Horticultural Society of Haarlem.

She found that worthy gentleman in a situation, which, to do justice to our story, we must not pass over in our description.

The President was drawing up a report to the Committee of the Society.

This report was written on large-sized paper, in the finest handwriting of the President.

Rosa was announced simply as Rosa Gryphus; but, as her name, well as it might sound, was unknown to the President, she was refused admittance.

Rosa, however, was by no means abashed, having vowed in her heart, in pursuing her cause, not to allow herself to be put down either by refusal, or abuse, or even brutaility.

" Announce to the President," she said to the servant, " that I want to speak to him about the black tulip."

These words seemed to be an " Open Sesame,"*for she soon found herself in the office of the President, Van Herysen, who gallantly rose from his chair to meet her.

He was a spare little man, resembling the stem of a flower, his head forming its chalice, and his two limp arms representing the double leaf of the tulip; the resemblance was rendered complete by his waddling gait, which made him even more like that flower, when it bends under a breeze.

" Well, miss," he said, " you are coming, I am told, about the affair of the black tulip."

To the President of the Horticultural Society the *Tulipa nigra* was a first-rate power, which, in its character as queen of the tulips, might send ambassadors.

" Yes, sir," answered Rosa, " I come, at least to speak of it."

" Is it doing well, then?" asked Van Herysen, with a smile of tender veneration.

" Alas! sir, I don't know," said Rosa.

" How is that? could any misfortune have happened to it?"

" A very great one, sir; yet not to it, but to me."

" What?"

" It has been stolen from me."

" Stolen! the black tulip!"

" Yes, sir."

" Do you know the thief?"

" I have my suspicions, but I must not yet accuse any one."

" But the matter may very easily be ascertained."

" How is that?"

" As it has been stolen from you, the thief cannot be far off."

" Why not?"

" Because I have seen the black tulip only two hours ago."

" You have seen the black tulip!" cried Rosa, rushing up to Mynheer Van Herysen.

" As I see you, miss."

" But where?"

" Well, with your master, of course."

" With my master?"

" Yes, are you not in the service of Master Isaac Boxtel?"

" I?"

" Yes, you."

" But for whom do you take me, sir?"

" And for whom do you take me?"

" I hope, sir, I take you for what you are, that is to say, for the honourable Mynheer Van Herysen, burgomaster of Haarlem, and President of the Horticultural Society."

" And what is it you told me just now?"

" I told you, sir, that my tulip has been stolen."

" Then your tulip is that of Mynheer Boxtel. Well, my child, you express yourself very badly. The tulip has been stolen, not from you, but from Mynheer Boxtel."

" I repeat to you, sir, that I do not know who this Mynheer Boxtel is, and that I have now heard his name pronounced for the first time."

" You do not know who Mynheer Boxtel is; and you also had a black tulip?"

" But is there any other besides mine?" asked Rosa, trembling.

" Yes—that of Mynheer Boxtel."

" How is it?"

" Black, of course."

" Without speck?"

" Without a single speck, or even point."

" And you have this tulip; you have it deposited here?"

" No, but it will be, as it has to be exhibited before the Committee, previous to the prize being awarded."

" Oh, sir!" cried Rosa, " this Boxtel, this Isaac Boxtel, who calls himself the owner of the black tulip——"

" And who is its owner——"

" Is he not a very thin man?"

" Yes."

" Bald?"

" Yes."

" With sunken eyes?"

" I think he has."

" Restless, stooping, and bow-legged?"

" In truth you draw Master Boxtel's portrait, feature by feature."

" And the tulip, sir? Is it not in a pot of white and blue earthenware, with yellowish flowers in a basket on three sides?"

" Oh, as to that, I am not quite sure; I looked more at the flower than at the pot."

" Oh, sir! that's my tulip, which has been stolen from me. I come here to reclaim it before you and from you."

" Oh! oh!" said Van Herysen, looking at Rosa. " What! you are here to claim the tulip of Master Boxtel? Well, I must say, you are cool enough."

" Honoured sir," said Rosa, a little put out by this apostrophe, " I do not say that I am coming to claim the tulip of Master Boxtel, but to reclaim my own."

" Yours?"

" Yes, the one which I have myself planted and nursed."

" Well, then, go, and find out Master Boxtel at the White Swan Inn, and you can then settle matters with him; as for me, considering that the cause seems to me as difficult to judge as that which was brought before King Solomon, and that I do not pretend to be as wise as he was, I shall content myself with making my report, establishing the existence of the black tulip, and ordering the hundred thousand guilders to be paid to its grower. Good-bye, my child."

" Oh, sir, sir!" said Rosa imploringly.

" Only, my child," continued Van Herysen, " as you are young and pretty, and as there may be still some good in you, I'll give you good advice. Be prudent in this matter, for we have a court of justice, and a prison here at Haarlem; and, moreover, we are exceedingly ticklish, as far as the honour of our tulips is concerned—go, my child, go. Remember, Master Isaac Boxtel at the White Swan Inn."

And Mynheer Van Herysen, taking up his fine pen, resumed his report, which had been interrupted by Rosa's visit.

CHAPTER TWENTY-SIX

A Member of the Horticultural Society

ROSA, BEYOND herself, and nearly mad with joy and fear at the idea of the black tulip being found again, started for the White Swan followed by the boatman, a stout lad from Frisia, who was strong enough to knock down a dozen Boxtels single-handed.

He had been made acquainted in the course of the journey with the state of affairs, and was not afraid of any encounter; only he had orders, in such a case, to spare the tulip.

But on arriving in the great market-place, Rosa at once stopped: a sudden thought had struck her, just as Homer's Minerva seizes Achilles by the hair at the moment when he is about to be carried away by his anger.*

" Good Heavens!" she muttered to herself, " I have made a grievous blunder; maybe I have ruined Cornelius, the tulip, and myself. I have given the alarm, and perhaps awakened suspicion. I am but a woman; these men may league themselves against me, and then I shall be lost. If I am lost, that matters nothing—but Cornelius and the tulip!"

She reflected for a moment.

" If I go to that Boxtel and do not know him; if that Boxtel is not my Jacob, but another fancier, who has also discovered the black tulip; or if my tulip has been stolen by someone else, or has already passed into the hands of a third person; if I do not recognise the man, only the tulip, how shall I prove that it belongs to me? On the other hand, if I recognise this Boxtel as Jacob, who knows what will come out of it? whilst we are contesting with each other, the tulip will die."*

In the meanwhile, a great noise was heard, like the distant

roar of the sea, at the other extremity of the market-place. People were running about, doors opening and shutting; Rosa alone was unconscious of all this hubbub among the multitude.

"We must return to the President," she muttered.

"Well, then, let us return," said the boatman.

They took a small street, which led them straight to the mansion of Mynheer Van Herysen, who with his best pen, in his finest hand, continued to draw up his report.

Everywhere on her way, Rosa heard people speaking only of the black tulip, and the prize of a hundred thousand guilders. The news had spread like wildfire through the town.

Rosa had not a little difficulty in penetrating a second time into the office of Mynheer Van Herysen, who, however, was again moved by the magic name of the black tulip.

But when he recognised Rosa, whom in his own mind he had set down as mad, or even worse, he grew angry, and wanted to send her away.

Rosa, however, clasped her hands, and said with that tone of honest truth which generally finds it way to the hearts of men—

"For Heaven's sake, sir, do not turn me away; listen to what I have to tell you, and if it be not possible for you to do me justice, at least you will not one day have to reproach yourself before God for having made yourself the accomplice of a bad action."

Van Herysen stamped his foot with impatience; it was the second time that Rosa interrupted him in the midst of a composition, which stimulated his vanity, both as a burgomaster and as the President of the Horticultural Society.

"But my report!" he cried; "my report on the black tulip!"

"Mynheer Van Herysen," Rosa continued, with the firmness of innocence and truth, "your report on the black tulip will, if you don't hear me, be based on crime or on falsehood. I implore you, sir, let this Master Boxtel, whom

I assert to be Master Jacob, be brought here before you and me, and I swear that I will leave him in undisturbed possession of the tulip if I do not recognise the flower and its holder."

" Well, I declare, here is a proposal," said Van Herysen.

" What do you mean?"

" I ask you what can be proved by your recognising them?"

" After all," said Rosa, in her despair, " you are an honest man, sir; how would you feel if one day you found out that you had given the prize to a man for something which he not only had not produced, but which he had even stolen?"

Rosa's speech seemed to have brought a certain conviction into the heart of Van Herysen, and he was going to answer her in a gentler tone, when at once a great noise was heard in the street, and loud cheers shook the house.

" What is this?" cried the burgomaster; " what is this? Is it possible? have I heard right?"

And he rushed towards his ante-room, without any longer heeding Rosa, whom he left in his cabinet.

Scarcely had he reached his ante-room, when he cried out aloud, on seeing his staircase invaded up to the very landing-place by the multitude, which was accompanying or rather following, a young man, simply clad in a coat of violet-coloured velvet, embroidered with silver; who, with a certain aristocratic slowness, ascended the shining white stone steps of the house.

In his wake followed two officers, one of the navy, and the other of the cavalry.

Van Herysen, having found his way through his frightneed domestics, began to bow, almost to prostrate himself before his visitor, who had been the cause of all this stir.

" Monseigneur!" he called out, " Monseigneur! What distinguished honour is Your Highness bestowing for ever on my humble house by your visit?"

" Dear Mynheer Van Herysen," said William of Orange, with a serenity which, with him, took the place of a smile, " I am a true Hollander; I am fond of the water, of beer, and of flowers, sometimes even of that cheese, the flavour of which seems so grateful to the French; the flower which I prefer to all others is, of course, the tulip. I heard at Leyden that the city of Haarlem at last possessed the black tulip; and, after having satisfied myself of the truth of the news which seemed so incredible, I have come to know all about it from the President of the Horticultural Society."

" Oh! Monseigneur, Monseigneur," said Van Herysen, " what glory to the Society, if its endeavours are pleasing to Your Highness!"

" Have you got the flower here?" said the Prince, who, very likely, already regretted having made such a long speech.

" I am sorry to say we have not."

" And where is it?"

" With its owner."

" Who is he?"

" An honest tulip-grower of Dort."

" His name?"

" Boxtel."

" His quarters?"

" At the White Swan; I shall send for him, and if, in the meanwhile, Your Highness will do me the honour of stepping into my drawing-room, he will be sure—knowing that Your Highness is here—to lose no time in bringing his tulip."

" Very well, send for him."

" Yes, Your Highness, but——"

" What is it?"

" Oh! nothing of any consequence, Monseigneur."

" Everything is of consequence, Mynheer Van Herysen."

" Well, then, Monseigneur, if it must be said, a little difficulty has presented itself."

" What difficulty?"

" This tulip has already been claimed by usurpers. It's true that it is worth a hundred thousand guilders."

" Indeed!"

" Yes, Monseigneur, by usurpers, by forgers."

" This is a crime, Mynheer Van Herysen."

" So it is, Your Highness."

" And have you any proofs of their guilt?"

" No, Monseigneur, the guilty woman——"

" The guilty woman, sir?"

" I ought to say, the woman who claims the tulip, Monseigneur, is here in the room close by."

" And what do you think of her?"

" I think, Monseigneur, that the bait of a hundred thousand guilders may have tempted her."

" And so she claims the tulip?"

" Yes, Monseigneur."

" And what proof does she offer?"

" I was just going to question her when Your Highness came in."

" Question her, Mynheer Van Herysen, question her; I am the first magistrate of the country; I will hear the case, and administer justice."

" I have found my King Solomon," said Van Herysen, bowing, and showing the way to the Prince.

His Highness was just going to walk ahead, but, suddenly recollecting himself, he said—

" Go before me, and call me plain Mynheer."

The two then entered the cabinet.

Rosa was still standing at the same place, leaning on the window, and looking through the panes into the garden.

" Ah! a Frisian girl," said the Prince, as he observed Rosa's gold brocade head-dress and red petticoat.

At the noise of their footsteps, she turned round, but scarcely saw the Prince, who seated himself in the darkest corner of the apartment.

All her attention, as may easily be imagined, was fixed on that important person who was called Van Herysen, so that she had no time to notice the humble stranger, who was following the master of the house, and who, for ought that she knew, might be somebody or nobody.

The humble stranger took a book down from the shelf, and made Van Herysen a sign to commence the examination forthwith.

Van Herysen, likewise at the invitation of the young man in the violet coat, sat down in his turn, and, quite happy and proud of the importance thus cast upon him, began—

" My child, you promise to tell me the truth, and the entire truth, concerning this tulip?"

" I promise."

" Well, then, speak before this gentleman; this gentleman is one of the members of the Horticultural Society."

" What am I to tell you, sir," said Rosa, " besides that which I have told you already?"

" Well, then, what is it?"

" I repeat the request which I have addressed to you before."

" Which?"

" That you will order Mynheer Boxtel to come here with his tulip; if I do not recognise it as mine I will frankly tell it; but if I do recognise it I will reclaim it, even if I must go before His Highness, the Stadtholder himself, with my proofs in my hands."

" You have, then, some proofs, my child?"

" God, who knows my good right, will assist me to some."

Van Herysen exchanged a look with the Prince, who, since the first words of Rosa, seemed to try to remember her, as if it were not for the first time that this sweet voice rang in his ears.

An officer went off to fetch Boxtel, and Van Herysen, in the meanwhile, continued his examination.

" And with what do you support your assertion that you are the real owner of the black tulip?"

" With the very simple fact of my having planted and grown it in my own chamber."

" In your chamber? Where was your chamber?"

" At Lœvestein."

" You are from Lœvestein?"

" I am the daughter of the jailer of the fortress."

The Prince made a little movement, as much as to say, " Well, that's it, I remember now."

And, all the while feigning to be engaged with his book, he watched Rosa even with more attention than he had done before.

" And you are fond of flowers?" continued Mynheer Van Herysen.

" Yes, sir."

" Then you are an experienced florist, I dare say?"

Rosa hesitated a moment; then with a tone which came from the depth of her heart, she said—

" Gentlemen, I am speaking to men of honour?"

There was such an expression of truth in the tone of her voice, that Van Herysen and the Prince answered simultaneously by an affirmative moment of their heads.

" Well, then, I am not an experienced florist; I am only a poor girl, one of the people, who, three months ago, knew neither how to read or write. No, the black tulip has not been found by myself."

" But by whom else?"

" By a poor prisoner of Lœvestein."

" By a prisoner of Lœvestein?" replied the Prince.

The tone of this voice startled Rosa, who was sure she had heard it before.

" By a prisoner of state, then," continued the Prince, " as there are none else there."

Having said this, he began to read again, at least in appearance.

" Yes," said Rosa, with a faltering voice, " yes, by a prisoner of state."

Van Herysen trembled as he heard such a confession made in the presence of such a witness.

" Continue," said William dryly, to the President of the Horticultural Society.

" Ah, sir," said Rosa, addressing the person whom she thought to be her real judge, " I am going to incriminate myself very seriously."

" Certainly," said Van Herysen, " the prisoners of state ought to be kept in close confinement at Lœvestein."

" Alas! sir."

" And from what you tell me you took advantage of your

position, as daughter of the jailer, to communicate with a prisoner of state about the cultivation of flowers."

" So it is, sir," Rosa murmured in dismay; " yes, I am bound to confess, I saw him every day."

" Unfortunate girl!" ecxlaimed Van Herysen.

The Prince, observing the fright of Rosa and the pallor of the President, raised his head, and said, in his clear and decided tone:

" This cannot signify anything to the members of the Horticultural Society; they have to judge on the black tulip, and have no cognisance to take of political offences. Go on; young women, go on."

Van Herysen, by means of an eloquent glance, offered, in the name of the tulip, his thanks to the new member of the Horticultural Society.

Rosa, reassured by this sort of encouragement, which the stranger was giving her, related all that had happened for the last three months, all that she had done, and all that she had suffered. She described the cruelty of Gryphus; the destruction of the first sucker; the grief of the prisoner; the precautions taken to ensure the success of the second sucker; the patience of the prisoner; and his anxiety during their separation: how he was about to starve himself, because he had no longer any news of his tulip; his joy when she went to see him again; and lastly, their despair when they found that the tulip, which had come into flower, was stolen just one hour after it had opened.

All this was detailed with an accent of truth, which, although producing no change in the impassible mien of the Prince, did not fail to take effect on Van Herysen.

" But," said the Prince, " it cannot be long since you knew the prisoner."

Rosa opened her large eyes and looked at the stranger, who drew back into the dark corner, as if he wished to escape her observation.

" Why, sir?" she asked him.

" Because it is not yet four months since the jailer Gryphus and his daughter were removed to Lœvestein."

" That is true, sir."

" Otherwise, you must have solicited the transfer of your father in order to be able to follow some prisoner who may have been transported from the Hague to Lœvestein."

" Sir," said Rosa, blushing.

" Finish what you have to say," said William.

" I confess, I knew the prisoner at the Hague."

" Happy prisoner!" said William, smiling.

At this moment, the officer who had been sent for Boxtel returned and announced to the Prince that the person whom he had been to fetch was following on his heels with his tulip.

CHAPTER TWENTY-SEVEN

The Third Sucker

BOXTEL'S RETURN was scarcely announced, when he entered in person the drawing-room of Mynheer Van Herysen, followed by two men, who carried in a box their precious burden, and deposited it on a table.

The Prince, on being informed, left the cabinet, passed into the drawing-room, admired the flower, and silently resumed his seat in the dark corner, where he had himself placed his chair.

Rosa, trembling, pale, and terrified, expected to be invited in her turn to see the tulip.

She now heard the voice of Boxtel.

" It is he!" she exclaimed.

The Prince made her a sign to go and look through the open door into the drawing-room.

" It is my tulip," cried Rosa, " I recognise it. Oh, my poor Cornelius!"

And saying this she burst into tears.

The Prince rose from his seat, went to the door, where he stood for some time with the full light falling upon his figure.

As Rosa's eyes now rested upon him, she felt more than ever convinced that this was not the first time she had seen the stranger.

" Master Boxtel," said the Prince, " come in here, if you please."

Boxtel eagerly approached, and finding himself face to face with William of Orange, started back.

" His Highness!" he called out.

" His Highness!" Rosa repeated in dismay.

Hearing this exclamation on his left, Boxtel turned round, and perceived Rosa.

At this sight the whole frame of the thief shook as if under the influence of a galvanic shock.

" Ah!" muttered the Prince to himself, " he is confused."

But Boxtel, making a violent effort to control his feelings, was already himself again.

" Master Boxtel," said William, " you seem to have discovered the secret of growing the black tulip?"

" Yes, Your Highness," answered Boxtel, in a voice which still betrayed some confusion.

It is true his agitation might have been attributable to the emotion which the man must have felt on suddenly recognising the Prince.

" But," continued the Stadtholder, " here is a young damsel who also pretends to have found it."

Boxtel, with a disdainful smile, shrugged his shoulders.

William watched all his movements with evident interest and curiosity.

" Then you don't know this young girl?" said the Prince.

" No, Your Highness!"

" And you, child, do you know Master Boxtel?"

" No, I don't know Master Boxtel, but I know Master Jacob."

" What do you mean?"

" I mean to say that at Lœvestein the man who here calls himself Isaac Boxtel went by the name of Master Jacob."

" What do you say to that, Master Boxtel?"

" I say that this damsel lies, Your Highness."

" You deny, therefore, having ever been at Lœvestein?"

Boxtel hesitated; the fixed and searching glance of the proud eye of the Prince prevented him from lying.

" I cannot deny having been at Lœvestein, Your Highness, but I deny having stolen the tulip."

" You have stolen it, and that from my room," cried Rosa, with indignation.

" I deny it."

" Now listen to me. Do you deny having followed me into the garden, on the day when I prepared the border where I was to plant it? Do you deny having followed me

198

into the garden when I pretended to plant it? Do you deny that, on that evening, you rushed, after my departure, to the spot where you hoped to find the bulb? Do you deny having dug in the ground with your hands—but, thank God, in vain; as it was but a stratagem to discover your intentions. Say, do you deny all this?"

Boxtel did not deem it fit to answer these several charges, but, turning to the Prince, continued:

" I have now for twenty years grown tulips at Dort. I have even acquired some reputation in this art; one of my hybrids is entered in the catalogue under the name of an illustrious personage. I have dedicated it to the King of Portugal. The truth in the matter is as I shall now tell Your Highness. This damsel knew that I had produced the black tulip, and, in concert with a lover of hers, in the fortress of Lœvestein, she formed the plan of ruining me, by appropriating to herself the prize of a hundred thousand guilders, which, with the help of Your Highness's justice, I hope to gain."

" Yah!" cried Rosa, beyond herself with anger.

" Silence!" said the Prince.

Then, turning to Boxtel, he said—

" And who is that prisoner to whom you allude as the lover of this young woman?"

Rosa nearly swooned, for Cornelius was designated as a dangerous prisoner, and recommended, by the Prince, to the especial surveillance of the jailer.

Nothing could have been more agreeable to Boxtel than this question.

" This prisoner," he said, " is a man whose name in itself will prove to Your Highness what trust you may place in his probity. He is a prisoner of state, who was once condemned to death."

" And his name?"

Rosa hid her face in her hands with a movement of despair.

" His name is Cornelius Van Baerle," said Boxtel, " and he is godson of that villain, Cornelius De Witte."

The Prince gave a start; his generally quiet eye flashed,

and a death-like paleness spread over his impassible features.

He went up to Rosa, and, with his finger, gave her a sign to remove her hands from her face.

Rosa obeyed, as if under mesmeric influence, without having seen the sign.

" It was then to follow this man that you came to me at Leyden, to solicit for the transfer of your father?"

Rosa hung down her head, and, nearly choking, said—

" Yes, Your Highness."

" Go on," said the Prince to Boxtel.

" I have nothing more to say," Isaac continued. " Your Highness knows all. But there is one thing which I did not intend to say, because I did not wish to make this girl blush for her ingratitude. I came to Lœvestein because I had business there. On this occasion I made the acquaintance of old Gryphus, and, falling in love with his daughter, made an offer of marriage to her; and, not being rich, I committed the imprudence of mentioning to them my prospect of gaining a hundred thousand guilders, in proof of which I showed to them the black tulip. Her lover, having himself made a show at Dort of cultivating tulips, to hide his political intrigues, they now plotted together for my ruin. On the eve of the day when the flower was expected to open, the tulip was taken away by this young woman. She carried it to her room, from when I had the good luck to recover it at the very moment when she had the impudence to dispatch a messenger to announce to the members of the Horticultural Society that she had produced the Grand Black Tulip. But she did not stop there. There is no doubt but that, during the few hours which she kept the flower in her room, she showed it to some persons, whom she may now call as witnesses. But, fortunately, Your Highness has now been warned against this impostor and her witnesses."

" Oh, my God! my God! what infamous falsehoods," said Rosa, bursting into tears, and throwing herself at the feet of the Stadtholder, who, although thinking her guilty, felt pity for her dreadful agony.

" You have done very wrong, my child," he said, " and

your lover shall be punished for having thus badly advised you. For you are so young, and have such an honest look, that I am inclined to believe the mischief to have been his doing, and not yours."

" Monseigneur! Monseigneur!" cried Rosa. " Cornelius is not guilty."

William started.

" Not guilty of having advised you; that's what you want to say, is it not?"

" What I wish to say, Your Highness, is, that Cornelius is as little guilty of the second crime imputed to him as he was of the first."

" Of the first? And do you know what was his first crime? Do you know of what he was accused and convicted? Of having, as an accomplice of Cornelius De Witte, concealed the correspondence of the Grand Pensionary and the Marquis De Louvois."

" Well, sir, he was ignorant of this correspondence being deposited with him; completely ignorant. I am as certain as of my life, that if it were not so, he would have told me; for how could that pure mind have harboured a secret without revealing it to me? No, no, Your Highness, I repeat it, and even at the risk of incurring your displeasure, Cornelius is not more guilty of the first crime than of the second; and of the second no more than of the first. Oh, would to Heaven that you knew my Cornelius, Monseigneur!"

" He is a De Witte!" cried Boxtel. " His Highness knows only too much of him, having once granted him his life."

" Silence!" said the Prince; " all these affairs of state, as I have already said, are completely out of the province of the Horticultural Society of Haarlem."

Then, knitting his brow, he added—

" As to the tulip, make yourself easy, Master Boxtel, you shall have justice done to you."

Boxtel bowed, with a heart full of joy, and received the congratulations of the President.

" You, my child," William of Orange continued, " you

were going to commit a crime. I shall not punish you; but the real evil-doer will pay the penalty for both. A man of his name may be a conspirator, and even a traitor, but he ought not to be a thief."

"A thief!" cried Rosa. "Cornelius a thief! Pray, Your Highness, do not say such a word; it would kill him if he knew it. If theft there has been, I swear to you, sir, no one else but this man has committed it."

"Prove it," Boxtel coolly remarked.

"I shall prove it. With God's help I shall."

Then, turning towards Boxtel, she asked—

"The tulip is yours?"

"It is."

"How many suckers were there of it?"

Boxtel hesitated for a moment, but, after a short consideration, he came to the conclusion that she would not ask this question if there were none besides the two bulbs of which he had known already. He, therefore, answered—

"Three."

"What has become of these suckers?"

"Oh! what has become of them? Well, one has failed; the second has produced the black tulip."

"And the third?"

"The third?"

"The third—where is it?"

"I have it at home," said Boxtel, quite confused.

"At home? Where? At Lœvestein, or at Dort?"

"At Dort," said Boxtel.

"You lie!" cried Rosa. "Monseigneur," she continued, whilst turning round to the Prince, "I will tell you the true story of those three suckers. The first was crushed by my father in the prisoner's cell, and this man is quite aware of it, for he himself wanted to get hold of it, and being baulked in his hope, he very nearly fell out with my father, who had been the cause of his disappointment. The second sucker, planted by me, has produced the Black Tulip; and the third and last "—saying this, she drew it from her bosom—" here it is, in the very same paper in which it was wrapped up together with the two others. When about to be led to the scaffold, Cornelius Van Baerle gave me all the three. Take it, Monseigneur, take it."

And Rosa, unfolding the paper, offered the bulb to the Prince, who took it from her hands and examined it.

"But, Monseigneur, this young woman may have stolen the bulb, as she did the tulip," Boxtel said, with a faltering voice, and evidently alarmed at the attention with which the Prince examined the bulb; and even more at the movements of Rosa, who was reading some lines written on the paper which remained in her hands.

Her eyes suddenly lighted up; she read, with breathless anxiety, the mysterious paper over and over again; and at last, uttering a cry, held it out to the Prince and said—

"Read, Monseigneur, for Heaven's sake, read!"

William handed the third sucker to Van Herysen, took the paper, and read.

No sooner had he looked at it than he began to stagger; his hand trembled, and very nearly let the paper fall to the ground; and the expression of pain and compassion in his features was really frightful to see.

It was that fly-leaf, taken from the Bible, which Cornelius De Witte had sent to Dort by Craeke, the servant of his brother John, to request Van Baerle to burn the correspondence of the Grand Pensionary with the Marquis de Louvois.

This request, as the reader may remember, was couched in the following terms:

"MY DEAR GODSON—Burn the parcel which I have entrusted to you. Burn it, without looking at it and without opening it, so that its contents may remain unknown to yourself. Secrets of this description are death to those with whom they are deposited. Burn it, and you will have saved John and Cornelius De Witte.

"Farewell, and love me,

"CORNELIUS DE WITTE."

"20th of August, 1672."

This slip of paper offered the proofs both of Van Baerle's innocence and of his claim to the property of the tulip.

Rosa and the Stadtholder exchanged one look only.

That of Rosa was meant to express: "Here, you see yourself."

That of the Stadtholder signified: "Be quiet, and wait."

The Prince wiped the cold sweat from his forehead, and slowly folded up the paper, whilst his thoughts were wandering in that labyrinth without a goal and without a guide, which is called remorse and shame of the past.

Soon, however, raising his head with an effort, he said, in his usual voice—

"Go, Mr. Boxtel, justice shall be done, I promise you."

Then, turning to the President, he added:

"You, my dear Mynheer Van Herysen, take charge of this young woman and of the tulip. Good-bye."

All bowed, and the Prince left, among the deafening cheers of the crowd outside.

Boxtel returned to his inn, rather puzzled and uneasy, tormented by misgivings about that paper which William had received from the hand of Rosa, and which His Highness had read, folded up, and so carefully put in his pocket. What was the meaning of all this?

Rosa went up to the tulip, tenderly kissed its leaves, and, with a heart full of happiness and confidence in the ways of God, broke out in the words:

"Thou knowest best for what end thou madest my good Cornelius teach me to read."*

CHAPTER TWENTY-EIGHT

The Hymn of the Flowers

WHILST THE events we have described in our last chapter were taking place, the unfortunate Van Baerle, forgotten in his cell in the fortress of Lœvestein, suffered, at the hands of Gryphus, all that a prisoner can suffer when his jailer has formed the determination of playing the part of hangman.

Gryphus, not having received any tidings of Rosa, nor of Jacob, persuaded himself that all that had happened was the devil's work. and that Doctor Cornelius Van Baerle had been sent on earth by Satan.

The result of it was, that one fine morning, the third after the disappearance of Jacob and Rosa, he went up to the cell of Cornelius in even a greater rage than usual.

The latter, leaning with his elbows on the window-sill, and supporting his head with his two hands, whilst his eyes wandered over the distant hazy horizon, where the windmills of Dort were turning their sails, was breathing the fresh air, in order to be able to keep down his tears, and to fortify himself in his philosophy.

The pigeons were still there, but hope was not; there was no future to look forward to.

Alas! Rosa, being watched, was no longer able to come. Could she not write? and if so, could she convey her letters to him?

No, no. He had seen, during the two preceding days, too much fury and malignity in the eyes of old Gryphus to expect that his vigilance would relax, even for one moment. Moreover, had not she to suffer even worse torments than those of seclusion and separation? Did this brutal, blaspheming, drunken bully take revenge on his daughter, like the ruthless fathers of the Greek drama? and when the

Genievre had heated his brain, would it not give to his arm, which had been only too well set by Cornelius, even double force?

The idea that Rosa might, perhaps, be ill-treated, nearly drove Cornelius mad.

He then felt his own powerlessness. He asked himself whether God was just in inflicting so much tribulation on two innocent creatures.

And certainly in these moments he began to doubt the wisdom of Providence. It is one of the curses of misfortune that it begets doubt.

Van Baerle had proposed to write to Rosa, but where was she?

He also would have wished to write to the Hague to be beforehand with Gryphus, who, he had no doubt, would, by denouncing him, do his best to bring new storms on his head.

But how should he write? Gryphus had taken the paper and pencil from him; and even if he had both, he could hardly expect Gryphus to dispatch his letter.

Then Cornelius resolved in his mind all those stratagems resorted to by unfortunate prisoners.

He had thought of an attempt to escape, a thing which never entered his head whilst he could see Rosa every day; but the more he thought of it, the more clearly he saw the impracticability of such an attempt. He was one of those choice spirits who abhor everything that is common, and who often lose a good chance through not taking the way of the vulgar, that high road of mediocrity which leads to everything.

" How is it possible," said Cornelius to himself, " that I should escape from Lœvestein, as Grotius has done the same thing before me? Has not every precaution been taken since? Are not the windows barred? Are not the doors of double and even of treble strength? and the sentinels ten times more watchful? And have not I, besides all this, an Argus*so much the more dangerous, as he has the keen eyes of hatred?* I am losing my patience, since I have lost the joy and company of Rosa, and especially since I have lost my tulip. Undoubtedly, one day or other, Gryphus will attack me in a manner painful to my self-respect, or to my love, or even threaten my personal safety. I don't know how it is, but since my imprisonment I feel a strange and almost irresistible pugnacity. Well, I shall get at the throat of that old villain, and strangle him."

Cornelius, at these words, stopped for a moment, biting his lips, and staring out before him; then, eagerly returning to an idea which seemed to possess a strange fascination for him, he continued:

" Well, and once having strangled him, why should not I take his keys from him; why not go down the stairs as if I had done the most virtuous action; why not go and fetch Rosa from her room; why not tell her all, and jump from her window into the Waal? I am expert enough as a swimmer to save both of us. Rosa! but, O Heavens, Gryphus is her father. Whatever may be her affection for me, she will never approve of my having strangled her father, brutal and malicious as he has been. It will not do, Cornelius, my fine fellow—it is a bad plan. But, then, what is to become of me, and how shall I find Rosa again?"

Such were the cogitations of Cornelius three days after the sad scene of separation from Rosa, at the moment when we find him standing at the window.

And at that very moment Gryphus entered.

He held in his hand a huge stick; his eyes glistening with spiteful thoughts, a malignant smile played round his lips, and the whole of his carriage, and even all his movements, betokened bad and malicious intentions.

Cornelius heard him enter, and guessed that it was he, but did not turn round, as he knew well that Rosa was not coming after him.

There is nothing more galling to angry people than the coolness of those on whom they wish to vent their spleen.

The expense being once incurred, one does not like to lose it; one's passion is roused, and one's blood boiling, so it would be labour lost not to have at least a nice little row.

Gryphus, therefore, on seeing that Cornelius did not stir, tried to attract his attention by a loud—

" Umph, umph."

Cornelius was humming between his teeth the " Hymn of Flowers,"*a sad, but very charming song.

" We are the daughters of the secret fire,
Of the fire which circulates through the veins of the earth;
We are the daughters of Aurora, and of the morning dew;
    We are the daughters of the air;
    We are the daughters of the water;
But we are, above all, the daughters of Heaven."

This song, the placid melancholy of which was still heightened by its calm and sweet melody, exasperated Gryphus.

He struck his stick on the stone pavement of the cell, and called out—

" Halloa! my warbling gentleman, don't you hear me?"

Cornelius turned round, merely saying—

" Good morning," and then began his song again.

" Men defile us, and kill us while loving us,
    We hang to the earth by a thread;
This thread is our root, that is to say, our life,
But we raise on high our arms towards Heaven."

" Ah, you accursed sorcerer! you are making game of me, I believe," roared Gryphus.

Cornelius continued:

" For Heaven is our home,
Our true home, as from thence comes our soul,
    As thither our soul returns,
    Our soul, that is to say, our perfume."

Gryphus went up to the prisoner, and said—

" But you don't see that I have taken means to get you under, and to force you to confess your crimes."

" Are you mad, my dear Master Gryphus?" asked Cornelius.

And as he now for the first time observed the frenzied features, the flashing eyes, and foaming mouth of the old jailer, he said—

" Bless the man, he is more than mad, it seems, he is furious."

Gryphus flourished his stick above his head, but Van Baerle moved not, and remained standing with his arms a-kimbo.

" It seems your intention to threaten me, Master Gryphus."

" Yes, indeed, I threaten you," cried the jailer.

" And with what?"

" First of all, look what I have in my hand."

" I think that's a stick," said Cornelius calmly, " but I don't suppose you will threaten me with that."

" Oh, you don't suppose—oh! why not?"

" Because any jailer who strikes a prisoner is liable to two penalties; the first laid down in Article 9 of the Regulations at Lœvestein:

" ' Any jailer, inspector, or turnkey, who lays hand upon a prisoner of state, will be dismissed.' "

" Yes, who lays hands," said Gryphus, mad with rage, " but there is not a word about a stick in the regulation."

"And the second," continued Cornelius, " which is not written in the regulation, but which is to be found elsewhere:

" ' Whosoever takes up the stick will be thrashed by the stick.' "

Gryphus, growing more and more exasperated by the calm and sententious tone of Cornelius, brandished his cudgel, but at the moment when he raised it, Cornelius rushed at him, snatched it from his hands, and put it under his own arm. Gryphus fairly bellowed with rage.

" Hush, hush, my good man," said Cornelius, " don't do anything to lose your place."

" Ah! you sorcerer, I'll pinch you worse," roared Gryphus.

" I wish you may."

" Don't you see that my hand is empty?"

" Yes, I see it, and I am glad of it."

" You know that it is not generally so, when I come upstairs in the morning."

" It's true, you generally bring me the worst soup, and the most miserable rations, one can imagine. But that's not a punishment to me; I eat only bread, and the worse the bread is to your taste, Gryphus, the better it is to mine."

" How so?"

" Oh, it's a very simple thing."

" Well, tell it me," said Gryphus.

" Very willingly. I know that in giving me bad bread, you think you do me harm."

" Certainly, I don't give it you to please you, you brigand."

" Well, then, I who am a sorcerer, as you know, change your bad into excellent bread, which I relish more than the best cake; and then I have the double pleasure of eating something that gratifies my palate, and of doing something that puts you in a rage."

Gryphus answered with a growl.

" Oh! you confess, then, that you are a sorcerer."

" Indeed, I am one; I don't say it before all the world, because they might burn me for it, but as we are alone, I don't mind telling you."

" Well, well, well," answered Gryphus, " but if a sorcerer can change black bread into white, won't he die of hunger if he has no bread at all?"

" What's that?" said Cornelius.

" Consequently, I shall not bring you any bread at all, and we shall see how it will be after eight days."

Cornelius grew pale.

" And," continued Gryphus, " we'll begin this very day! As you are such a clever sorcerer, why, you had better change the furniture of your room into bread; as to myself, I shall pocket the eighteen sous which are paid to me for your board."

" But that's murder," cried Cornelius, carried away by the first impulse of the very natural terror with which this horrible mode of death inspired him.

" Well," Gryphus went on in his jeering way, " as you are a sorcerer, you will live notwithstanding."

Cornelius put on a smiling face again, and said—

" Have not you seen me make the pigeons come here from Dort?"

" Well?" said Gryphus.

" Well, a pigeon is a very dainty morsel, and a man who eats one every day would not starve, I think."

" And how about the fire?" said Gryphus.

" Fire! but you know that I'm in league with the devil. Do you think the devil will leave me without fire? why, fire is his proper element."

" A man, however healthy his appetite may be, would not eat a pigeon every day. Wagers have been laid to do so, and those who made them gave them up."

" Well, but when I am tired of pigeons, I shall make the fish of the Waal and of the Meuse come up to me."

Gryphus opened his large eyes, quite bewildered.

" I am rather fond of fish," continued Cornelius; " you never let me have any. Well, I shall turn your starving me to advantage, and regale myself with fish."

Gryphus nearly fainted with anger and with fright, but he soon rallied, and said, putting his hand in his pocket—

" Well, as you force me to it," and, with these words, he drew forth a clasp-knife and opened it.

" Halloa, a knife!" said Cornelius, preparing to defend himself with his stick.

CHAPTER TWENTY-NINE

In Which Van Baerle, before Leaving Lœvestein, Settles Accounts with Gryphus

THE TWO remained silent for some minutes, Gryphus on the offensive, and Van Baerle on the defensive.

Then, as the situation might be prolonged to an indefinite length, Cornelius, anxious to know something more of the causes which had so fiercely exasperated his jailer, spoke first, by putting the question—

" Well, what do you want, after all?"

" I'll tell you what I want," answered Gryphus; " I want you to restore to me my daughter Rosa."

" Your daughter?" cried Van Baerle.

" Yes, my daughter Rosa, whom you have taken from me by your devilish magic. Now, will you tell me where she is?"

And the attitude of Gryphus became more and more threatening.

" Rosa is not at Lœvestein?" cried Cornelius.

" You know well she is not. Once more, will you restore her to me?"

" I see," said Cornelius, " this is a trap you are laying for me."

" Now, for the last time, will you tell me where my daughter is?"

" Guess it, you rogue, if you don't know it."

" Only wait, only wait," growled Gryphus, white with rage, and with quivering lips, as his brain began to turn. " Ah, you will not tell me anything? Well, I'll unlock your teeth!"

He advanced a step towards Cornelius, and said, showing him the weapon which he held in his hand—

" Do you see this knife? Well, I have killed more than

fifty black cocks with it, and I vow I'll kill their master the devil, as well as them."

" But, you blockhead," said Cornelius, " will you really kill me?"

" I shall open your heart, to see in it the place where you hide my daughter."

Saying this, Gryphus in his frenzy rushed towards Cornelius, who had barely time to retreat behind his table to avoid the first thrust; but as Gryphus continued, with horrid threats, to brandish his huge knife, and as, although out of the reach of his weapon, yet, as long as it remained in the madman's hand, the ruffian might fling it at him— Cornelius lost no time, and, availing himself of the stick, which he held tight under his arm, dealt the jailer a vigorous blow on the wrist of that hand when held the knife.

The knife fell to the ground, and Cornelius put his foot on it.

Then, as Gryphus seemed bent upon engaging in a struggle which the pain in his wrist, and shame for having allowed himself to be disarmed, would have made desperate, Cornelius took a decisive step, belabouring his jailer with the most heroic self-possession, and deliberately aiming his blows at him.

It was not long before Gryphus begged for mercy. But, before begging for mercy, he had lustily roared for help, and his cries had roused all the fuctionaries of the prison. Two turnkeys, an inspector, and three or four guards made their appearance all at once, and found Cornelius still using the stick, with the knife under his foot.

At the sight of these witnesses, who could not know all the circumstances which had provoked and might justify his offence, Cornelius felt that he was irretrievably lost.

In fact, appearances were sadly against him.

In one moment Cornelius was disarmed, and Gryphus raised and supported; and, bellowing with rage and pain, he was able to count on his back and shoulders the bruises which were beginning to swell like the hills dotting the slopes of a mountain-ridge.

A protocol of the violence practised by the prisoner

against his jailer was immediately drawn up, and as it was made on the depositions of Gryphus, it certainly could not be said to be too tame; the prisoner being charged with neither more nor less than with an attempt to murder, for a long time premeditated, with open rebellion.

Whilst the charge was made out against Cornelius, Gryphus, whose presence was no longer necessary, after having made his depositions, was taken down by his turn-keys to his lodge, groaning, and covered with bruises.

During this time, the guards who had seized Cornelius busied themselves in charitably informing their prisoner of the usages and customs of Lœvestein, which, however, he knew as well as they did. The regulations had been read to him, at the moment of his entering the prison, and certain articles in them remained fixed in his memory.

Among other things, they told him, that this regulation had been carried out to its full extent in the case of a pri-soner named Mathias,* who in 1668, that is to say, five years before, had committed a much less violent act of rebellion than that of which Cornelius was guilty. He had found his soup too hot, and thrown it at the head of the chief turnkey, whom in consequence of this ablution, had been put to the inconvenience of having his skin come off as he wiped his face.

Mathias was taken within twelve hours from his cell, then led to the jailer's lodge, where he was registered as leaving Lœvestein, then taken to the Esplanade, from which there is a very fine prospect over a wide expanse of country. There they fettered his hands, bandaged his eyes, and let him say his prayers.

Hereupon he was invited to go down on his knees, and the guards of Lœvestein, twelve in number, at a sign from a sergeant, very cleverly lodged a musket ball each in his body.

In consequence of this proceeding, Mathias incontinently* did then and there die.

Cornelius listened with the greatest attention to this delightful recital, and then said—

" Ah! ah! within twelve hours, you say?"

" Yes, the twelfth hour had not even struck, if I remember right," said the guard who had told him the story.

" Thank you," said Cornelius.

The guard still had the smile on his face, with which he accompanied, and, as it were, accentuated his tale, when footsteps and a jingling of spurs were heard ascending the staircase.

The guard fell back to allow an officer to pass, who entered the cell of Cornelius, at the moment when the clerk of Lœvestein was still making out his report.

" Is this No. 11?" he asked.

" Yes, Captain," answered a non-commissioned officer.

" Then this is the cell of the prisoner Cornelius Van Baerle?"

" Exactly, Captain."

" Where is the prisoner?"

" Here I am, sir," answered Cornelius, growing rather pale, notwithstanding all his courage.

" You are Doctor Cornelius Van Baerle?" asked he, this time addressing the prisoner himself.

" Yes, sir."

" Then follow me."

" Oh! oh!" said Cornelius, whose heart felt oppressed by the first dread of death. " What quick work they make here in the fortress of Lœvestein. And the rascal talked to me of twelve hours!"

" Ah! what did I tell you?" whispered the communicative guard into the ear of the culprit.

" A lie."

" How so?"

" You promised me twelve hours."

" Ah, yes; but here comes to you an aide-de-camp of His Highness, even one of his most intimate companions, Van Decken. Zounds! they did not grant such an honour to poor Mathias."

" Come, come!" said Cornelius, drawing a long breath. " Come, I'll show to these people that an honest burgher, godson of Cornelius De Witte, can, without flinching, receive as many musket-balls as that Mathias."

Saying this, he passed proudly before the clerk, who, being interrupted in his work, ventured to say to the officer—

"But, Captain Van Decken, the protocol is not yet finished."

"It is not worth while finishing it," answered the officer.

"All right," replied the clerk, philosophically putting up his paper and pen into a greasy and well-worn writing case.

"It was written," thought poor Cornelius, "that I should not, in this world, give my name either to a child, to a flower, or to a book, the three things by which a man's memory is perpetuated."

But repressing his melancholy thoughts, he followed the officer with a resolute heart, and carrying his head erect.

Cornelius counted the steps which led to the Esplanade, regretting that he had not asked the guard how many there were of them, which the man in his officious complaisance would not have failed to tell him.

What the poor prisoner was most afraid of during this walk, which he considered as leading him to the end of the journey of life, was to see Gryphus and not to see Rosa. What savage satisfaction would glisten in the eyes of the father, and what sorrow dim those of the daughter!*

Indeed, the poor tulip-fancier needed all his courage and resolution not to burst into tears at the thought of the latter, and of her foster-daughter the black tulip.

Although he looked to the right and to the left, he saw neither Rosa nor Gryphus.

On reaching the Esplanade, he bravely looked about for the guards who were to be his executioners, and in reality saw a dozen soldiers assembled. But they were not standing in line, or carrying muskets, but talking together so gaily, that Cornelius felt almost shocked.

All at once, Gryphus, limping, staggering, and supporting himself on a crooked stick, came forth from the jailer's lodge; his old eyes, gray as those of a cat, were lit up by a gleam in which all his hatred was concentrated. He then began to pour forth such a torrent of disgusting imprecations against Cornelius that the latter, addressing the officer, said—

" I do not think it very becoming, sir, that I should be thus insulted by this man, especially at a moment like this."

" Well! hear me," said the officer, laughing; " it is quite natural that this worthy fellow should bear you a grudge—you seem to have given it him very soundly."

" But, sir, it was only in self-defence."

" Never mind," said the Captain, shrugging his shoulders like a true philosopher, " let him talk; what does it matter to you now?"

The cold sweat stood on the brow of Cornelius at this answer, which he looked upon somewhat in the light of brutal irony, especially as coming from an officer of whom he had heard it said that he was attached to the person of the Prince.

The unfortunate tulip-fancier then felt that he had no more resources, and no more friends, and resigned himself to his fate.

" God's will be done," he muttered, bowing his head; then, turning towards the officer who seemed complacently to wait until he had finished his meditations, he asked—

" Please, sir, tell me now, where am I to go?"

The officer pointed to a carriage drawn by four horses, which reminded him very strongly of that which, under similar circumstances, had before attracted his attention at the Buitenhof.

" Enter," said the officer.

" Ah!" muttered Cornelius to himself, " it seems they are not going to treat me to the honours of the Esplanade."

He uttered these words loud enough for the chatty guard, who was at his heels, to overhear him.

That kind soul very likely thought it his duty to give Cornelius some new information; for, approaching the door of the carriage, whilst the officer, with one foot on the step, was still giving some orders, he whispered to Van Baerle:

" Condemned prisoners have sometimes been taken to their own town, to be made an example of, and they have then been executed before the door of their own house. It's all according to circumstances."

Cornelius thanked him by signs, and then said to himself:

" Well, here is a fellow who never misses giving consolation whenever an opportunity presents itself. In truth, my friend, I'm very much obliged to you. Good-bye."

The carriage drove away.

" Ah! you villain, you brigand!" roared Gryphus, clenching his fists at the victim, who was escaping from his clutches; " is it not a shame that this fellow gets off without having restored my daughter to me?"

" If they take me to Dort," thought Cornelius, " I shall see, in passing my house, whether my poor borders have been much spoiled."

CHAPTER THIRTY

*Wherein the Reader begins to Guess the Kind of Execution
that was Awaiting Cornelius Van Baerle*

THE CARRIAGE rolled on during the whole day; it passed
on the right of Dort, went through Rotterdam, and
reached Delft. At five o'clock in the evening, at least
twenty leagues had been travelled.

Cornelius addressed some questions to the officer, who
was at the same time his guard and his companion; but,
cautious as were his inquiries, he had the disappointment
of receiving no answer.

Cornelius regretted that he had no longer by his side
that chatty soldier, who would talk without being questioned.

That obliging person would, undoubtedly, have given
him as pleasant details, and exact explanations, concerning
this third strange part of his adventures, as he had done
concerning the two first.

The travellers passed the night in the carriage. On the
following morning, at dawn, Cornelius found himself
beyond Leyden, having the North Sea on his left, and the
Zuyder Zee on his right.

Three hours after, he entered Haarlem.

Cornelius was not aware of what had passed at Haarlem,
and we shall leave him in ignorance of it until the course of
events enlighten him.

But the reader has a right to know all about it, even
before our hero, and, therefore, we shall not make him wait.

We have seen that Rosa and the tulip, like two orphan
sisters, had been left, by the Prince William of Orange, at
the house of the President Van Herysen.

Rosa did not hear again from the Stadtholder until the
evening of that day on which she had seen him face to face.

About evening, an officer called at Van Herysen's house. He came from His Highness, with a request for Rosa to appear at the Town Hall.

There, in the large council room, into which she was ushered, she found the Prince writing.

He was alone, with a large Frisian greyhound at his feet, which looked at him with a steady glance, as if the faithful animal were wishing to do what no man could do—read the thoughts of his master in his face.

William continued his writing for a moment; then, raising his eyes, and seeing Rosa standing near the door, he said, without laying down his pen—

" Come here, my child."

Rosa advanced a few steps towards the table.

" Sit down" he said.

Rosa obeyed, for the Prince was fixing his eyes upon her; but he had scarcely turned them again to his paper, when she bashfully retired to the door.

The Prince finished his letter.

During this time, the greyhound went up to Rosa, surveyed her, and began to caress her.

" Ah! ah!" said William to his dog, " it's easy to see that she is a countrywoman of yours, and that you recognise her."

Then, turning towards Rosa, and fixing on her his scrutinising, and, at the same time, impenetrable glance, he said—

" Now, my child."

The Prince was scarcely twenty-three, and Rosa eighteen or twenty. He might, therefore, perhaps, better have said, " my sister."

" My child," he said, with that strangely-commanding accent, which chilled all those who approached him, " we are alone; let us speak together."

Rosa began to tremble: and yet there wa nothing but kindness in the expression of the Prince's face.

" Monseigneur," she stammered.

" You have a father at Lœvestein?"

" Yes, Your Highness."

" You do not love him?"

" I do not—at least, not as a daughter ought to do, Monseigneur."

" It is not right not to love one's father, but it is right not to tell a falsehood."

Rosa cast her eyes to the ground.

" What is the reason of your not loving your father?"

" He is wicked."

" In what way does he show his wickedness?"

" He ill-treats the prisoners."

" All of them?"

" All."

' But don't you bear him a grudge for ill-treating some-one in particular?"

" My father ill-treats in particular Mynheer Van Baerle, who——"

" Who is your lover?"

Rosa started back a step.

" Whom I love, Monseigneur," she answered proudly.

" Since when?" asked the Prince.

" Since the day when I first saw him."

" And when was that?"

' The day after that on which the Grand Pensionary John and his brother Cornelius met with such an awful death."

The Prince compressed his lips and knit his brow, and his eyelids dropped so as to hide his eyes for an instant. After a momentary silence, he resumed the conversation.

" But to what can it lead to love a man who is doomed to live and die in prison?"

" It will lead, if he lives and dies in prison, to my aiding him in life and in death."

" And would you accept the lot of being the wife of a prisoner?"

" As the wife of Mynheer Van Baerle, I should, under any circumstances, be the proudest and happiest woman in the world; but——"

" But what?"

" I dare not say, Monseigneur."

" There is something like hope in your tone—what do you hope?"

She raised her moist and beautiful eyes, and looked at William with a glance full of meaning, which was calculated to stir up in the recesses of his heart the clemency which was slumbering there.

" Ah! I understand you," he said.

Rosa, with a smile, clasped her hands.

" You hope in me?" said the Prince.

" Yes, Monseigneur."

" Umph!"

The Prince sealed the letter which he had just written, and summoned one of his officers, to whom he said—

" Captain Van Decken, carry this despatch to Loevestein; you will read the orders which I give to the Governor, and execute them as far as they regard you."

The officer bowed, and, a few minutes afterwards, the gallop of a horse was heard resounding in the vaulted archway.

" My child," continued the Prince, " the feast of the tulip will be on Sunday next, that is to say, the day after to-morrow. Make yourself smart with these five hundred guilders, as I wish that day to be a great day for you."

" How does Your Highness wish me to be dressed?" faltered Rosa.

" Take the costume of a Frisian bride," said William. " it will suit you very well indeed."

CHAPTER THIRTY-ONE

Haarlem

THE FIFTEENTH of May, 1673,* was a great day for the good
city of Haarlem. It had to celebrate a three-fold festival.
In the first place, the black tulip had been produced;
secondly, the Prince William of Orange, as a true Hollander, had promised to be present at the ceremony of its
inauguration; and, thirdly, it was a point of honour with
the States to show to the French, at the conclusion of such
a disastrous war as that of 1672, that the flooring of the
Batavian Republic* was solid enough for its people to dance
on it, with the accompaniment of the cannon of their fleets.

The Horticultural Society of Haarlem had shown itself
worthy of its fame, by giving a hundred thousand guilders
for the bulb of a tulip. The town, which did not wish to
remain behindhand, voted a like sum, which was placed
in the hands of that notable body to solemnise the auspicious
event.

And, indeed, on the Sunday fixed for this ceremony,
there was such a stir among the people, and such an
enthusiasm among the townsfolk, that even a Frenchman,
who laughs at everything at all times, could not have
helped admiring the character of those honest Hollanders,
who were equally ready to spend their money for the con-
struction of a man-of-war—that is to say, for the support
of national honour, as they were to reward the grower of
a new flower, destined to bloom for one day, and to serve
during that day to divert the ladies, the learned, and the
curious.

At the head of the Notables and of the Horticultural
Committee shone Mynheer Van Herysen, dressed in his
richest habiliments.

The worthy man had done his best to resemble his

favourite flower, in the sombre and stern elegance of his garments; and we are bound to record, to his honour, that he had perfectly succeeded in his object.

Dark crimson velvet, dark purple silk, and jet-black cloth, with linen of dazzling whiteness, composed the festive dress of the President, who marched at the head of his Committee, carrying an enormous nosegay, like that which, a hundred and twenty-one years later, Monsieur de Robespierre displayed at the festival of " The Supreme Being."*

There was, however, a little difference between the two: very different from the French tribune, whose heart was so full of hatred and ambitious vindictiveness, the honest President carried in his bosom a heart as innocent as the flowers which he held in his hand.

Behind the Committee, who were as gay as a meadow, and as fragrant as a garden in spring, marched the learned societies of the town, the magistrates, the military, the nobles, and the boors.

The people, even among the respected republicans of the Seven Provinces, had no place assigned to them in the procession: they merely lined the streets.

This is the place for the multitude which, with true philosophic spirit, waits until the triumphal pageants have passed, to know what to say of them, and sometimes also to know what to do.

This time, however, there was no question either of the triumph of Pompey or of Caesar; neither of the defeat of Mithridates, nor of the conquest of Gaul.* The procession was as placid as the passing of a flock of lambs, and as inoffensive as a flight of birds sweeping through the air.

Haarlem had no other triumphers, except its gardeners. Worshipping flowers, Haarlem idolised the florist.

In the centre of this pacific and fragrant *cortège* the black tulip was seen, carried on a litter which was covered with white velvet and fringed with gold.

It was arranged that the Prince Stadtholder himself should give the prize of a hundred thousand guilders, which interested the people at large, and it was thought that, perhaps, he would make a speech which interested more particularly his friends and enemies.

The whole population of Haarlem, swelled by that of the neighbourhood, had arranged itself along the beautiful avenues of trees, with the fixed resolution, this time, to applaud neither the heroes of war, nor those of science, but merely the conqueror of Nature, who had forced her to produce the black tulip.

Nothing, however, is more fickle than such a resolution of the people. When a crowd is once in the humour to cheer, it is just the same as when it begins to hiss. It never knows when to stop.*

It, therefore, in the first place, cheered Van Herysen and his nosegay, then the corporations, then followed a cheer for the people; and at last, and for once with great justice, there was one for the excellent music with which the gentlemen of the town council generously treated the assemblage at every halt.

All eyes were on the look-out for the hero of the day— of course we mean the grower of the tulip.

This hero made his appearance at the conclusion of the reading of the report, which we have seen Van Herysen drawing up with such conscientiousness; and he produced almost a greater sensation than the Stadtholder himself.

There he walked, covered with flowers down to his girdle; well combed and brushed and entirely dressed in scarlet, a colour which contrasted strongly with his black hair and yellow complexion.

This hero, radiant with rapturous joy, who had the distinguished honour of making the people forget the speech of Van Herysen, and even the presence of the Stadtholder, was Isaac Boxtel, who saw, carried on his right before him, the black tulip, his pretended daughter; and on his left, in a large purse, the hundred thousand guilders in glittering gold pieces, towards which he was constantly squinting, fearful of losing sight of them for one moment.

Another quarter of an hour and the Prince will arrive, and the procession will halt for the last time; after the tulip is placed on its throne, the Prince, yielding precedence

to this rival for the popular adoration, will take a mag-
nificently-emblazoned parchment, on which is written the
name of the grower; and His Highness, in a loud and
audible tone, will proclaim him to be the discoverer of a
wonder: that Holland, by the instrumentality of him,
Boxtel, had forced nature to produce a black flower,
which shall henceforth be called *Tulipa nigra Boxtellea*.

From time to time, however, Boxtel withdrew his eyes
for a moment from the tulip and the purse, timidly looking
among the crowd, for, more than anything, he dreaded to
descry there the pale face of the pretty Frisian girl.

She would have been a spectre spoiling the joy of the
festival for him, just as Banquo's ghost did that of Macbeth.

And yet, if the truth must be told, this wretch, who had
stolen what was the boast of a man, and the dowry of a
woman, did not consider himself as a thief. He had so
intently watched this tulip, followed it so eagerly from the
drawer in Cornelius's dry-room to the scaffold of the
Buitenhof, and from the scaffold to the fortress of Lœvestein,
he had seen it bud and grow in Rosa's window, and so
often warmed the air round it with his breath, that he felt
as if no one had a better right to call himself its producer
than he had; and any one who would now take the black
tulip from him, would have appeared to him as a thief.

Yet he did not perceive Rosa; his joy, therefore, was not
spoiled.

In the centre of a circle of magnificent trees, which were
decorated with garlands and inscriptions, the procession
halted, amidst the sounds of lively music; and the young
damsels of Haarlem made their appearance to escort the
tulip to the raised seat which it was to occupy on the platform, by the side of the gilded chair of His Highness the
Stadtholder.

And the proud tulip, raised on its pedestal, soon overlooked the assembled crowd of people, who clapped their
hands, and made the old town of Haarlem re-echo with
their tremendous cheers.

CHAPTER THIRTY-TWO

A Last Request

IN THIS solemn moment, and whilst the cheers still resounded, a carriage was driving along the road on the outskirts of the green on which the scene occurred; it pursued its way slowly, on account of the flocks of children who were pushed out of the avenue by the crowd of men and women.

This carriage, covered with dust, and creaking on its axles, the result of a long journey, enclosed the unfortunate Van Baerle, who was quite dazzled and bewildered by this festive splendour and bustle.

Notwithstanding the little readiness which his companion had shown in answering his questions concerning his fate, he ventured once more to ask what all this meant.

" As you may see, sir," replied the officer, " it is a feast."

" Ah, a feast," said Cornelius, in the sad tone of indifference of a man to whom no joy remains in this world.

Then, after some moments' silence, during which the carriage had proceeded a few yards, he asked once more—

" The feast of the patron saint of Haarlem? as I see so many flowers."

" It is indeed a feast in which flowers play a principal part."

" Oh, the sweet scents! oh, the beautiful colours!" cried Cornelius.

" Stop, that the gentleman may see," said the officer, with that frank kindliness which is peculiar to military men, to the soldier who was acting as postilion.

" Oh, thank you, sir, for your kindness," replied Van Baerle, in a melancholy tone; " the joy of others pains me —please spare me this pang."

" Just as you wish. Drive on! I ordered the driver to

stop because I thought it would please you, as you are said to love flowers, and especially that, the feast of which is celebrated to-day."

" And what flower is that?"

" The tulip."

" The tulip!" cried Van Baerle: " is to-day the feast of the tulip?"

" Yes, sir; but as this spectacle displeases you, let us drive on."

The officer was about to give the order to proceed, but Cornelius stopped him, a painful thought having struck him. He asked, with faltering voice:

" Is the prize given to-day, sir?"

" Yes, the prize for the black tulip."

Cornelius's cheek flushed, his whole frame trembled, and the cold sweat stood on his brow.

" Alas! sir," he said, " all these good people will be as unfortunate as myself, for they will not see the solemnity which they have come to witness, or at least they will see it incompletely."

" What is it you mean to say?"

" I mean to say," replied Cornelius, throwing himself back in the carriage, " that the black tulip will not be found, except by one whom I know."

" In this case," said the officer, " the person whom you know has found it, for the thing which the whole of Haarlem is looking at at this moment is neither more nor less than the black tulip."

" The black tulip!" cried Van Baerle, thrusting half his body out of the carriage-window. " Where is it? where is it?"

" Down there, on the throne; don't you see?"

" I do see it."

" Come along, sir," said the officer. " Now, we must drive off."

" Oh! have pity, have mercy, sir," said Van Baerle, " don't take me away. Let me look once more. Is what I see down there the black tulip? Quite black? Is it possible? Oh, sir, have you seen it? It must have specks, it must be imperfect, it must only be dyed black; ah, if I were there! I should see it at once. Let me alight, let me see it close, I beg of you."

" Are you mad, sir? How could I allow such a thing?"

" I implore you?"

" But you forget that you are a prisoner."

" It is true I am a prisoner, but I am a man of honour, and I promise you on my word that I will not run away, I will not attempt to escape—only let me see the flower."

" But my orders, sir, my orders." And the officer again made the driver a sign to proceed.

Cornelius stopped him once more.

" Oh, be forbearing, be generous, my whole life depends upon your pity. Alas! perhaps it will not be much longer. You don't know, sir, what I suffer. You don't know the struggle going on in my heart and mind; for after all," Cornelius cried in despair, " if this were my tulip, if it were the one which has been stolen from Rosa! Oh! I must alight, sir! I must see the flower. You may kill me afterwards if you like, but I will see it; I must see it."

" Be quiet, unfortunate man, and come quickly back into the carriage, for here is the escort of His Highness the Stadtholder, and if the Prince observed any disturbance or heard any noise, it would be ruin to me, as well as to you."

Van Baerle, more afraid for his companion than himself, threw himself back into the carriage, but he could only keep quiet for half a minute, and the first twenty horsemen had scarcely passed when he again leaned out of the carriage-window, gesticulating imploringly towards the Stadtholder at the very moment when he passed.

William, impassible and quiet as usual, was proceeding to the green to fulfil his duty as chairman. He held in his hand the roll of parchment, which, on this festive day, had become his baton.

Seeing the man gesticulate with imploring mien, and perhaps also recognising the officer who accompanied him, His Highness ordered his carriage to stop.

In one instant his snorting steeds stood still, at a distance of about six yards from the carriage in which Van Baerle was caged.

" What is this?" the Prince asked the officer, who at the first order of the Stadtholder had jumped out of the carriage, and was respectfully approaching him.

" Monseigneur," he cried, " this is the prisoner of state whom I have fetched from Lœvestein, and whom I have brought to Haarlem according to Your Highness's command."

" What does he want?"

" He entreats for permission to stop here for a moment."

" To see the black tulip, Monseigneur," said Van Baerle, clasping his hands, " and when I have seen it, when I have seen what I desire to know, I am quite ready to die, if die I must; but in dying I shall bless Your Highness's mercy for having allowed me to witness the glorification of my work."

It was, indeed, a curious spectacle to see these two men, at the windows of their several carriages; the one, surrounded by his guards, and all powerful, the other a prisoner and miserable; the one going to mount a throne, the other believing himself to be on his way to the scaffold.

William, looking with his cold glance on Cornelius, listened to his anxious and urgent request.

Then, addressing himself to the officer, he said:

" Is this person the mutinous prisoner who has attempted to kill his jailer at Lœvestein?"

Cornelius heaved a sigh and hung his head. His good-tempered honest face turned pale and red at the same instant. These words of the all-powerful Prince, who, by some secret messenger, unavailable to other mortals, had already been apprised of his crime, seemed to him to forebode not only his doom, but also the refusal of his last request.

He did not try to make a struggle, or to defend himself; and he presented to the Prince the affecting spectacle of despairing innocence, like that of a child; a spectacle which was fully understood and felt by the great mind and the great heart of him who observed it.

" Allow the prisoner to alight, and let him see the black tulip; it is well worth being seen once."

" Thank you, Monseigneur, thank you," said Cornelius, nearly swooning with joy, and staggering on the steps of his carriage; had not the officer supported him, our poor friend would have made his thanks to His Highness prostrate on his knees with his forehead in the dust.

After having granted this permission, the Prince proceeded on his way over the green, amidst the most enthusiastic acclamations.

He soon arrived at the platform, and the thunder of cannon shook the air.

CHAPTER THIRTY-THREE

Conclusion

VAN BAERLE, led by four guards, who pushed their way through the crowd, sidled up to the black tulip, towards which his gaze was attracted with increasing interest the nearer he approached to it.

He saw it; that unique flower, which he was to see once, and no more. He saw it at the distance of six paces, and was delighted with its perfection and gracefulness; he saw it surrounded by young and beautiful girls who formed, as it were, a guard of honour for this queen of excellence and purity. And yet the more he ascertained with his own eyes the perfection of the flower, the more wretched and miserable he felt. He looked all around for some one to whom he might address only one question; but his eyes everywhere met strange faces, and the attention of all was directed towards the chair of state, on which the Stadtholder had seated himself.

William rose, casting a tranquil glance over the enthusiastic crowd, and his keen eye rested by turns on the three extremities of a triangle, formed opposite to him by three persons of very different interests and feelings.

At one of the angles, Boxtel, trembling with impatience, and quite absorbed in watching the Prince, the guilders, the black tulip, and the crowd.

At the other, Cornelius, panting for breath, silent, and his attention, his eyes, his life, his heart, his love, quite concentrated on the black tulip.

And, thirdly, standing on a raised step among the maidens of Haarlem, a beautiful Frisian girl, dressed in fine scarlet woollen cloth, embroidered with silver, and covered with a lace veil, which fell in rich folds from her head-dress of gold brocade; in one word, Rosa, who, faint and with swimming eyes, was leaning on the arm of one of the officers of William.

The Prince then slowly unfolded the parchment, and said, with a calm clear voice, which, although low, made itself perfectly heard amidst the respectful silence, which all at once arrested the breath of fifty thousand spectators:

" You know what has brought us here.

" A prize of one hundred thousand guilders has been promised to whosoever should grow the black tulip.

" The black tulip has been grown; here it is before your eyes, coming up to all the conditions required by the programme of the Horticultural Society of Haarlem.

" The history of its production, and the name of its grower, will be inscribed in the book of honour of the city.

" Let the person approach to whom the black tulip belongs."

In pronouncing these words, the Prince, to judge of the effect they produced, surveyed, with his eagle eye, the three extremities of the triangle.

He saw Boxtel rushing forward. He saw Cornelius make an involuntary movement; and, lastly, he saw the officer, who was taking care of Rosa, lead, or rather, push her forward towards him.

At the sight of Rosa, a double cry arose on the right and left of the Prince.

Boxtel, thunderstruck, and Cornelius, in joyful amazement, both exclaimed—

" Rosa! Rosa!"

" The tulip is yours, is it not, my child?" said the Prince.

" Yes, Monseigneur," stammered Rosa, whose striking beauty excited a general murmur of applause.

" Oh!" muttered Cornelius, " she has then belied me, when she said this flower was stolen from her. Oh! that is why she left Lœvestein. Alas! am I then forgotten, betrayed by her whom I thought my best friend on earth?"

" Oh!" sighed Boxtel, " I am lost."

" This tulip," continued the Prince, " will therefore bear the name of its producer, and figure in the catalogue under the title, *Tulipa nigra Rosa Barlaeensis*, which will henceforth be the name of this damsel."

And at the same time William took Rosa's hand, and placed it in that of a young man, who rushed forth, pale and beyond himself with joy, to the foot of the throne, greeting alternately the Prince and his bride; and who, with a grateful look to Heaven, returned his thanks to the Giver of all this happiness.

At the same moment, there fell at the feet of the President Van Herysen another man, struck down by a very different emotion.

Boxtel, crushed by the failure of his hopes, lay senseless on the ground. When they raised him, and examined his pulse and his heart, he was quite dead.

This incident did not much disturb the festival, as neither the Prince nor the President seemed to mind it much.

Cornelius started back in dismay, when in the thief, in the pretended Jacob, he recognised his neighbour Isaac Boxtel, whom, in the innocence of his heart, he had not for one instant suspected of such a wicked action.*

Then, to the sound of trumpets, the procession marched back without any change in its order, except that Boxtel was now dead, and that Cornelius and Rosa were walking triumphantly side by side, and hand in hand.

On their arriving at the Hotel de Ville, the Prince, pointing with his finger to the purse with the hundred thousand guilders, said to Cornelius—

" It is difficult to say by whom this money is gained, by you or by Rosa; for if you have found the black tulip, she has nursed it, and brought it into flower. It would, therefore, be unjust to consider it as her dowry: it is the gift of the town of Haarlem to the tulip."

Cornelius wondered what the Prince was driving at. The latter continued—

" I give to Rosa the sum of a hundred thousand guilders, which she has fairly earned, and which she can offer to you. They are the reward of her love, her courage, and her honesty. As to you, sir—thanks to Rosa again, who has furnished the proofs of your innocence——"

And, saying these words, the Prince handed to Cornelius that fly-leaf of the Bible on which was written the letter of Cornelius De Witte, and in which the third sucker had been wrapped.

"As to you, it has come to light that you were imprisoned for a crime which you had not committed. This means, that you are not only free, but that your property will be restored to you; as the property of an innocent man cannot be confiscated. Cornelius Van Baerle, you are the godson of Cornelius De Witte, and the friend of his brother John. Remain worthy of the name you have received from one of them, and of the friendship you have enjoyed with the other. The two De Wittes, wrongly judged, and wrongly punished in a moment of popular error, were two great citizens, of whom Holland is now proud."

The Prince, after these last words, which, contrary to his custom, he pronounced with a voice full of emotion, gave his hands to the lovers to kiss, whilst they were kneeling before him.

Then, heaving a sigh, he said—

"Alas! you are happy, who, dreaming only of what perhaps is the true glory of Holland, and forms especially her true happiness, do not attempt to acquire for her anything beyond the true colours of a tulip."

And, casting a glance towards that point of the compass where France lay, as if he saw new clouds gathering there, he entered his carriage and drove off.*

Cornelius, on his part, started on the same day to Dort with Rosa, who sent her lover's old housekeeper as a messenger to her father, to apprise him of all that had taken place.

Old Gryphus was by no means ready to be reconciled to his son-in-law. He had not yet forgotten the blows which he received in that famous encounter. To judge from the weals which he counted, their number, he said, amounted to forty-one; but, at last, in order, as he declared, not to be less generous than His Highness the Stadtholder, he consented to make his peace.

Appointed to watch over the tulips, the old man made

the rudest keeper of flowers in the whole of the Seven Provinces.

It was indeed a sight to see him watching the obnoxious moths and butterflies, killing slugs, and driving away the hungry bees.

As he had heard Boxtel's story, and was furious at having been the dupe of the pretended Jacob, he destroyed the sycamore behind which the envious Isaac had spied into the garden; for the plot of ground belonging to him had been bought by Cornelius, and taken into his own garden.

Rosa, growing not only in beauty but in wisdom also, after two years of her married life, could read and write so well that she was able to undertake by herself the education of two beautiful children which she had borne in 1674 and 1675, both in May, the month of flowers.

As a matter of course, one was a boy, the other a girl, the former being called Cornelius, the other Rosa.

Van Baerle remained faithfully attached to Rosa, and to his tulips. The whole of his life was devoted to the happiness of his wife and the culture of flowers, in the latter of which occupations he was so successful, that a great number of his Varieties found a place in the catalogue of Holland.

The two principal ornaments of his drawing-room were those two leaves from the Bible of Cornelius De Witte, in large golden frames; one of them containing the letter in which his godfather enjoined him to burn the correspondence of the Marquis de Louvois, and the other his own will, in which he bequeathed to Rosa his suckers under condition that she should marry a young man of from twenty-six to twenty-eight years, who loved her, and whom she loved, a condition which was scrupulously fulfilled, although, or rather because, Cornelius did not die.

And to ward off any envious attempts*of another Isaac Boxtel, he wrote over his door the lines which Grotius had, on the day of his flight, engraved on the wall of his prison:

" One has sometimes suffered enough to have a right ever afterwards to say, I am too happy."*

EXPLANATORY NOTES

3   *seven United Provinces*: the federative state created in January
1579 by the treaty of Utrecht. The seven Provinces (Holland,
Zeeland, Utrecht, Gelderland, Friesland, Groningen, and
Overijssel) made up the Republic of Holland which
remained a strong commercial power until the beginning of
the eighteenth century, after which it declined. It ceased to
exist when overrun by French revolutionary forces in 1795.

the Buitenhof: though Dumas thinks of the Buitenhof as a
building, it was in fact an open space in front of the
Binnenhof, the seat of the government of the province of
Holland. Cornelius was held first in the Kastelnij jail before
being transferred to the Gevangenpoort, a small prison
between the Buitenhof and the Square.

Tyckelaer: see Introduction, pp. xv–xvi.

Cornelius De Witte: born in 1623 at Dordrecht (Dort in this
translation, 10 miles south of Rotterdam) of which he
became burgomaster in 1666. He twice accompanied the
Dutch fleet in actions against the English and was the most
dependable ally of his brother, John de Witte, in the running
of the Republic. The chief magistrate of every town was
called a 'pensionary': the 'Grand Pensionary' was the equivalent of a prime minister.

the States of Holland: each province administered its own
internal affairs and sent mandated deputies to the States
General which dealt mainly with foreign affairs. The States
of Holland met in the Binnenhof.

John De Witte: born in 1625 at Dordrecht of which he was
elected Pensionary in 1650. Three years later he became
Grand Pensionary of Holland, in which position he continued to oppose the claims of the House of Orange. In 1654,
he forced through the Act of Exclusion which stated that no
member of the House of Orange should be allowed to
become Stadtholder, the supreme office which gave effective
command of the armed forces and all branches of government. Certain provinces were allowed to express reservations,

237

and it was not until 1667 that the 'Perpetual' or 'Eternal Edict' made the exclusion complete, a move which, though it was not initiated by John (as Dumas says here), angered the Orangist party. When Louis XIV invaded Holland in 1672, many believed that their only chance of retaining Dutch independence was to reinstate the Stadtholderate in the person of William of Orange.

4 *William of Orange*: son of William II of Orange (1626–50) and Mary (1631–60), eldest daughter of Charles I of England. French editions add: 'whom his contemporaries christened "the Taciturn"—a name which has come down to our own day.' Here Dumas, with customary carelessness, confuses the future William III with William I, 'the Silent' (assassinated in 1585), an error which he both repeated and corrected: see notes to pp. 41 and 207. By the summer of 1672, feeling against John de Witte was intense and the Orange cause was revived on a wave of popular enthusiasm. William was named Stadtholder on 9 July, six weeks before the events recounted in the first four chapters. The Dutch were then so hard-pressed by Louis XIV that their position seemed hopeless, but under William's firm leadership the war was intelligently prosecuted and the treaty of Nimeguen which concluded it in 1678 brought advantage and honour to the United Provinces. In 1677, William married Mary, daughter of the future James II of England whom he succeeded in 1689. Views of William's part in the murder of the De Witte brothers vary. In 1726 Jacques Basnage, one of Dumas's sources, affirmed that there was an Orangist conspiracy but concluded that William had no knowledge of it, a view which has received much support from later historians. However, in 1787 Benjamin Franklin stated categorically that William 'excited insurrections, spilled a great deal of blood, murdered the De Wittes, and got the powers reinvested in the Stadtholder'. Dumas at first sides with the republicans; in the last chapter he projects an altogether more sympathetic view of William. The ambiguity stems from his own uncertain political sympathies: a democratic republican by temperament, he dearly loved associating with royalty.

humoured Louis XIV: in 1665 Louis had laid claim to the

Spanish Netherlands by the Law of Devolution, a local law which awarded inherited property to the female children of a first marriage, and by 1667, Charleroi, Tournay, and Lille had become French. In 1672 he invaded Dutch territory by land and sea with 100,000 men and took less than three months (May–June) to overcome three provinces and forty cities. For the translator's 'campaign' a few lines later on, read 'crossing of the Rhine', a famous exploit which occurred on 12 June 1672.

insulted or ridiculed him: Louis was indeed a favourite target of satirists and included offensive prints and medals among his reasons for declaring war. As Dumas rightly points out, Holland was already a haven for French refugees denied free expression in their own country.

Mithridates: Mithridates VI of Pontus (132–63 BC), one of the most tenacious and able of the enemies of Rome. Had it not been for the superior skills and forces of generals such as Lucullus and Pompey, he would probably have driven the Romans out of Asia.

5 *his tutor*: after the introduction of the 'Perpetual Edict' in 1667 John de Witte took personal charge of William's education, with a view to turning him away from Catholic royalism towards the values of Protestantism and republicanism.

repealing the 'Perpetual Edict': revoked on 3/4 July 1672.

only yielded to force: on 29 June Cornelius declared that he would not sign. However, at the insistence of his wife and children, who feared the anger of the mob, he gave his qualified assent in the manner described here. When the crowd learned what he had written, he was obliged to strike out the letters indicating that he had been 'constrained by force'.

after an attempt . . . to stab him: for 'after', read 'before'. On 21 June John was set upon by four Orangist supporters as he walked from the Binnenhof to his house in the Kneuterdijk, and left for dead. It was a month before he recovered, by which time the Perpetual Edict had been repealed and William had been sworn in as Stadtholder (9 July).

by calumny: when he had recovered from his wounds, John de Witte rebutted the slanders made against him by satirists, and on 23 July the States of Holland issued a statement confirming that his honesty and probity were above suspicion.

6 *Justum ac tenacem*: Horace, *Odes*, III. 3: 'Justum et tenacem propositi virum' (the just and unwavering man), a line which Dumas often used to indicate his approval of the moral conduct of his characters. But records of the proceedings show that Cornelius did indeed repeat this line (and, when the torture was over, another: 'Nil conscire sibi, nulla pallascere culpa': 'To be guilty of no wrong, to grow pale for no guilt'). In the following paragraphs Dumas also correctly indicates the horror felt by the torturer (who, on his deathbed, wrote to Cornelius's wife to ask for forgiveness), and reproduces the exact terms of the sentence.

republic for ever: Dumas's original text had stated his sympathies more clearly: 'The insane passions of the people, to whose best interests Cornelius de Witte had ever been conscientiously devoted, were to some extent appeased by this judgement against one who was an entirely innocent as well as a great man; but, as we shall see, it failed to content them.' References to Dumas's original text in these notes are taken from the unabridged translation of 1850.

7 *Aristides*: surnamed 'the Just', one of the ten Athenian leaders at the Battle of Marathon (490 BC). In 483 BC the envious Themistocles had him banished, but when Xerxes headed the Persian invasion three years later, he offered his services and contributed to the success of Themistocles at the Battle of Salamis. He died in 468 BC so poor that he had to be buried at the expense of the state.

resigned his office of Grand Pensionary: on 6 August 1672.

guerdon: reward, profit. Dumas's idealistic view of public service, elsewhere exemplified by his valiant Musketeers, is clearly stated here.

an active part in it: the Orangist party regarded the De Witte brothers as a threat to their interests and it is accepted that the mob was strongly seeded with agitators who orchestrated events.

8 *Marquis de Louvois*: Michel Le Tellier (1641–91), Marquis de
Louvois, as French Under-Secretary of War, had been
responsible for reorganizing the French Army and, with
Pomponne, was one of Louis's chief ministers in the Dutch
War. After the French invasion of early June, John became
the butt of pamphleteers who accused him of complicity with
Louvois and of selling his country for money. It was said that
he had betrayed his country to prevent William coming to
power, certain in the knowledge that after the French victory
he would continue to rule under Louis. The compromising
correspondence which later connects Van Baerle with docu-
mented history is no more than a fictional device. After
John's death his papers were seized by the States of Holland,
which subsequently reported that they contained 'nothing
but honour and virtue'.

9 *get off so cheaply*: the judges had been unable to return a
capital sentence; see Introduction, p. xvi.

Schevening: in 1672 a fishing village about two miles north of
The Hague.

Count Tilly: the French-born Count Claude de Tilly, com-
mander of the cavalry, refused to give way to the armed and
hostile burghers and remained at his post. By afternoon,
rumours came from Delft that looting peasants were moving
on the capital and orders were rushed to Tilly to defend the
bridges leading to the town against them. But he refused to
accept oral orders. Written orders were obtained and, as a
professional soldier, Tilly obeyed him, though he did so
reluctantly. Dumas's account of his honourable part in events
is accurate.

burgher-guard: local militia forces, raised by all large Dutch
cities, carried out local civil and military duties. However,
their independence made their links with the national military command difficult.

11 *Gryphus*: the name of Cornelius's jailer is not recorded, but
eye witnesses spoke of his attempts to shield the De Wittes,
allowing himself to be maltreated rather than lead the mob
to their cell. A 'maid', whom Dumas turns into the jailer's
daughter, was sent to John's house.

Frisian women: or Friesian. Rosa hails from Friesland, one of the northern provinces, and Dumas makes much of her picturesque costume which, however, he describes in the vaguest way. She wears a golden brocade cap, tipped with lace, and red petticoats: see pages 90, 192.

12 *except for the contrary*: this puzzling afterthought does not figure in Dumas's French and should be ignored.

14 *ask for a meanness*: the 1850 translation, though no more elegant, is clearer: 'go to the Town-Hall and seek to procure the perpetration of a dastardly act . . .'.

15 *torture extraordinary*: torture, in varying degrees, was part of the civil-law procedures of most European countries in the seventeenth century. The 'question' used the rack and involved crushing thumbs, feet, legs, or head in a wooden or iron apparatus. The 'extraordinary' form required burning the sides, arms, and fingernails with fire or red-hot irons and pincers. The records show that Cornelius was left not only 'with broken wrists and crushed fingers', but also with mutilated feet and legs which prevented him from walking.

16 *the pond*: that is, the Vijver, the ornamental lake fronting the Buitenhof.

17 *Scheldt to Antwerp*: the reference seems to be rather to John's celebrated exploit of June 1665 when he personally assisted nine Dutch ships, pursued by two English frigates, through shallow water into the Texel roadstead. Cornelius Tromp (1629–91), a confirmed Orangist, was deprived of his command in 1666 for over-eagerness in pursuing an advantage. He was reinstated by William in 1673, fought gloriously for the Dutch cause, and in 1676 became lieutenant admiral-general of the United Provinces.

the defeats of Rees, Orsay, Wesel, and Rheirberg: Dumas mentions four of the six Dutch-held fortified towns in Cleves in Rhenish Prussia which were the advanced positions of the United Provinces. Orsoy and Wezel fell in the early days of June, Rees capitulated to Turenne on 10 June and Rheinberg (*sic*) surrendered on 12 June. Louis XIV crossed the Rhine at Tolhuis on 12 June.

18 *Van Baerle*: John de Witt had an extended family and made

a point of keeping in touch with them, but he had no godson. Dumas may have borrowed the name from the Latin scholar, Caspar van Baerle (1584–1648).

19 *my servant Craeke*: another invented name. Dumas gave suitably 'Dutch' names to many minor characters. These notes refer only to historical figures: the rest are fictitious.

22 *Hoogstraat*: runs from the Square behind the Gevangenpoort to the Stadhuis, or Town Hall.

Lavater: the old art of reading character in a person's face had been made fashionable in the 1780s by Johann Kaspar Lavater (1741–1801).

of the pirate?: it is said that a pirate, brought before Alexander the Great, protested that he saw no difference between himself and his judge. While he looted and pillaged with a single boat and was called a criminal, Alexander, who acted no differently but had a fleet of ships, was hailed as a conqueror.

23 *the deputy Bowelt*: read 'van Boschveld', one of only two deputies still at their post when the mob arrived at the Stadthuis. See following note.

24 *Mynheer d'Asperen*: Phillip Jacob van Boetselaer van Asperen, a senior deputy in the States of Holland. He and van Boschveld signed the order to Tilly.

28 *leave by the postern*: the prison had a rear exit but the jailer advised against its use and the waiting carriage drove off. The De Wittes left through the front door where they were cut down by the mob which did not wait for them to be tied to stakes and shot. Dumas's account of their attempt to flee by carriage and pass through the locked city gates is not historical, but it allows him to establish William as a figure of political ruthlessness.

33 *to close the town-gates?*: no such order was given and the brothers' attempted flight is a fiction.

large street: the Korte Voorhout.

34 *commutation of the punishment*: the sentence passed on Cornelius—loss of office and exile—had not been commuted.

38 *for he it was*: on 20 August William was 15 miles away in

Alphen, near Leyden. The councillors of the States of Holland sent word to him by express urging him to come in person to calm the situation which was getting out of hand, but he refused to come: it is this message which William anticipates on page 41. By inventing this secret visit to The Hague Dumas exaggerates William's part in events which, whether he orchestrated them or not, significantly improved his hand by the removal of the De Witte brothers. The States subsequently asked him to bring the murderers to justice. The burghers opposed any such action, and William responded by granting an amnesty, though those responsible were not merely pardoned but rewarded: Tichelaer was given a pension and became Ruart of Putten in 1675 (a post once held by Cornelius), while the ringleader of the mob became the equivalent of mayor of the Hague.

41 *Leyden road*: Leyden, 9 miles NW of The Hague and 5 from the North Sea, was then a thriving town with a population of near 100,000.

have been served: in the original text William continues to gloat over the reactions of Louis, the Sun-King: '"O thou Sun! thou Sun! as surely as I am called William the Taciturn, thou Sun, thou hadst best look to thy radiance!" And away upon his mettled steed sped this young Prince, the relentless rival of the great king; this Stadtholder in embryo, who had been, but the day before, very uncertainly established in his new-born power, but for whom the burghers of the Hague had built a staircase with the bodies of John and Cornelius, two princes as noble as he in the eyes of God and man.' On 'William the Taciturn' see note to p. 207.

42 *to Dort*: the original text adds: 'making their way under skilful guidance by the shortest possible routes through the windings of the stream, which held in its embrace so many fascinating little islands, edged with willows and rushes and abounding in luxuriant vegetation, whereon flocks of fat sheep were browsing sleepily and peacefully.' Dumas's attempts at injections of local colour, so beloved of the Romantics, rarely rise above this level of generality.

43 *rara avis*: Juvenal, *Satires*, VI. 164: 'Rara avis in terris, nigroque simillima cygno': 'A Black Swan is not half so rare a bird', in Dryden's version.

a sort of purse: that is, to fund his household expenses.

44   *De Ruyter's flagship*: Michael Adrianzoon de Ruyter (1607–75), one of the greatest seventeenth-century admirals. When war broke out in 1672, accompanied by Cornelius de Witte as adviser in his flagship the *Zeven Provinciën*, he engaged an Anglo-French force indecisively at Southwold (or Sole) Bay, 49 miles NE of Ipswich, on 7 June. Dumas's original text makes the implicit anti-war message plainer, for it continues: '. . . "The Seven Provinces", the flagship of a fleet of one hundred and thirty-nine sail, with which the famous admiral set out to contend single-handed against the combined forces of France and England. When, guided by the pilot Léger, he had come within musket-shot of the *Prince*, with the Duke of York (the English King's brother) aboard, upon which De Ruyter, his Mentor, made so sharp and well-directed an attack that the Duke, perceiving that his vessel would soon have to strike, made the best of his way aboard the *Saint Michael*; when he had seen the *Saint Michael*, riddled and shattered by the Dutch broadside, drift out of the line; when he had witnessed the sinking of the *Earl of Sandwich*, and the death by fire or drowning of four hundred sailors; when he realized that the result of this destruction—after twenty ships had been blown to pieces, three thousand men killed and five thousand injured—was that nothing was decided, that both sides claimed the victory, that the fighting would soon begin again, and that just one more name, that of Southwold Bay, had been added to the list of battles; when he had estimated how much time . . .'. This account of the battle, which involved heavy loss of life, is substantially correct, though Ruyter's force was about half the size mentioned by Dumas and the Earl of Sandwich was not a ship but one of the English commanders. However, it was not the Cornelius who is 'the hero of this story' but Cornelius de Witte who sailed with De Ruyter. Moreover, by giving January 1672 as the date of the battle (see p. 57), Dumas dislocates the historical chronology. Later he adds to the confusion by informing us that Van Baerle's withdrawal from public life occurred 'seven years' before these events (p. 181), which suggests that he may have had in mind Cornelius de Witte's famous role in the victory of Chatham of 1667. Dumas's grasp of historical detail fails him badly at this point.

44 *wrote a treatise*: the treatise, like the character and his contribution to 'the catalogue of Holland' (p. 236), is an invention.

come from the East: probably from Persia—see Introduction and note to p. 45. Dumas's interest in horticulture had been stimulated by the detailed plans he had made for the gardens of the Château de Monte Cristo which he had built at Marly in 1847.

Mons: in Belgium, capital of the province of Hainault.

45 *Alexandria*: a city of lower Egypt, famed for its library, said to have contained 700,000 scrolls. It was stormed by a mob of fanatical Christians in AD 391 and many of its treasures destroyed.

catalogues of the times: we have not traced these and other varieties (see pp. 52, 61) which Dumas either invented or indeed found 'in the catalogues of the times'. Even after the collapse of Tulipmania in 1637, the Dutch trade in bulbs remained strong. Commercial seed and bulb catalogues, often elaborate and illustrated by artists like Judith Leyster, a pupil of Franz Hals, continued to be issued, and it is to these that Dumas refers.

to Dort for three months: on the contrary, Cornelius de Witte was on the move, working closely with his brother, and in March led the Dutch negotiators in Brussels.

46 *Isaac Boxtel*: an invention, taken perhaps from the town of that name, near Eindhoven, where Louis XIV set up his headquarters in July. French readers would certainly have caught the Jewish implications of the character's first name, as of the Jacob which he subsequently adopts.

the word tulips: the original version continues: 'mere mention of the word "tulban" which (as we are assured by the "Floriste français", the most highly-considered authority in matters relating to this flower) is the first word of the Cingalese tongue which was ever used to designate that masterpiece of floriculture which is now called the tulip.' Charles La Chesnée Monstereul's *Le Floriste françois* (1654), on which Dumas drew heavily, mistakenly claimed that the tulip was brought to Portugal from Ceylon (modern Sri Lanka) in about 1530 and Dumas repeats his error throughout the novel. The tulip does not occur naturally in Ceylon and reached Europe in the sixteenth century from Turkey or Persia. The name derives from the Persian *dulban*, and refers to the turban to which the shape of the flower was compared.

a tulip: dropping names as a way of showing his scientific credentials, Dumas, in the original version, here adds passing references to Linnaeus (1707–78), who established the modern classification of tulips, and Joseph-Pitton de Tournefort (1656–1708), whose botanical system lasted until it was improved by Linnaeus.

Don Alphonso VI: king of Portugal, born 1643, deposed 1667. Terceire is one of the Azores. Louis de Bourbon, Prince of Condé (1621–86), known as the 'Great Condé', was detained for a year (1650–1) at the Chateau de Vincennes.

48 *Dow . . . Meiris*: Gerard Douw (1613–75), painter of everyday subjects. Frans Van Mieris (1635–81), born at Leyden and a pupil of Douw, was also known for genre pictures and for portraits.

49 *Porus*: a prince of the Hydaspes (Jhelum), overcome after a fierce battle in 326 BC.

50 *Haarlem*: 10 miles west of Amsterdam, in the seventeenth century a flourishing commercial city already famous for its trade in flowers, especially in tulips, hyacinths, and other bulbs.

52 *shade of the same*: Dumas's original list of blooms also includes the 'Colombin obscur' and the 'Colombin clair terni'. The flower is said to be 'feathered' when the colour is confined to the edges of the petals.

54 *Tulip Society of Haarlem*: Dumas clearly has in mind the horticultural societies—he uses the term elsewhere—of his own day. Though there were syndicates of Dutch tulip-growers in seventeenth-century Holland which offered prizes for new varieties and methods of cultivation, the 100,000 guilders mentioned here is a preposterous sum, especially in an economic climate which was still dominated by the war.

in those days: 'Felix ille tamen, corvo quoque rarior albo' (Juvenal, *Satires*, VII. 202); 'As rare as a white Crow, or sable Swan' in Dryden's translation.

dark brown: the blackest blooms have been produced not from darkening browns but by deepening purples. Dumas was hardly an expert, but in the original text had airily filled a paragraph with pseudo-expertise: 'It might be interesting to explain to the gentle reader the beautiful chain of theories which go to prove that the tulip borrows its colours from the elements; perhaps we should give him pleasure if we were to maintain and establish that nothing is impossible for a florist who avails himself with judgement and discretion and patience of the sun's heat, the clear water, the juices of the earth, and the cool breezes. But this is not a treatise upon tulips in general; it is the story of one particular tulip which we have undertaken to write, and to that we limit ourselves, however alluring the subject which is so closely allied to ours.'

57   *Southwold Bay*: see note to p. 44.

58   *Delphi of old*: a sacred city, believed by the Greeks to be the centre of the earth.

foot there: Dumas adds: 'as the great Racine, who flourished at this time, might have put it.' The French just makes a classical Alexandrine at this point.

cabinet with a glass front: not a piece of furniture but a 'many-windowed drying-room'.

59   *with the Marquis de Louvois*: see note to p. 8.

60   *with a storm*: at this point the French text summarizes the story so far and adds: 'And now here are all the branches of our tale planted in the rich tract of country which stretches from Dort to the Hague. Let him follow them who will, in the chapters which follow: we have kept our word, and have demonstrated that neither John nor Cornelius de Witte had at that time in all Holland so relentless a foe as Van Baerle had at his own door in Dort in the person of Isaac Boxtel.'

1675: an error for 1673.

62   *Ceylon*: one of a number of sites, which include Chaldea, Kashmir and Armenia, proposed as the original Garden, a myth shared by many religions. But Cornelius would not have found tulips there: see note to p. 46.

or Maximilian: that is, Alexander the Great, Julius Caesar, and Maximilian I (1449–1519), Emperor of Germany and grandfather of Charles V.

65   *Van Spenne*: both the character and the name—Van Spennen in the original—were invented by Dumas.

66   *long enough for that*: since William was named Stadtholder on 9 July 1672, six weeks previously, there seems to be no reason why his authority should be questioned in this way.

68   *the brothers de Witte being arrested*: again Dumas is careless. Only Cornelius was officially charged.

70   *bronze lions at Venice*: a reference to the lion's mouth into which denunciations addressed to the state inquisitors were thrown.

75   *Tol-Hek*: the brothers were in fact killed outside the Gevangenpoort, near the scaffold on the Buitenhof.

76   *cresset*: a lantern or torch.

77   *arquebuses*: European armies had in fact by now gone over to the lighter musket.

78   *huge placard*: Dumas's placard is an invention, though signs were attached to the corpses: 'Land Prince' for John, and 'Water Prince' for Cornelius (a reference to his participation in the actions at Chatham and Southwold Bay). An official medal, struck to commemorate the event, bore the following inscription: 'The brothers De Witte, both equally well-intentioned, cursed, hated, loved, raised upon high and cast down low, are here minted and represented in their natural likenesses: they both met their end in the same way and serve as an example to all Great Men.'

87   *Tarquin the Elder*: Tarquinius Priscus (616–578 BC), fifth King of Rome. But Gabii was taken by Tarquinius Sextus who, uncertain how to proceed, sent a messenger to his father, Tarquinius Superbus (534–10 BC), seventh and last King of Rome, who, in reply, removed the poppy heads in his garden with a stick, indicating his view that his son should execute the chief citizens in the town. On the Great Condé, see note to p. 46.

91   *Sybarite*: the inhabitants of Sybaris, an ancient Greek city on the Gulf of Tarentum, enjoyed such luxury that in the ancient world their name became a byword for easy living.

92   *seven months*: really nine. Cf. p. 109, 'which for the last five

months . . .', where 'five' should be 'seven', another instance of Dumas's carelessness with chronology.

95 *taken down*: late on 20 August 1672, the States of Holland ordered what was left of the bodies to be assembled and removed. They were buried quietly the next night in the Nieuwe Kerk.

98 *Chalais . . . de Thou*: Henri de Talleyrand, Comte de Chalais, was decapitated in 1626, but only after the axe-man had tried thirty times to sever his head. François-Auguste de Thou was beheaded at Lyons in 1642, also clumsily, for plotting with Spain.

99 *granted him his life*: though this episode is a fiction, the commuting of Van Baerle's sentence is consistent with the policy of William who arrived at the Hague on 21 August, two days before Van Baerle writes his will (see p. 108). The new Stadtholder was anxious to calm reactions to events from which he had greatly benefited. The unmodified translation adds a long amplification which ends with a splendid example of Dumas's famous padding: Cornelius looks around him in relief and enjoys the experience 'of exercising the muscles of that part of the body, which the Greeks called the τράχηλος (*trachelos*), but to which we French have given the name of "le col" (the neck)'.

Madame de Sévigné: Marie de Rabutin-Chantal, Marquise de Sévigné (1626–96), who thought of her correspondence as so many 'conversations at a distance'.

Loevenstein: Lovenstein, a castle near Gorkum (Gorinchem), 25 miles south-east of Rotterdam and a few miles upstream from Dordrecht; a small, secure jail for prisoners of state on an island where, as Dumas says, the Meuse joins the Waal.

100 *after the death of Barneveldte*: Hugo van Groot (1583–1645), known as Grotius, the leading jurist of his day, was a supporter of Jan van Oldenbarneveldt (1547–1619) who defended republican principles against Maurice de Nassau when, as Stadtholder, he was bent on reducing the power of the States. In 1618, Barneveldt and Grotius were arrested. Barneveldt was sentenced to death and executed the following year, while Grotius was ordered to be detained for life at Lovenstein. His wife contrived his escape by having him

carried out of the castle in a chest used for transporting books and linen while she remained in his cell.

stivers: the basic unit of Dutch currency was the guilder (or gulden), the equivalent of 20 *stuivers*. To 'guilder', Dumas regularly prefers the alternative 'florin' which was worth about 2 shillings in contemporary English money. Some idea of values may be judged from the following. Around the middle of the century, agricultural workers were paid a daily wage of 15–20 stuivers, urban workers in towns 20 stuivers, and certain artisans (such as shipwrights) up to 36 stuivers. The satirical pamphlets to which the Dutch were addicted normally fell within the 3–5 stuiver range. A tankard of beer cost 2 stuivers, though in Antwerp a 'tankard' meant 8–9 litres. Against the price of tulips may be set the 1,600 gulden which Rembrandt was paid for *The Nightwatch*.

102   *unguibus et rostro*: a Latin tag, meaning literally 'with fingernails and beak'.

104   *the hardest of all metals*: Dumas's display of scientific knowledge is not reassuring, though he always paraded it with panache: see note to p. 149.

flower for him: the French text adds, unhelpfully: 'There are certain calamities which the pen of a writer, who is but human, is powerless to describe, but which he must leave to his readers' imagination, contenting himself with a bare statement of the facts.'

other side of the Channel: English pugilists were famous in Dumas's time, not in the seventeenth century.

105   *a set of serpents*: the French text makes no mentions of envy and Dumas clearly had in mind the Gorgon Medusa, whose hair was transformed into a nest of snakes by Athene as punishment for submitting to the desires of Poseidon in the temple. Perseus managed to cut off her head.

106   *lost to him for ever*: here, Dumas's original version strengthened the piety of the characters: 'Fortunately, honest Van Baerle was mistaken. God, who had His eyes upon him with the smile of a loving father when he was walking to the scaffold, God had destined him to lead even in his prison-cell, the former abode of Grotius, the most adventurous life which ever fell to the lot of a tulip-fancier.'

108   *envious neighbour*: again, Dumas had bolstered the role of religion: 'God, who with a single breath scattered on 21 August the grain upon the walls of time-worn castles, and fertilizes it here and there with a drop of rain, decreed in His infinite goodness that Van Baerle's nurse should receive the letter.' In the same pious spirit he adds, a few paragraphs later: 'Chance, or rather God, for we see the hand of God in everything, had willed that Cornelius Van Baerle should happen to hit upon one of these very pigeons.'

113   *Master Harbruck*: probably a name invented by Dumas. Pamphleteers referred to the executioner as Master Tobias.

115   *your bulbs*: Dumas has forgotten that Cornelius instructed Rosa to plant them in August (p. 92). She has not obeyed and will not do so until late April (p. 138). Cornelius is strangely unperturbed and happily plants his at the start of April. He must be one of the 'experienced gardners' who, Dumas tells us confidently (p. 143), always plant in April. Readers who believe him will be disappointed—October and November are the recommended months.

118   *trespassing*: committing a punishable offence.

122   *mistrustful of herself*: in the original French version Dumas had explained why—'since she had discovered how a prisoner's breath may set a maiden's heart on fire.'

      on her father: here, Dumas's original text adds a paragraph reflecting the romantic infatuation with genius and its corresponding dislike of the vulgar: 'On that account, the very life of Van Baerle, the learned doctor of science, the picturesque artist, the man of genius—of Van Baerle, who could in all probability claim to be the discoverer of that *chef d'oeuvre* of creation which was to be called, in accordance with previous arrangement, "Rosa Barlaensis",—the life, yes, more than the life, the happiness of this man, depended absolutely on the mere whim of another man: and that other man was a being on a lower scale, and of the meanest capacity—a jailer, rather less intelligent than the lock in which he turned the key, and harder than the bolt he drew. It resembled the episode of Caliban in the *Tempest*—a struggle between a man and a brute.' For similar reflections about vulgarity and the mediocre, see p. 206.

129   *to greater anxieties*: the unmodified text reinforces the Romantic theme of destiny: 'When one's evil destiny is about to be fulfilled, it rarely happens that the victim is not forewarned of its approach, on the same principle of generosity which prompts the bully to give his adversary leisure to put himself on guard.

    'Almost invariably such warnings which are due to the human instinct, or to the complicity of inanimate objects, which are often not so inanimate as they are generally believed to be—almost always such warnings are neglected. The whistle has sounded, and has fallen upon an inattentive ear, which should have taken alarm, and, having taken alarm should have been forewarned.'

131   *Pellisson's spider*: on the fall of Nicolas Fouquet in 1661, one of his most loyal supporters, Paul Pellisson (1624–93), was sent to the Bastille where he remained for five years. The prisoner tamed a spider which, when he played the flute, emerged and fed in his hand. The governor, de Baisemeaux, asked to see the spider. Pellisson summoned it with his flute. Baisemeaux picked it up, dropped it on the floor, and crushed it. Then he left the cell without saying a word.

138   *source of good to us*: the unmodified text is more explicit: '. . . and the source of wealth to us! Watch over it! And even if the lightning should strike Loewenstein, give me your oath, Rosa, that you will seize and save this last of the bulbs which encloses the possibility of a black tulip in preference to your rings or your jewels or the pretty golden head-dress which frames your lovely features; swear it, Rosa!' Cornelius has no very practical idea of how many jewels a jailer's daughter normally wore.

140   *she wept*: originally, Dumas made the reasons for her tears much clearer. While Rosa might well be 'a high-spirited creature, of no mean perception and a noble heart', she was poor and low-born, and therefore perhaps no more to Cornelius 'who belonged to the merchant-bourgeoisie' than 'a pleasant companion for the dreary hours of his captivity . . . Thus Rosa understood Cornelius's preference of the tulip to herself, but was only so much more the unhappy therefor.'

141   *a vague uneasiness*: caused, Dumas had written, by 'the fear lest Rosa might not come in the evening as usual'.

149   *too late to plant it*: even so, Rosa, with Dumas's help, is able to plant a bulb in April which flowers in early May. See note to p. 115.

     ladies of Haarlem and Dort: though Dumas mocks, certain bulbs may be grown in water. The unmodified text adds pompously that water is two-thirds hydrogen and one-third oxygen.

152   *my heart beats*: Cornelius's speech, in which he confesses that he loves Rosa more than the black tulip, was, in Dumas's French text, fuller and much more cloying.

155   *the light of love*: the unmodified text furnishes another example of Dumas's lyrical manner: 'Love was blooming there, and causing everything about it to bloom as well—love, that heavenly flower with a radiance and a perfume far different from all the flowers on earth!'

     friend Cerberus: the three-headed dog which, in Greek mythology, stood guard at the mouth of Hades.

157   *whom the world has seen*: Semiramis, mythical queen of Nineveh; Anne of Austria (1602–66), the daughter of Philip III of Spain, who became Queen of France in 1615 and mother of Louis XIV in 1638.

165   *beyond herself with happiness*: and so, in a lengthy amplification in Dumas's original, is Cornelius. After snatching a kiss (his mouth met hers 'not by chance or stratagem but as Saint-Preux's was to meet the lips of Julie a hundred years later'), he opens the window and thanks God who has not abandoned him after all: 'I see Thee in all thy wondrous glory in the mirror of thy Heavenly abode, and more clearly still in the mirror of my grateful heart.' And, though still a prisoner, 'the wretched captive was free once more'. The reference to Rousseau's novel, *La Nouvelle Héloïse* (1762), the pathetic fallacy, and the theme of happiness in prison, are typical of Romantic sensibility.

167   *Van Herysen*: this name appears only in the pirated Belgian text. In Dumas's original the character is called Peters van Systens.

169   *Genièvre*: that is, gin. Texel is a northerly island of North

Holland, on the Zuyder Zee; the phrase means 'from one end of Holland to the other'.

171 *Mieris and Metzys*: on Mieris, see note to p. 48. The French text has 'Metzu', and Dumas refers here not (as the translator indicates) to the Flemish portraitist Quentin Metzys (1466–1530), but to Gabriel Metzu (1630–70), also born in Leyden.

172 *renowned tulip-grower*: Dumas forgets that Boxtel's 'name had disappeared forever'—see p. 50.

173 *a reclamation*: that is, a claim.

179 *Delft*: 10 miles north-west of Rotterdam.

182 *exceedingly circuitous*: the unmodified translation continues: 'But none but birds can fly as the crow flies in Holland—a country which is more cut up by rivers and brooks and streams and canals than by any other in the world.' Dumas's descriptions of the Dutch landscape never rise above such non-specific glimpses in which stock features of 'Dutch picturesque'—windmills, dykes, canals, and the like—figure prominently.

183 *like an adventuress*: the original edition adds cultural references (of which Dumas was particularly fond), 'like Bradamante or Clorinda' respectively heroines of Ariosto and Tasso.

184 *Open Sesame*: Dumas's was an enthusiastic reader of *The Arabian Nights*, which was still known only in the translation (1704–17) made by the Orientalist Antoine Galland.

188 *by his anger*: Homer, *Iliad*, I. 197. In Pope's translation: 'Minerva swift descended from above. | Sent by the sister and the wife of Jove: | (For both the princes claim'd her equal care.) | Behind she stood, and by the golden hair | Achilles seiz'd . . .'.

    tulip will die: Dumas inserts another pious note: 'Oh, Holy Virgin! grant me strength and inspiration; the happiness of my whole life is at stake—to say nothing of the unhappy captive who may be breathing his last at this moment. Having uttered this heartfelt prayer Rosa waited for the inspiration from on high which she had besought.'

204 *teach me to read*: the unmodified text gives a pious confirmation: 'Yes, God did know, for it is He who chastises and rewards mankind according to their deserts.'

206   *Argus*: in Greek myth, the herdsman of Hera, said to have had a hundred eyes, of which fifty remained open all the time. The word came to designate an ever-watchful guard.

     eyes of hatred: originally Dumas had stoked up the suspense and significantly increased Van Baerle's uncertainties: '. . . his eyes are made keen by hatred—old Gryphus himself? Finally, is there not one circumstance which takes away all my spirit—I mean Rosa's absence? But I suppose I should waste ten years of my life in making a file to file off my bars or in braiding cords to let myself down from the window, or in sticking wings on my shoulders to fly, like Daedalus? But luck is against me now. The file would get dull, the rope would break, or my wings would melt in the sun; I should surely kill myself; I should be picked up maimed and crippled; I should be labelled, put on exhibition in the museum of the Hague between the blood-stained doublet of William the Taciturn and the female walrus captured at Stavesen, and the only result of my enterprise will have been to procure me a place among the curiosities of Holland. But no; and it is much better so. Some fine day, Gryphus will commit some atrocity. I am losing my patience . . .' Daedalus and his son Icarus, imprisoned by Minos, escaped with the aid of wings made of wax and bird's feathers; but Icarus flew too near the sun, the wax melted, and he fell. The reference to William 'the Taciturn', assassinated in 1584, makes nonsense of Dumas's applying this label to the Stadtholder (see note to p. 41). For Stavesen, read Staveren, though Dumas seems to refer to the 'sea-woman' of Edam who appeared through the dyke in 1403 and, it is said, learned to spin.

208   *Hymn of Flowers*: the poem is Romantic in manner and was most likely written by Dumas himself.

210   *burn me for it*: Dumas's original text had included two of his favourite reference points, 'at the stake, like Gaufredy or Urbain Grandier'. Louis Gaufredy, a Marseilles priest, died at the stake for witchcraft in 1611. Urbain Grandier (1590–1634) was also burnt as a sorceror.

214   *Mathias*: we have been unable to identify 'Mathias'.

     incontinently: immediately.

216   *the daughter!*: the unmodified text adds further interior mono-

256

logue to increase the suspense: 'How Gryphus would glory in his punishment! Punishment? Rather, savage vengeance for an eminently righteous deed, which Cornelius had the satisfaction of having performed as a bounden duty.

'But Rosa, poor girl! must he die without a glimpse of her, without an opportunity to give her one last kiss, or even to say one last word of farewell?

'And worst of all, must he die without any intelligence of the black tulip, and regain his consciousness in heaven with no ideas in what direction he should look to find it?

'In truth to restrain his tears at such a crisis the poor wretch's heart must have been encased in more of the *aes triplex*—"the triple brass"—than Horace bestows upon the sailor who first visited the terrifying Acroceraunian shoals.' The reference is to Horace, *Odes*, I. 3. line 9.

223 *fifteenth of May, 1673*: in his original text, Dumas had opened Chapter 31 with a long and none-too specific description of Haarlem as the tulip capital of Holland. There is no indication that at this time the population was concerned by the continuing war (see next note). On this date the fleet was at sea, Condé was trying to find a way through the inundations, and the siege of Maastricht (at which the real d'Artagnan died of a bullet in the throat) was imminent. It is unlikely that war-exhausted Haarlem should have organized such an occasion and equally implausible that William could spare three days to award the prize. The festival is pure invention.

Batavian Republic: hostilities had not ceased, as Dumas states, but were merely suspended when the dykes had been opened in mid-June 1672. The inundations made it impossible for the French to advance. The war continued until the Peace of Nimeguen in 1678. The terms 'Batavian people' and 'Batavian Republic' derive from the Batavi, a Germanic people who, in Roman times, occupied the *Batavorum insula*, an area between the Rhine and the Waal.

224 *The Supreme Being*: Dumas was no admirer of Maximilian Robespierre (1759–94), creator of the Revolutionary Terror, who on 7 May 1793 persuaded the National Convention to proclaim the existence of the Supreme Being—Reason, infinitely superior to the old religion which had been over-

thrown—and decreed that a ceremony be held annually to celebrate its glories.

conquest of Gaul: Pompey defeated Mithridates in 65 BC and was in turn overcome by Caesar, the conqueror of Gaul, at the Battle of Pharsalia in 49 BC.

225   *never knows when to stop*: a comment which indicates the limits of Dumas's democratic principles, which in the original version he had expressed more fully than this translation allows: 'This public display of the tulip was an act of homage rendered by a whole nation, uncultured and unrefined, to the refinement and culture of its illustrious and devout leaders, whose blood it had shed upon the foul pavement of the Buitenhof, reserving the right at a future day to inscribe the names of its victims upon the fairest stone of the Dutch Pantheon.' But Dumas also expresses his reservations about politicians: 'For in the most insignificant speeches of men of political prominence their friends and their opponents always try to detect, and hence think they can interpret, something of their real thoughts. As if your true politician's hat were not always a bushel under which he hides his light!'

234   *a wicked action*: the unmodified text adds a moral paragraph: 'This sudden stroke of apoplexy was a blessing from God for Boxtel, in so far, at any rate, as it saved him from having any longer to contemplate things so painful to his pride and avarice.'

235   *and drove off*: in paying due tribute to those 'two great citizens', the De Witte brothers, William is now shown to have become a statesman to Dumas's taste. His humanity is evident in his insistence on righting the wrong done to Van Baerle and he leaves, conscious of the weight of the heroic solitude which the poet Vigny attributed to all truly great leaders. His rehabilitation is complete.

236   *envious attempts*: in a phrase cut from this translation, Dumas undermines the happy outcome with a sober warning by commenting: '. . . whom Providence might not have had leisure to rid him of as it had of Mynheer Isaac Boxtel . . .'.

. . . *too happy*: for 'ever', read 'never'.